Touched by This Place

Touched by This Place

Theology, Community, and the Power of Place

BENJAMÍN VALENTÍN

ORBIS  BOOKS

Maryknoll, New York 10545

Founded in 1970, Orbis Books endeavors to publish works that enlighten the mind, nourish the spirit, and challenge the conscience. The publishing arm of the Maryknoll Fathers and Brothers, Orbis seeks to explore the global dimensions of the Christian faith and mission, to invite dialogue with diverse cultures and religious traditions, and to serve the cause of reconciliation and peace. The books published reflect the views of their authors and do not represent the official position of the Maryknoll Society. To learn more about Maryknoll and Orbis Books, please visit our website at www.orbisbooks.com.

Manufactured in the United States of America

Library of Congress Cataloging-in-Publication Data

Names: Valentin, Benjamin, author.
Title: Touched by this place : theology, community, and the power of place / Benjamín Valentín.
Description: Maryknoll, NY : Orbis Books, [2024] | Includes bibliographical references and index. | Summary: "Explores the ways in which geographic places influence and are influenced by human life, thought, and action"— Provided by publisher.
Identifiers: LCCN 2023051916 (print) | LCCN 2023051917 (ebook) | ISBN 9781626985735 (trade paperback) | ISBN 9798888660294 (epub)
Subjects: LCSH: Memory—Social aspects. | Place attachment. | Place (Philosophy)
Classification: LCC BF371 .V2546 2024 (print) | LCC BF371 (ebook) | DDC 153.1/2—dc23/eng/20231218
LC record available at https://lccn.loc.gov/2023051916
LC ebook record available at https://lccn.loc.gov/2023051917

*In loving memory of my dad, the Rev. Ángel M. Valentín—
one of the elder siblings of Spanish Harlem*

Contents

Acknowledgments

This book was written amid and in the face of considerable difficulties: the first year of the Covid-19 pandemic; statewide Covid-19 stay-at-home orders; almost a year of isolation from family and friends due to the pandemic; the death of my mother-in-law, Sylvia Rodríguez, due to Covid complications; the death of my father, the Rev. Ángel M. Valentín, due to Covid complications; my own brush with death due to a horrific truck crash; a couple of minor but still stressful health scares; the need to relocate and look after my grieving mother; a move and transition from Yale University to Boston College; and the anguish connected to a looming marital separation. These are among the difficult life challenges I endured while writing this book. That I could finish it at all is nothing short of remarkable. I am thankful to be alive in the first place, thankful to still be sane (I think!), and thankful to have been able to complete this work in the span of three years despite all this.

The last two feats, however, would not have been possible without the steadfast love and support of many cherished people, and without the vital assistance and backing of esteemed organizations and institutions. I can honestly say that these acknowledgments have taken on added meaning for me given the circumstances of the last three years.

And so, it is with "great pleasure," gratefulness, and a sense of indebtedness that I say thank you to the following persons and groups. I am thankful to the God of life and mystery for putting me and keeping me on this Earth. I am thankful to my mom and dad—Luz Belen Santa Valentín and the Rev. Ángel Manuel Valentín—for showing me the meaning of love, care, devotion, resilience, humility, and faithfulness. I am thankful for my native place, my native town, Spanish Harlem, for all that it taught me about the beauty of life, community, and inner strength and joy despite the injustices of this world and the cruel circumstances of life. From the very bottom of my heart, I want to thank my brother, Elieser "Eli" Valentín; his wife, Maria; and his children, my beautiful nephews Justin, Gabriel, and Benjamin, for being there for me through thick and thin. I love you, *familia*! My brother, Eli, deserves a special shout-out for being someone I can always rely on to be helpful and supportive. He was even instrumental in recommending Orbis Books for the publication of this work.

I am also thankful for the unfailing love, companionship, and support of Anthony Pinn and Mayra Rivera over many years. Long ago they ascended the realm of friendship to become "true family." I love you to pieces!

Much love as well to my sister Bethsaida Valentín; her husband, Reinaldo Ruiz; and her daughter, my adorable niece, Aracelis Marie. They too have always been there for me.

I am thankful for the constant presence and support of my extended family for life: Alba Karina Valentín, Jackie Rodríguez, Felix "Junior" Meléndez, Aaron and Alexander Meléndez, Bert Rodriguez, and Sofia Carolina.

Another friend who has been like family to me through the years is Robert "Bobby" Rivera. Thanks for always being there for me, bro! A special thanks to Juan Carlos Rosales, Gloria Jeanette Rosales, and Sofia Rosales, and to Elias and Emily Ortiz, for treating me like family, for bringing joy to my life, and for being by my side all these years. A special thank you as well to Ulrike Guthrie for being in my corner from very early on in my career, offering editorial help, writing advice, and guild-related counsel. I am also grateful to Orlando Espín, Milagros Peña, Luis N. Rivera-Pagán, Fernando F. Segovia, Daisy L. Machado, Carmen Nanko-Fernández, Joanne Rodríguez, the Hispanic Theological Initiative Consortium, and the Hispanic Summer Program for all that they have meant to me through the years. I extend a special thank you to Orlando Espín for suggesting that I approach Orbis Books with this work, and for taking the initiative of contacting the folks there on my behalf to facilitate publication of this work. Likewise I am thankful for all of the wonderful people of the American Theological Society and the Constructive Theology Workgroup for providing healthy, creative dialogical and thinking space and not only career support but at times even emotional support over the span of years.

I extend a thank you to my colleagues and friends at Yale Divinity School for providing me with supportive space in which to work from 2015 to 2020. It isn't lost on me that this book began to take shape during my last year at Yale Divinity School. The good people there and the rich intellectual environment of the place played an important part in its formation without a doubt. I will forever be grateful to colleagues and friends at Andover New-ton Theological School for their friendship and support over many years and for teaching me much about what it means to be "a colleague," "a faculty member," and a "Christian scholar" early on in my career. I especially thank Robert Pazmiño, Wanda Pazmiño, Sarah Drummond, S. Mark Heim, Gregory Mobley, Nayda Aguila, and Rose Costas.

I feel extremely lucky to find myself in a new and equally invigorating and supportive "academic home" here at Boston College, and at Boston College's School of Theology and Ministry specifically. I thank the administrators of Boston College's School of Theology and Ministry for granting me a one-semester research leave at the beginning of my professorship in 2020. This allowed me to carry out research and to write the second chapter of this work. And already I am thankful for the friendship and support of some of my new or newer colleagues and friends there. I extend a special thank you to Dean Thomas Stegman, Dean Michael McCarthy, Callid Keefe-Perry, Hosffman Ospino, Jennifer Bader, Thomas Groome, Colleen Griffith, Heather DuBois, Theresa O'Keefe, Ernesto Valiente, Andrew Davis, Kris-tin Heyer, Maura Colleary, and Karen Smith.

And, finally, I thank Robert Ellsberg, publisher at Orbis Books, for believing in this project. I also thank Thomas Hermans-Webster and all the wonderful people at Orbis Books for their help in making this book a real-ity. *Thank you, everyone!*

Introduction

I have been interested in the significance of place for quite a while now but had no conscious idea of it. A question asked of me at my doctoral dissertation defense many years ago got me thinking about the dialectical relationship that exists between matters of thought and mind and the physical environments in which they evolve. What I gained that day was a curiosity, not yet the language or the conceptual framework of place. The truth is that it wasn't until 2018 that I discovered the scholarly field of place studies and the exciting discussions and ideas surrounding the emergence of critical inquiry about place. This in itself is noteworthy.

What this means is that somehow I had not only managed to get an education in theological and religious studies but also to pursue my career as an academic theologian and religious studies scholar without any knowledge of the so-called *spatial turn* that had been taking shape in other areas of the humanities and in the social sciences. I take responsibility for the obliviousness certainly. It is not as if I have been insular in my studies and work. I have always "tried" to read broadly and to incorporate an array of disciplines into my writings as far as possible. And yet, despite all that, I was unaware of the increasing attention that was being granted to the agency of place.

Since the late 1970s, scholars across the humanities and social sciences have been highlighting the ways in which knowledge, identity, and belief are structurally wedded to the physical geographies of life.[1] So, why was I

---

1. For examples of some works that explore or highlight this connection (listed chronologically), see Vine Deloria Jr., *God Is Red: A Native View of Religion* (New York: Putnam Publishing Group, 1973); Yi-Fu Tuan, *Topophilia: A Study of Environmental Perception, Attitudes and Values* (Englewood, NJ: Prentice Hall, 1974); Edith Cobb, *The Ecology of Imagination in Childhood* (New York: Columbia University

unaware of their important work? Why did it take me so long to discover a thriving cross-disciplinary field of study that would, in time, provide the necessary language and conceptual basis for my slowly developing interest in the significance of place and place experience?

In large measure, I simply have to admit that I missed the boat on the place and spatial turn development. Despite my attempts at cross-disciplinary learning, I failed to take note of this emergent and expanding intellectual trend and subject field. But the matter of a lack of exposure early on in my formative academic years played a part in my obliviousness, too. As it happens, there weren't many theological and religious studies works (especially books!) taking up the subject of place when I was completing my graduate studies in the mid-to-late 1990s. Not yet at least. The sparsity was even more apparent in theology, especially in the subfields of systematic and constructive theology and the theological discourses focusing on matters of

Press, 1977); Donna J. Haraway, "Situated Knowledges: The Science Question in Feminism and the Privilege of Partial Perspective," in *Feminist Studies* 14, no. 3 (Fall 1988): 575–99; Carol Bigwood, *Earth Muse: Feminism, Nature, and Art* (Philadelphia: Temple University Press, 1993); Gaston Bachelard, *The Poetics of Space* (Boston: Beacon Press, 1994); Winifred Gallagher, *The Power of Place: How Our Surroundings Shape Our Thoughts, Emotions, and Actions* (New York: HarperPerennial, 1994); Andrew Pickering, *The Mangle of Practice* (Chicago: University of Chicago Press, 1995); David Abram, *The Spell of the Sensuous* (New York: Vintage, 1996); Keith Basso, *Wisdom Sits in Places: Landscape and Language among the Western Apache* (Albuquerque: University of New Mexico Press, 1996); Kathleen M. Kirby, *Indifferent Boundaries: Spatial Concepts of Human Subjectivity* (New York: Guilford Press, 1996); William Vitek and Wes Jackson, eds., *Rooted in the Land: Essays on Community and Place* (New Haven, CT: Yale University Press, 1996); David Sack, *Homo Geographicus* (Baltimore, MD: Johns Hopkins University Press, 1997); Heidi J. Nast and Steve Pile, eds., *Places through the Body* (New York: Routledge, 1998); Jeff Malpas, *Place and Experience: A Philosophical Topography* (Cambridge, UK: Cambridge University Press, 1999); Nancy Tuana, "Material Locations," in *Engendering Rationalities*, eds. Nancy Tuana and S. Morgan (Albany, NY: SUNY Press, 2001); Christopher J. Preston, *Grounding Knowledge: Environmental Philosophy, Epistemology, and Place* (Athens: University of Georgia Press, 2003); Sarah Menin, ed., *Constructing Place: Mind and the Matter of Place-Making* (New York: Routledge, 2003); Wendy Schissel, ed., *Home/Bodies: Geographies of Self, Place, and Space* (Calgary, Canada: University of Calgary Press, 2006); bell hooks, *Belonging: A Culture of Place* (New York: Routledge, 2009); and Esther M. Sternberg, *Healing Spaces: The Science of Place and Well-Being* (Cambridge, MA: Belknap Press, 2009). This isn't a comprehensive list of books and articles on the subject of place and knowledge, identity, and belief. It simply gives some examples of works that can be considered on this particular subject, and it hints at the cross-disciplinary character of the conversation just on the basis of the authors and editors represented.

justice and liberation, which happened to be the areas of study and conversation to which I was mostly tied.

Things started to change in the early 2000s with the emergence of a steadier stream of monographs and other writings on theology and place. And, since then, a good number of titles that explore the subject matter have been published in the field.[2] But, even to this day, we can't exactly say that there has been a large-scale influx of writings on the issue and issues of place in the field of theology. There is an appreciable number, yes! A large and consistent influx? No! Not yet at least. And, in my formative years as a graduate student and during my first few years in the field of theological studies, it was still a mere sprinkling. You can understand, then, how, as a theologian, I could be unaware of the enthusiasm transpiring in the arts, humanities, and social sciences with respect to the study of place, places, and their epistemic influence.

Thank goodness for the nudge of that defense question! As a result of it, I discovered the placed origin of my thinking. I have become more aware of how indebted my thinking and my writing are to Spanish Harlem, my home. I can see in them vital connections with the region of my upbringing, vital connections to which I had paid little attention previously, connections that I had underestimated and underappreciated. This realization has awak-

---

2. Familiar works on place and/or the built environment that come to mind within the field of theology are (in alphabetical order by last name): Craig G. Bartholomew, *Where Mortals Dwell: A Christian View of Place for Today* (Grand Rapids, MI: Baker Academic, 2011); Sigurd Bergmann, *Religion, Space, and the Environment* (New York: Routledge, 2017); Sigurd Bergmann, ed., *Theology in Built Environments: Exploring Religion, Architecture, and Design* (New York: Routledge, 2017); T. J. Gorringe, *A Theology of the Built Environment: Justice, Empowerment, Redemption* (Cambridge, UK: Cambridge University Press, 2002); T. J. Gorringe, *The Common Good and the Global Emergency: God and the Built Environment* (Cambridge, UK: Cambridge University Press, 2011); Leonard Hjalmarson, *No Home Like Place: A Christian Theology of Place* (Farnham, UK: Ashgate Publishing, 2003); Leonard Hjalmarson, *The Soul of the City: Mapping the Spiritual Geography of Eleven Canadian Cities* (Skyforest, CA: Urban Loft Publishers, 2018); John Inge, *A Christian Theology of Place* (Farnham, UK: Ashgate Publishing, 2003); Eric O. Jacobsen, *The Space Between: A Christian Engagement with the Built Environment* (Grand Rapids, MI: Baker Academic, 2012); David P. Leong, *Race and Place: How Urban Geography Shapes the Journey to Reconciliation* (Downers Grove, IL: InterVarsity Press, 2017); Murray A. Rae, *Architecture and Theology: The Art of Place* (Waco, TX: Baylor University Press, 2017); Philip Sheldrake, *Spaces for the Sacred: Place, Memory, and Identity* (London: SCM Press, 2001); and Philip Sheldrake, *The Spiritual City: Theology, Spirituality, and the Urban* (Malden, MA: Wiley-Blackwell, 2014).

ened me to the ways in which place contributes to critical knowledge and to keep in view how it is out of my interactions with place (specifically Spanish Harlem) that I construct my knowledge, beliefs, and ways of thinking.[3] In other words, I've learned to include places among the epistemic locations that persons bring to their knowledge claims.

This alone would be worth the price of admission, I like to say. But I have also come to understand that place is important as a central and meaningful component in human life and as a primary basis for existence more generally. Indeed, human life is impossible without place, inasmuch as life always requires emplacement in the world. We might as well direct attention to the places that emplace us, then, since life is always fashioned, produced, experienced, and expressed in and through particular places. So, those seemingly unimportant, mundane, humdrum, customary, taken-for-granted, and/or easy-to-ignore places in which we live? Those places in which we live, move, and have our being?[4] They're a big deal.

Much of our sense of identity is derived from, or mediated through, the actual places we inhabit. No wonder we ask on first meeting, "Where are you from?" or "Where do you come from?" And, whether the place we name is a town, a city, a neighborhood, a state, or a region more generally, the point remains the same: we ourselves and others work out our self-identity in relation to the places in which we live, whether we are fully aware of it or not.

That has been part of my discovery, too. But what I have discovered besides is that places matter in a social and more widespread manner. Places shape our destinies, influencing the fates of individuals and groups. Place is an individual and social factor that influences a people's life chances because it commonly determines the access or the lack of access that persons will have to educational, social, economic, and environmental resources. The quality of one's educational opportunities; the types of jobs available in an area; the quality of public amenities like parks, libraries, and cultural and recreational centers; the availability of reliable or first-rate medical services; the effectiveness of public servants; and the degree of exposure to violence, gangs, toxic hazards, and clean air—all of this depends on where one lives. This is one of the many points at which the issues of justice and of place intersect.

This suggests that place matters a great deal and in a whole host of ways. Few topics and actualities are as crucial, as multifaceted, and as wide-rang-

---

3. My phrasing here is inspired by the work of Christopher Preston. See especially Preston's *Grounding Knowledge*, esp. pp. 100–117.

4. These words appear in a well-known passage from Acts 17:28.

ing or all-encompassing as place. There is no current existential, cognitive, emotional, social, political, justice, global, religious, or environmental, land-related, or nature-related issue that doesn't intersect with place in some way or another. That is why I have decided to call for "even more" place consideration and place inquiry than already exists in the field of theology. We might call it a "return-to-place moment" or intervention, and I hope such a return will reorient our thinking toward the idea and actuality of place.

I hope through this book to shine a light on the multidimensional significance of places, and to encourage fellow scholars of religion and theology to continue to delve into and, if possible, to further the work of highlighting their manifold importance, especially their epistemological, existential, social, and political importance in connection with matters of social and environmental justice. I focus mostly on the subject of recognizing the epistemic significance or the epistemic contributions of places, but I don't ignore the existential, social, and political aspects of place's importance.

What do I mean when I speak of "places"?

By "places" I refer to the different physical spaces and locations that we invest with meaning in the context of power.[5] I mean the actual, physical, geographical places that register in our memories and to which we have emotional and practical commitments, even if subconsciously or unperceptively at times. I'm talking about the regions, towns, villages, cities, city blocks, neighborhoods, buildings, homes, rooms, and all of the other kinds of possible material settings within which we conduct our lives and produce and consume meaning. As can be seen, my focus here is mostly on what is often referred to as the built environment—the human-made surroundings that support and give particular shape to human activity. I don't ignore the importance of land and natural environments in all of this. I see these as integral parts of the marvelously dynamic, complex, and multifaceted place-world that deserves continuous attention in any and all discussion of epistemic locations and experiential contexts. It just so happens that, in this work, I will be homing in on one of the facets or constituents of our place-world, focusing on our constructed places, particularly on the affective agency of neighborhoods.

These meaningful material locales that we call "places" aren't neutral, static backdrops to human life. They influence and shape life. They affect and

---

5. For this definition of place and places, I am depending on the work of Tim Cresswell. See especially his *Place: An Introduction* (Malden, MA: Wiley Blackwell, 2015), esp. 1–21.

mold human thought, experience, memory, identity, and activity. They often even even affect the opportunities we are afforded or denied in social life. Every aspect of our personal and social lives is touched, influenced, and shaped by the particular geographical places in which we live and move and have our being. Places, one could say, are contextual entities *and* agential entities. This is why we should count them among the influences on our understandings of thought, knowledge, and belief as well as on the contours of every other aspect of our lives.

Theology stands to make a bigger deal of and to make further room for this influence of place, I believe, which brings me to my placial or place-based appeal.

My appeal takes shape in three chapters. Chapter 1, "Finding a Place for Place," explores theology's slow, patchy, or somewhat episodic consideration of place. It begins with reflection on some of the factors that could be contributing to the overlooking or bypassing of place in theology and moves from there to reflect on some of the important ways in which place and experience of place matter. Here, I dwell on the points that place matters as a necessary condition for life; that place provides us with a sense of who we are; that place has an impact on the products of the mind; that places shape our destinies, influencing the fates of individuals and groups; and that place matters by reason of the grievous experience of displacement endured by numerous individuals and groups. With all this in view, the chapter ends with an appeal for more theological work to be done on place and an appeal for a particular kind of writing about place—one that doesn't limit itself to talking about place in the abstract but tries instead to immerse itself in the particularity of a place in the process of talking about place—endeavoring to give us a feel and taste, or a "narratory sampling," of place, including but not limited to the history and materiality of place. This sensitivity to the distinctiveness and particularity of actual geographical places facilitates the process of perceiving the unique role that places play in structuring the ways we think and the ways we view and experience the world.

Chapter 2, "A Place Called Spanish Harlem: Spanish Harlem Remembered," takes up this challenge. Since I am writing about place connections and the epistemic significance of place experiences in particular places and communities all while making a case for contextual or context-specific description of the history and materiality of places in theological place writing, it is appropriate for me to say something about the place from which I came and in which I grew up. Accordingly, I grapple with the complex history and multifaceted materiality of the place I called home for twenty-seven years of life—a place known variously as East Harlem, Spanish Harlem, or El Barrio. This extended neighborhood, located on the upper northeastern corner of Manhattan in New York City, echoes through my subconscious and informs my understandings of thought and belief.

Chapter 3, "Theological Writing and the Power of Place," highlights three emphases, themes, and traits that can be clearly traced to my place beginnings in Spanish Harlem and to my experiences in and with it. I refer to these as (1) a critical social justice orientation that stays focused on matters of economic inequality; (2) a perceptible pragmatist tenor; and (3) an unequivocal Latino identification. In this way, I throw light on the placed origin and character of my thinking and writing and, more importantly, on the knowledge that resides in and is imparted by places. This chapter highlights the agential contributions of the places from which we come. My hope in doing so is to spur others to more attention to the affective agency of the physical environments we inhabit.

If asked for a categorization of what this work offers, I would begin with a word on what it is not. I don't seek to offer here a full-fledged theology of place, nor do I propose a constructive reformulation of any of the traditional themes of theology from the perspective or concept of place. There is still open room in the field of theology for both of these endeavors, but my interests are more modest and lie elsewhere for now.[6] I offer, first, a call—a call to continue to build on and to extend the work that has already begun within theology on critical place-based learning and inquiry.[7]

The call goes out to the realm of theological studies more broadly, and it is especially directed to the varied progressivist, liberationist, and justice-focused theological camps that inhabit the wide left side of the theological spectrum in the United States. Strangely enough, few works have directly

---

6. Three works that come close to offering a full-fledged theology of place in my view are Gorringe, *A Theology of the Built Environment*; Rae, *Architecture and Theology*; and Sheldrake's *The Spiritual City*.

7. For a helpful work that outlines the characteristics of critical place-based inquiry, see Eve Tuck and Marcia McKenzie, *Place in Research: Theory, Methodology, and Methods* (New York: Routledge, 2015). Three great introductory texts on place-studies are Tim Creswell, *Place: An Introduction*; Tim Edensor, Ares Kalandides, and Uma Kothari, eds., *The Routledge Handbook of Place* (New York: Routledge, 2020); and Phil Hubbard and Rob Kitchin, eds., *Key Thinkers on Space and Place* (London: SAGE Publications, 2011).

taken up matters of place as core components of their presentation in this side of the theological spectrum, and this despite the clear connections that exist between the issues of justice and of place and despite the sensibilities that exist among theological scholars in this side of the spectrum toward in-depth contextualization, materiality, and the active processes of materialization. On that account, one of the distinctive features of this work lies in its placement of the conversation of place within the bounds of U.S. liberation theology and in relation to Puerto Rican and Latino/a life in the United States, as will be seen especially in chapters 2 and 3.

On occasion, I zoom out a little bit to speak of or allude to the trans-American intellectual movement we know as liberation theology more generally; and, on other occasions, I zoom out even further to reflect on the field of theology more widely, as in chapter 1. For the most part, however, my primary reflective and discursive context for theology and matters of theological method and construction is U.S. liberation theology. On the whole, I hope, through the whole of this book, to help spread the excitement regarding the centrality of place in human experience and regarding the potential contributions of place-based studies within theology as widely as possible. This could help to draw further attention to the work that has already been done on place in theology, fostering present and future reengagement of that work as well as expansion of the conversation and further exploration of the concept of place from various perspectives and backgrounds in the field.

In addition to tendering this call, *Touched by This Place* puts forward a model of place writing in theology. It's a novel, experimental, and, in some ways, unconventional model—one that brings theology into play as a form of critical cultural approach and discourse and that combines it with personal narrative, with stories and depictions of a particular place (Spanish Harlem), with various types of writing styles, and with insights obtained from the wider fields of social theory, cultural studies, humanistic geography, environmental philosophy and epistemology, and Puerto Rican and Latinx studies. It is a particular blend no doubt and one that I wouldn't hesitate to characterize as a kind of experimental or exploratory place-writing practice. But I humbly offer it here as a model of theological place writing that highlights place and the experience of place, seeking to arouse or inspire more curiosity for the significance, agency, intelligence, and touch or influence of the vital materiality of particular places; arousing or inspiring, even, more care and affection for the particular physical, geographical places in which we live and move and have our being.

So let the exploration and explorations continue! I'll begin this one with a retelling of the day and way in which my curiosity about place was awakened, followed by a relaying of discoveries I have made about the history of my old neighborhood and the vital connections that exist between it and the character of my thinking and writing. I invite you to read on, in so doing also allowing yourself the space to reflect both on the ways in which you yourself have been touched by a place and on the effectual significance and reverberations of that touch.

• 1 •

Finding a Place for Place

We do think different thoughts in different places.
—Alberto Pérez-Gómez[1]

Ben, in the rest of our time together we will surely explore deeper and more interesting questions regarding content, thought process, sources, methodology, and the like. But I am curious, can you tell us, *where* exactly was this work born?

I still remember the question as if it were asked yesterday. It was the first one asked at my doctoral dissertation defense many years ago at Drew University. The late Ada María Isasi-Díaz, a well-known ethicist, theologian, and activist, renowned for being the original architect of mujerista theology, asked it.[2] The late Otto Maduro, a prominent Latin American sociologist of religion, and Catherine Keller, one of the most distinguished and acclaimed feminist theologians of our time, were with us. I thought I was ready for the first question. I thought I understood it.

Thinking that she was asking me about the intellectual sources of inspiration that had influenced me, I proceeded to rough out a genealogy of ideas

---

1. Alberto Pérez-Gómez, "Place and Architectural Space," in *The Intelligence of Place: Topographies and Poetics*, ed. Jeff Malpas (New York: Bloomsbury Academic, 2015), 158.

2. For the first public appearance of the term "mujerista theology," see Ada María Isasi-Díaz, "Mujeristas: A Name of Our Own*," The Christian Century* (May 24–31, 1989): 560–62. For a book-length elaboration of the traits and emphases of mujerista theology, see Isasi-Díaz, *En la Lucha/In the Struggle: Elaborating a Mujerista Theology* (Minneapolis, MN: Fortress Press, 1993), and *Mujerista Theology: A Theology for the Twenty-First Century* (Maryknoll, NY: Orbis Books, 1996).

that demonstrated my intellectual development on the subject of my dissertation. Honestly, I thought I had hit it out of the park with my response. So, I was surprised when Isasi-Díaz responded, "Ben, this is a thoughtful and helpful response. But it doesn't exactly get us to where I was hoping. Perhaps we will have the chance to come back to my question later on." We moved on, but we never did return to Isasi-Díaz's opening question; not on that day at least.

About a month later, life granted me a chance to talk with Professor Isasi-Díaz again, and, this time, we were alone. A few days before commencement at Drew, I was walking to my car in one of the university's parking lots, and I saw Isasi-Díaz struggling with her car. I approached her and offered my help, but our efforts at starting her car proved futile. I offered to drive her to her home, which wasn't too far from where I was living at the time.

The drive from Madison, New Jersey, to the Washington Heights area in New York City granted us a good fifty to sixty minutes to talk and revisit the question she had asked me at the start of my dissertation defense. What Isasi-Díaz had actually wanted to know was how my growing up in Spanish Harlem had possibly influenced my ideas and conclusions, and maybe even my choices about what to study and write about. There actually was a geographic *where* in Isasi-Díaz's question. She really was asking me about the neighborhood I had called my homeplace for much of my life and how it played into all that I had said in and through the pages of my dissertation. In short, the question had been *where* my work was born not *how* it had been born.

Isasi-Díaz knew that I was born and raised in a neighborhood of New York City known as East Harlem or Spanish Harlem or "El Barrio," which was home to the oldest and largest Puerto Rican community in the continental United States. She further knew that, after having lived for various years in other locales in the Northeast, I had returned to live in this neighborhood for the final two years of my doctoral program, during which I wrote my dissertation. Isasi-Díaz was curious as to if and how East Harlem had played any part in it.

Though she didn't use these terms, the question she posed to me the afternoon of my dissertation defense was the question of place. More precisely, it was a question about the importance and influence of places. For almost two decades, I've reflected long and hard on this complicated question. I've increasingly come to realize its salience and centrality in relation to a whole host of other topics, issues, and concerns.

That Isasi-Díaz would ask me this question about the significance of place is understandable and even predictable. She was a thinker, writer, and activist who studied experience as it is lived through questions of sociality, community, and different contexts; through human situations of struggle in the face of socioeconomic oppression; racial, cultural, and ethnic degradation; patriarchal domination; hierarchies based on sexual orientation; and the manifold manifestations of colonialist aggression. She was especially keen on what I call narrative inquiry. I have in mind her penchant for the examination of personal experience stories, shared stories, and oral stories, all in the attempt to understand how individuals and groups of people come to know, understand, and make meaning in the social world, while also making themselves known, understood, and meaningful in this world. Latinas and the experiences of Latinas in the United States were usually the focus of her work. But her concerns, methods, and conceptualizations applied more broadly. In fact, these sorts of interests, concerns, and commitments led Isasi-Díaz to experiment with the use of interviews and ethnography in her writings.[3] These research methods were mostly unheard of or overlooked when she began to write in the broad field of theological studies.

The point here is that Isasi-Díaz always showed an interest in the root or grounding details of life as she tried to understand the larger context in which thought and action occur. It is understandable that she wanted to know more about the role that Spanish Harlem may have played in the formation of my thoughts and ideas. And yet, it is also somewhat surprising that Isasi-Díaz asked me the question. It is surprising because liberation theology—the stream of theology that nourished Isasi-Díaz's thinking, vision, and praxis as well as my own—hadn't asked it.[4] It still hasn't.

The paradox residing in its inattentiveness to the issue of place deserves some consideration for what it says about how easy it is to overlook the importance and influence of places when one is considering matters of human thought, experience, identity, and belief. The paradox deserves some consideration, also, for what it says about how even the best of us or the best of our intellectual renderings can fall prey to this sort of placial[5] oversight.

---

3. For example, see Isasi-Díaz, *Hispanic Women: Prophetic Voice in the Church* (Minneapolis, MN: Fortress Press, 1992).

4. In using the term "praxis," I have in mind the interrelationship of thought and action and also the goal of principled action in support of social transformation or change. This is the broader sense in which many liberationist theologians tend to use the term, and the way in which Isasi-Díaz herself employs the term.

5. Philosopher Edward Casey has used the term "platial" as a kind of play on the term "spatial," and to give emphasis to the aspect of place and the importance of place.

All Contexted Up and No Place to Go

The word "paradox" fits here. It is paradoxical, ironic even, that an intellectual movement like liberation theology could overlook the importance of places. I say this on account of its preference and penchant for situated orientations in reflective deliberation.

One of the central aspects of this influential trans-American intellectual movement is its contextualist sensibility and approach—that is, its attentiveness to the various contexts within which individual meanings and social practices are produced, understood, and negotiated, and its willingness to examine these various contexts and to draw from them in an intentional manner.[6] This latter readiness has been especially important when or where the experiences and perspectives of marginalized and oppressed individuals and communities have been ignored, sidelined, or put down. To be sure, I wouldn't dare to distract from the most important contribution that liberation theology has made to intellectual consciousness and to the world at large, namely, its manifold contributions to the quest for justice.

For almost fifty years now, we have read or heard about this movement's strivings to root out and contend with patterns of injustice; to empower ordinary people; and to promote progressive social movements for change in different spheres of life and in different areas of the Americas.[7] It has attempted to do this while putting forward religious theories or theologies that can orient human activity toward new personal meaning, social adjustment, and political struggle in the name of greater social justice.

This intervention on behalf of the poor—on behalf of oppressed and marginalized groups and on behalf of all those who have been dehumanized

---

I prefer the term "placial," however, because it allows for a closer connection or resemblance to the word "place." For Casey's use of the term "platial," see Edward Casey, *The Fate of Place: A Philosophical History* (Berkeley: University of California Press, 1997), esp. 285–330.

6. For two works that highlight and explore the contextualist character of liberation theologies, see Angie Pears, *Doing Contextual Theology* (New York: Routledge, 2010); and Stephen B. Bevans, *Models of Contextual Theology* (Maryknoll, NY: Orbis Books, 2002), esp. 70–87.

7. For a thorough intellectual history of liberation theology, see Lilian Calles Barger, *The World Come of Age: An Intellectual History of Liberation Theology* (New York: Oxford University Press, 2018). See also Luis N. Rivera-Pagán, "God the Liberator: Theology, History, and Politics," in *In Our Own Voices: Latino/a Renditions of Theology,* ed. Benjamín Valentín (Maryknoll, NY: Orbis Books, 2010), 1–20.

on the margins of society—is liberation theology's most important offering to the world.

Even so, the advancement of a greater level of context sensitivity or context awareness in the realms of religious and theological studies is important and is centrally related to the justice-seeking venture. For example, it comes into play in that sphere of action whenever one has to uncover and protest "the disguised particularisms—the masculinism, the white-Anglo ethnocentrism, the heterosexism—lurking behind what parades as universal."[8] That such supposed universalistic claims can, at times, convey outmoded, misguided, myopic, and inaccurate information is bad enough. Sometimes, their menace can be greater. Sometimes, they convey biased, prejudiced, stereotypical, chauvinistic, and supremacist outlooks that are stunting, repressive, oppressive, disrespectful, and denigrating. So, they need to be contested and resisted whenever and wherever they appear. This, too, is part of the multifaceted quest for justice, at least in its cultural dimension or form and in relation to the struggle against harmful and unjust patterns of representation, interpretation, and communication in culture and society. For now, I am interested in the epistemological aspect of liberation theology's insistence that scholars of religion and theology pay more attention to the influence of context upon individual and communal knowledge processes.

Knowledge, thought, values, attitudes, and beliefs are always arrived at from vantage points that incorporate many dimensions of distinction or particularity—our historical context; our personal history and experiences; our race and ethnicity, economic class, gender, sexual orientation or identity; our national and cultural heritage; our religion, physical ability, and age. These are all part of our knowledge-producing, thought-engendering, meaning-making, and identity-forming vantage points. These all play a part in directing what we see, know, value, and believe. We can think of these as the epistemic locations that a person brings to his or her claims.

That knowledge claims don't simply emerge from the mind or the biological brain is the point here. As environmental philosopher Christopher Preston puts it, "Knowledge is neither hyper-pure nor alienated from the world in the glassy essence of a person's mind."[9] It is always in the world, contex-

8. Nancy Fraser, *Justice Interruptus: Critical Reflections on the "Postsocialist" Condition* (New York: Routledge, 1997), 5.

9. Christopher J. Preston, *Grounding Knowledge: Environmental Philosophy, Epistemology, and Place* (Athens: University of Georgia Press, 2003), 42.

tually located in the world, and available, then, for historical, sociological, cultural, and material analysis. Knowledge, thought, values, attitudes, and beliefs are never the products of the mind alone but always expressions of its integration and participation with the physical and sociocultural world that lies around it and with our situated and context-conditioned experiences in and with that multilayered world. With Preston, we can say that "humans blend their sense experience with their reasoning powers to form beliefs about the world"[10] and about everything they encounter within it.

The sociocultural and socioeconomic factors I mentioned before function as more than epistemic locations that influence our views of things. They also influence our experiences. One could say that the cultural factors of embodiment and the categories of social distinction just enumerated function as epistemic *and* social locations that sow the seeds for different knowledge claims and for different experiences among different groups of individuals. The experiential side of this equation is due to the existence of patterns of cultural value or status hierarchies that develop around these factors and distinctions. Societies usually establish systems of cultural value that apportion worth, power, and privilege in varying ways. In many parts of the world, and certainly here in the United States and throughout most of the Americas, this has often been based on people's race/ethnicity, class, gender, sexual orientation or identity, national and cultural ancestry, religion, ability, age, or some combination of them.

Given our recorded history with regard to detrimental proclivities and conflicted impulses, whether these be toward self-centeredness, callousness, provincialism, narrow-mindedness, chauvinism, prejudice, insecurity, gullibility, the misappropriation of human difference, or some other foible, it should not surprise us that the institutionalization of hierarchies of cultural value constructed around these factors of embodiment and social identification have transpired over time in our societies. The result has been the siring of an enormously complex system of interlocking and self-perpetuating relations of domination and subordination, of privilege and disadvantage. In everyday life, all of this simply means that people experience the world differently by reason of the impact of these cultural status hierarchies and social systems of power, privilege, and inequality. Some individuals and groups of individuals gain easier, greater, and less obstructed access to various resources, including wealth, property, and gainful employment. Their property consists of suitable accommodations for dwelling, work, and play

---

10. Preston, *Grounding Knowledge*, 3.

that are in cleaner and safer neighborhoods than others. Their employment happens in safe working environments and often provides access to quality health care. Significantly, these benefits also contribute to an unhampered voice in public deliberations, fair representation in public decision-making, and validation in public cultural representations. Others find it more difficult, even impossible, to achieve such things while also contending with recurrent instances of discrimination, denigration, exploitation, deprivation, exclusion, marginalization, misrepresentation, non-recognition, harassment, and violence or the threat of it. Context matters in many powerful, life-shaping, and life-changing ways.

This has been liberation theology's teaching from the start. "Context makes a difference" has been its lesson and warning. It matters as a matter of epistemology, seeing that our forms of knowledge, perspectives, values, attitudes, and beliefs are always context specific. And it matters in an experiential manner, since human experience always transpires in and is influenced by a network of contexts, locations, or positions based in history, economic class, race, and gender, for instance. Context matters in all of these ways. This is why liberation theology has urged scholars of religion and theology to reflect upon the dynamic wholeness of the life-world experience. It has challenged scholars of religion and theology to account for as much of the context of human life as they possibly can. This comes into play when interpreting the history, texts, ideas, convictions, and practices of the religious traditions and communities we study. This also comes into play when putting forward constructive religious theories or theologies that aspire to orient human activity toward existential empowerment and toward a more inclusive and more salutary engagement with the world at large. Liberation theology's goal all along has been the realization of a theology or discourse of location—a theology or discourse that recognizes the location of the knower and the known in relation to multiple contexts of experience, meaning, identity, power, and privilege.

Undoubtedly, this is a worthy goal, and its implementation has been influential in academia, especially in the field of theological studies. It has helped to bring our theology down to earth, so to speak, to have us deal theologically with the foibles of human life, and to challenge us to project theologically realizable possibilities in pressing predicaments of inequity here on Earth. It has also helped to keep at bay the fallacy of the "zero point epistemology" of which decolonial theorist Walter Mignolo speaks—that of assuming that thought, knowledge, and belief can be discounted from the stuff of the world and presented as universal and neutral.[11] By situating thought, knowledge, and belief in our very human experience, liberation theology has taught us that we are better off ridding ourselves of any pretense to the view from nowhere, foregrounding instead our context-related perspectives, biases, and values and then proceeding from there. Liberation theology's contextual sensibility and approach have also made us more aware of the many factors that affect daily living, all while enhancing the prospects of our being able to appreciate the difference of human beings responding to different circumstances, especially in the context of the Americas.

There is much to like with regard to liberation theology's contextualist agenda, then, but it has misplaced place. It has ignored the significance and influence of physical places, glossing over the important role that places play in shaping the configurations of our thought and experience.

If we take a closer look at the version of contextuality with which most liberation theologians work, we notice that it has mostly allowed for three forms of location, those being historical, social, and cultural location. These forms of location have rightfully been assumed to give different shape to the knowledge claims and social experiences of different groups of individuals. For this reason, liberation theologians usually consider the historical, social, and cultural contexts of individuals and communities to be in a better position to understand how these levels of situatedness influence and inform any words, texts, claims, views, and beliefs produced by them. Moreover, liberation theologians take into account their own historical, social, and cultural locations to try to be more mindful of and upfront about the factors of influence and the potential biases that filter into their work. These are important levels of situatedness to have in mind, but the matter of physical and geographical location have been missing from the equation. The recognition that "life always takes place," as geographer and environmental design expert David Seamon likes to put it, has been missing.[12]

Life always transpires in the context of particular places of dwelling, and these particular places influence life. I have in mind the actual, physical, geographical places that register in our memories and to which we have emotional and practical commitments, even if subconsciously or unperceptively at times. I'm talking about the regions, towns, villages, cities, city blocks,

---

11. See Walter D. Mignolo, *The Darker Side of Western Modernity: Global Futures, Decolonial Options* (Durham, NC: Duke University Press, 2011), 80.

12. David Seamon, *Life Takes Place: Phenomenology, Lifeworlds, and Place Making* (New York: Routledge, 2018), 1.

neighborhoods, buildings, homes, and all of the other kinds of possible material settings within which we conduct our lives and produce and consume meaning.

These meaningful material locations that we call "places" are not neutral, static backdrops to human life. They influence and shape life. They affect and have a say in the shaping of human thought, experience, memory, identity, and activity. They often affect the opportunities we are afforded or denied in social life. Every aspect of our personal and social lives is touched by, influenced by, and shaped by the broad, multilayered, multifaceted context we call place—by the particular geographical places in which we "live and move and have our being."[13]

Indeed, I will note that the factors of cultural embodiment and social identification to which liberation theologians give much importance need to be considered in relation to particular places. Class, race, gender, and ethnicity, for instance, don't materialize in a vacuum or in a conceptual bubble. They transpire in, are experienced within, and sometimes play out differently in the context of different geographical places. Places are important to our understandings of human agency in all of its dimensions and manifestations. Places are not only contextual entities but also agential entities, one could say. Hence, they should be counted among the factors of influence that affect and shape life. They should be one of those influential contexts, one of those consequential forms of location, one of those fundamental levels of situatedness.

The turn to place that I am suggesting has not taken place in liberation theology, not fully at least. Liberation theology has generally taken place for granted, looking past the formative presence of physical geographical places in people's lives. At the very least, until now, liberation theology has shown a tendency to focus more intently on "people-materialities" than on "thing-materialities."[14] Consequently, we may observe that the experiences, thoughts, histories, stories, and cultural practices tied to and generated and observed within "communities" receive considerable attention in these theologies. These human, community-based elements make up a crucial aspect

---

13. Acts 17:28; in this New Testament text, these words are used in reference to God. They operate as a kind of definition of or as a way of envisioning God. I am using them in a creative or analogical manner and in reference to the places we inhabit, on which we depend, and by which we are shaped.

14. My language here is inspired by the work of Jane Bennett. See especially Bennett, *Vibrant Matter: A Political Ecology of Things* (Durham, NC: Duke University Press, 2010), esp. vii–xix.

of "place," but this does not yet account for all of the other vital physical realities that constitute the particular physical environments in which we live, nor does it account for the contributions these environments make to human experience, subjectivity, and agency. Broader material phenomena constitute places as much as communal, ethnic, social, and cultural patterns of humanity. Basic natural factors such as air type and quality, geographic characteristics, and water are generally recognized for their contributions to the character of a place. Within these categories, trees and other plants interact with water, soil, and rocks. Local animal life, including human life, is shaped by these plant relationships. Weather patterns and broader climate factors shape and are shaped by these living creatures and nonliving features. In addition to the natural environment, myriad elements of the built environment shape the place itself and how humans interact with and in a place. Buildings, building construction, and internal and external design choices prioritize cultural and economic values. Sidewalks, paths, and roads connect persons and communities, sometimes embedding the human within the broader world and sometimes further isolating the human from the natural characteristics of places mentioned above. Signs, murals, and public art organize societal patterns, including patterns of thought and imagination. Finally, how the built environment produces, designates, and deals with waste significantly impacts the character of a place.

Furthermore, these other particular constituent elements of a "place" can be as shaping and reshaping of conscious experiences, nonconscious cognitions, thought processes, knowledge forms, feelings, identities, hopes, and beliefs as the histories, narratives, and cultural practices we can generate and put into action in a place. This coming together of the cultural and the material in a place or this blending of cultural materialism and physical materialism in a place is among the reasons why places carry much affective weight. The latter part of this equation, the side that incorporates the physical dimension of our physical environments and that includes the broader material fragments, elements, features, and aspects of the place-world[15] and of the place-world experience, has not been intimately explored and featured in the annals of the different liberation theologies.[16] This may be due to a stronger

---

15. In my use of this term, I am attempting to bring together the following: place (i.e., our constructed environments that we invest with meaning in the context of social structures and power dynamics), land, and our natural environments.

16. As noted in the book's introduction, in this critical observation, I mostly have in mind the different theologies of justice and liberation developed within the United

focus on "people-materialities," on the cultural dimension of human experience, or on the circumstances and activities of the members of human collectives in a geographical place than on the physical realities and the emplaced experiences of the physical surroundings in which those circumstances and activities are formed. As I see it, this placial oversight has left the different liberation theologies that form this stream of theology all contexted up with no place to go. It has left them stressing the importance of historical, social, and cultural location in the name of proper contextualization, all while missing out on an orienting, grounding, and salutary sense of place.

Clearly, there is a loss that can already be talked about here—the forfeiture of a fuller and more cognizant or reflective sense of place. I want to

States (e.g., Black theology of liberation, feminist theology of liberation, Latino/a theology of liberation, Asian American theology of liberation, and LGBTQIA+ theology of liberation). That said, I believe that my critical observation could be extended to include Latin American liberation theology as well, seeing that the corpus of writings that forms that stream of liberation theology displays the same tendency to pay special attention to "people materialities," to communities, and to the cultural dimension in a place as opposed to and/or independently from the experience being generated or formed by the history and materiality of a place and as opposed to and/or independently from a consideration of the physical qualities, aspects, and properties of a place and of their affective influence on the people and communities living in the place. People may bring up or wonder about the case of a work such as Ernesto Cardenal's *The Gospel in Solentiname*, often considered a classic of Latin American liberation theology, which offers a collection of dialogues and/or commentaries on the Gospels from the perspective of a group of peasants in a remote archipelago in Lake Nicaragua. But I will note that, despite the mentioning of a geographical place by name in the title and within the book, it is quite clear that the focus of this work is the agency of "the people of Solentiname." The community is the focal point in other words and not the geographic location and/or the physical place more broadly. The structural, experiential, and epistemological relevance and influence of the geographical place isn't being considered here. Consequently, the role that the complex and multiformed history and materiality of Solentiname is playing in shaping the lived experience, the cognitive processes, the knowledge, the beliefs, and the perceptual skills of the people of Solentiname isn't being put up for consideration in the work. The physical geographical place (i.e., Solentiname) remains passive in this case, and the community retains all of the perceptual and epistemic agency. Another way of putting it is that the complex, dialectical relationship that exists between agents of knowledge and the physical geographical locations in which they reside is going unnoticed in the book. This bypassing of the formative presence of physical geographical places in people's lives can be seen elsewhere and more widely in Latin American liberation theology. For this one stated example, see Ernesto Cardenal, *The Gospel in Solentiname* (Maryknoll, NY: Orbis Books, 1976).

focus on two vitiating outcomes or negative "side-effects" that result from the placial oversight that I bemoan. I begin with reference to the restricted, diminished depiction of context that results.

As I see it, the contextualist's agenda revolves around the task of situating human agency in the context of the full range of contexts that give shape to it. If that's the goal, then we would want to give some thought to such things as the variables of historical and social location; the specificity of cultural heritage; the particularities of bodies; the heterogeneity of our places of dwelling; and the different natural landscapes and environmental settings that surround us. These different but interrelated contextual connections are likely to have cognitive and experiential consequences in people's lives. For that reason, they should be taken into account when attempting to detail the different aspects of a person's context.

Our different liberation theologies have historically done well when reflecting on the difference that historical, social, and cultural contexts make. More recently, they have begun to take the materiality and agency of the human body more seriously.[17] So, bodies have, rightfully, become a context to consider. The same cannot be said for the "place-world,"[18] however, because liberation theologians haven't identified the places we create and inhabit, and the natural environments upon which we rely, as being among the epistemic and experiential contexts that can make a difference in the

---

17. For example, see Karen Baker Fletcher, *Sisters of Dust, Sisters of Spirit: Womanist Wordings on God and Creation* (Minneapolis, MN: Fortress Press, 1998); Marcella Althaus Reid, *Indecent Theology: Theological Perversions in Sex, Gender, and Politics* (London: Routledge, 2000); and Marcella Althaus Reid, *Liberation Theology and Sexuality* (Farnham, UK: Ashgate Publishing, 2006); M. Shawn Copeland, *Enfleshing Freedom: Body, Race, and Being* (Minneapolis, MN: Fortress Press, 2009); and Dwight N. Hopkins, *Black Theology: Essays on Gender Perspectives* (Eugene, OR: Cascade Books, 2017). See also the articles that appear in a volume edited by Anthony B. Pinn and Dwight N. Hopkins, *Loving the Body: Black Religious Studies and the Erotic* (New York: Palgrave Macmillan, 2004). Many of the contributors to this volume identify as liberation theologians. Although he may not identify as a liberation theologian, due to methodological differences and religious orientation, Anthony Pinn would certainly admit that he has been influenced by the vision and the justice-centered impulse of liberation theology. For that reason, I include his important work on the body here. See especially Pinn's *Embodiment and the New Shape of Black Theological Thought* (New York: NYU Press, 2010). The same is true of Mayra Rivera. Thus, I include her splendid work on this topic. See Mayra Rivera, *Poetics of the Flesh* (Durham, NC: Duke University Press, 2015).

18. Edward Casey, *Getting Back into Place: Toward a Renewed Understanding of the Place-World* (Bloomington: Indiana University Press, 2009).

realm of meaning and experience. This despite the fact that they influence how we know and live. As a result, the whole realm of our physical environment, including our built environment and our natural environment, is being left out of consideration in this process of accounting for context and subjectivity.

We're talking about place, land, and environment here. That's a rather large, primary, formative, and vibrant context to leave out of consideration. And its exclusion from a more deliberative process of reflection is a reason why we liberationists have been left to work with a narrow version of context. A more comprehensive and improved version must include the complex, multifaceted place-world.

My focus in this work happens to be on the places that we humans build, live in, and make meaningful. Neighborhoods, villages, towns, cities, and city blocks or areas: these are the kind of places in which I am interested and from which I come. We could refer to these as examples of our built environment or as the human-made material setting for the social relations I gather.

I don't ignore the importance of land and natural environments, however. I see these as integral parts of the broader place-world that deserves attention in any discussion of epistemic locations and experiential contexts. These are all interrelated and intertwined, as land, environment, and our constructed places come together to constitute a part of the singular, yet marvelously complex and multifaceted material world that envelops us and runs through and across us. We can certainly choose to focus on one or another of these facets of our place-world, be it our constructed places, or land, or the broader natural environment. We just need to bear in mind that these relate, intersect, and unite to form the material world that surrounds and acts on us. A big part of the active and affective context for meaning and experience is being left out if we ignore the realm of our physical, geographical location— if we ignore the place-world.

The placial oversight to which I'm calling attention is also implicated in another casualty: the loss of some degree of materiality. The neglect of our broader physical places of dwelling in distinction to just our "communal settings of dwelling" can be seen as a missed discursive opportunity to engage more fully with one of the material contexts that gives shape to the conditions of our everyday lives. This points us in the wrong direction since, in recent time, we have begun to recognize and to open up to "the vital materialities that flow through and around us."[19] Thanks to the work of theorists

---

19. Bennett, *Vibrant Matter*, x.

in the natural sciences, the humanities, and the social sciences since around the late 1990s, we have witnessed a greater level of interest in the analysis of our daily interactions with the materiality of the world, including its social and natural forms.[20]

It's not news that we humans inhabit a material world, that we live our everyday lives surrounded by and immersed in matter, and that we ourselves are made of matter. Our growing recognition that agency arises as the effect of manifold ad hoc configurations of human and nonhuman material forces or that processes of materialization bear upon the nature of life and experience is relatively new, however. Increasingly, we are recognizing that, "at every turn, we encounter physical objects fashioned by human design and endure natural forces whose imperatives structure our daily routines for survival."[21] Diana Coole and Samantha Frost capture something of this vital materiality when they note that

> Our existence depends from one moment to the next on myriad micro-organisms and diverse higher species, on our own hazily understood bodily and cellular reactions and on pitiless cosmic motions, on the material artifacts and natural stuff that populate our environment, as well as on socioeconomic structures that produce and reproduce the conditions of our everyday lives.[22]

In this case, we can highlight or add that places are a part of the vital materiality on which we depend, in which we have a hand, and by which we

---

20. Worth noting here is the work of the so-called new materialists, spearheaded by thinkers such as Karen Barad, Rosi Braidotti, Elizabeth Grosz, Jane Bennett, Vicki Kirby, Manuel DeLanda, Nick Fox, Pam Alldred, Diana Coole, and Samantha Frost. See Karan Barad, *Meeting the Universe Halfway: Quantum Physics and the Entanglement of Matter and Meaning* (Durham, NC: Duke University Press, 2007); Rosi Braidotti, *Posthuman Knowledge* (Cambridge, UK: Polity Press, 2019); Elizabeth Grosz, *The Incorporeal: Ontology, Ethics, and the Limits of Materialism* (New York: Columbia University Press, 2018); Bennett, *Vibrant Matter*; Vicki Kirby, *Quantum Anthropologies: Life at Large* (Durham, NC: Duke University Press, 2011); Manuel DeLanda, *Materialist Phenomenology: A Philosophy of Perception* (New York: Bloomsbury Academic, 2021); Nick Fox and Pam Alldred, *Sociology and the New Materialism: Theory, Research, Action* (London: SAGE Publications, 2017); and Diana Coole and Samantha Frost, eds., *New Materialisms: Ontology, Agency, and Politics* (Durham, NC: Duke University Press, 2010).

21. Coole and Frost, *New Materialisms*, 1.

22. Coole and Frost, *New Materialisms*, 1.

are affected. They are a big part of it, both as the material settings for a multiplicity of natural and social interactions and as a material force affecting situations and events. To inquire into the nature, particularity, and agency of these places—the places in which we live and carry out our lives—would allow our discourses to delve deeper into the material world we inhabit, with which we interact, and to which we contribute. The alternative is the delivery of discourses that are light in the areas of physicality, materiality, and concreteness. On top of the measure of contextuality that is being lost in the case of placial oversight, I think that this is quite a lot to risk or surrender. But I fear that this has already happened in liberation theology.

Such a risk, let alone a possible surrender, is ironic for one wouldn't expect a discursive tradition that makes much of context, location, experience, and situated orientations to misplace one of the more important and influential contexts of human thought and experience—the place-world of all things. But if a theological movement that has been so alert to the influence of context can overlook the salience and agency of places, we can expect other streams of theology to be doing the same.

And, sure enough, placial oversight looms in other sectors of the theological realm, including among the varied progressivist theologies that span the wide left side of the theological spectrum in the United States. The scattering of theological works that have taken up matters of place as core components of their presentation have not come from this side of the theological spectrum, though, puzzlingly, calls for a reappraisal of material reality and material causality have been coming mostly from this "left" side of the expanse. One could suppose that theologians who have been influenced by the recent new materialist turn in academia, emphasizing the active processes of materialization in their works, would want to attend to the saliency and agency of places and to the ineluctable placial dimension of existence. But this hasn't been the case.

This placial inattention could be affixed to the field of theology more generally. As noted previously, although we have seen the emergence of a steadier stream of monographs and other writings that explore this general subject matter in the field since the early 2000s, we can't say yet that there has been a large-scale influx of writings that focus directly on the concept and issue of place in the field of theology. We might call it a scattering or an appreciable number perhaps, but not quite a great influx as of yet.[23] Theological studies needs more consideration of the place-world.

---

23. For works in the field of theology that deal specifically with the concept and

Why has this topic been passed over, spared, or undersold by theologians? Well, for one, the most obvious things can be the hardest ones to see. Places seem to have become transparent to us. Because we are regularly immersed in them and are always surrounded by them, and because we repeatedly walk over and through them, we, generally, do not take notice of them. We take them for granted, basically. Every once in a while, something may happen that forces us to take notice of our places of dwelling. For example, extreme weather events like hurricanes, storms, floods, earthquakes, tornadoes, and fires can bring attention to the importance of place when we are forced to reckon with the devastation of particular places or when we or other people are uprooted from environments made up of meaningful places as a result of these kinds of events. In cases like these, we may mourn the loss, destruction, or the damaging of locales that we or other people have made meaningful. We may come to miss them, too, if we are uprooted from them or can't return to them for some length of time. Right there and then, we may awaken to the reality, gravity, beauty, and love of place. Having to or choosing to move from one place to another, be it from one country, city, region, town, or home to another, can also trigger a recognition of place, especially if or when we come to miss something about a former dwelling place or have to adjust to different patterns of life in a new place of living. Sometimes, a simple slowdown in our pace of life can bring about the same thing. In other cases, shifting to cycling or walking instead of driving to get around a particular place, or choosing to exercise by way of jogging or a brisk walk through a neighborhood instead of on a treadmill or an elliptical machine in a gym, can trigger a recognition of place.

Pattern changes like these can bring us to recognize the physical reality of a place in a new way or for the first time. All of a sudden, we may find that we are moved to recognize the sights, sounds, textures, rhythms, and smells of a place. Most of the time, however, we take places for granted as daily living proceeds matter-of-factly and uneventfully, and they end up receding into

---

issue of place, see the titles I mention in n. 2 of this book's introduction. There are works that take up the matter of land in relation to biblical studies. One of Walter Brueggeman's works comes to mind here: *The Land: Place as Gift, Promise, and Challenge in Biblical Faith* (Minneapolis, MN: Fortress Press, 2002). And there are other works that focus specifically on the concept of "sacred space and/or sacred places." These works are rooted either in the field of biblical studies or in the field of religious studies and spirituality. They aren't rooted in the field of theology or theological studies per se. Hence, it is mostly the thirteen works I mentioned in the introduction that can be seen as book-length works on theology and place at this time.

the background, like the scenery in a play. We who get paid to think about things are not immune to these sorts of oversight.

In like manner, we should not underestimate the effect that long-standing disciplinary habits and patterns can have on a course of study. In this case, I am thinking about theology's documented practice of focusing on figures and events. The writings of figures and the religious practices of communities have, historically, registered high on the list of this regimented study. On the whole, the focus of study in theology has remained on these four things: figures, events, writings, and practices.

At some level of consciousness, we who study theology know that these figures, events, writings, and practices emerged, developed, and took place in particular places. We even intuit that places played a role in their existence, eventuation, and development. And yet, even with these inklings, those places are rarely featured in the articles, reports, and books that emerge from the study of these figures, events, writings, and practices. It is as if the myopic reflex of human agency and history has become so ingrained in our field that it causes us to skim over or to completely pass over the agential contributions of places in people's lives, thoughts, and practices.

The influence of the broader Western intellectual tradition is evident here. Philosopher Edward Casey has written extensively about the idea of place in the history of Western philosophy or more specifically its gradual disappearance.[24] In his book *The Fate of Place*, Casey relates that, in the wake of classical antiquity, the idea of place began to be submerged under a rise in thought about the concept of space.[25] From the High Middle Ages onward, Western thinkers became increasingly enchanted with notions of the absolute and the infinite and with ideas about the immense and the indefinitely extended. Consequently, the concept of space became attractive to them and, then, proceeded from there to take on the aspect of the final, or the ultimate, and most desired frontier of wonder and regard.

Things only grew worse, becoming more complicated for the idea of place over time, as Western thinkers ventured on another long-term love affair in the modern period. The object or topic of their affection this time was time itself. And, just like that, place found itself far down in the hierarchy of topics of interest. Space and time, it would mostly be among Western thinkers and writers, with place struggling to garner their attention.

In retrospect, place stood little chance against the charms of space and

---

24. See especially Casey, *The Fate of Place* and *Getting Back into Place*.
25. Casey, *The Fate of Place*, esp. ix–xv and 75–193.

time in the context of the High Middle Ages and throughout the period of modernity particularly. On account of its being associated with impressions of introverted particularity, static identity, finite historicity, and hum-drum, circumscribed locality, place found it difficult to remain attractive to thinkers who were showing a growing fondness for the notions of transcendence, infinitude, and boundlessness. Of course, place is much more than boundedness.

Places are always relational, prospectively open, and changing entities marked by a mixture of wider and more local social and material relations, involving the human world and the broader physical world.[26] Places are complex sites that gather elements from a world that lies at once beyond them and yet also within them; interesting sites that are made up of "constantly evolving networks which are social, cultural, and natural/environmental."[27] They can even be thought of as wondrous and surprising events in the sense that they are a product of manifold objects and wide-ranging relationships, processes, and practices all coming together and taking form in a specific physical locale over time. They are never truly complete, finished, or static but are always becoming or in process.[28] In short, place does not equal narrow provincialism, rigid rootedness, and static or fixed essence, though it was perceived like this. And this perception or misrepresentation had much to do with a thinking process that had taken root by the time of the High Middle Ages.

The thinking process in the High Middle Ages retained much of the broader direction that prevailed in the later stages of the Hellenistic world (approx. 200 BCE to 400 CE). In particular, it held onto an unfavorable interpretation of human history and the material world and onto the goal

---

26. I am influenced here by the work of Doreen Massey. See Massey, *Space, Place, and Gender* (Minneapolis: University of Minnesota Press, 1994), and *For Space* (London: SAGE, 2005), esp. 130–76.

27. Tim Creswell, *Place: An Introduction* (Malden, MA: Wiley Blackwell, 2015), 75.

28. For more on this point and on this more dynamic way of viewing places, see Allan Pred, "Place as Historically Contingent Process: Structuration and the Time-Geography of Becoming Places," *Annals of the Association of American Geographers* 74 (1984): 279–97; Massey, *Space, Place, and Gender*; Nigel Thrift, "Inhuman Geographies: Landscapes of Speed, Light, and Power," in *Writing the Rural: Five Cultural Geographies,* ed. Paul J. Cloke and Marcus A. Doel (London: SAGE, 1994), 191–248; Nigel Thrift, *Non-Representational Theory: Space, Politics, Affect* (New York: Routledge, 2007); and Arturo Escobar, "Culture Sits in Places: Reflections on Globalism and Subaltern Strategies of Localization," *Political Geography* 20 (2001): 139–74.

of discovering a transcendent realm of value and reality that escaped the vagaries and finiteness of human life and the limiting and changing circumstances of the tangible world. During this period, the material world was seen as susceptible to change and deterioration, and human life and history were understood as uncertain and finite. Understandably, in face of this wider intellectual and cultural perception, thinkers of the High Middle Ages carried on with the long-standing goal of setting forth a theory of reality and knowledge based on notions of a changeless, transcendent, eternal realm that preceded and was superior to the temporal and empirically visible world. The inclination, in other words, was toward notions of immutability, transcendence, and eternity. This set the stage for the eventual interest in space by reason of its association with the features of otherness, constancy, vastness, undelimitable outspread, and seeming endlessness.

The fascination grew deeper in the modern era, with such things as scientific discovery, the birth of modern scientific discourse, a yearning for exploration, and the gravitation toward abstract and universalistic ways of thinking all contributing to "an ever-lengthening shadow of preoccupation with space" and an eclipsing of concern for place.[29] A new-fashioned interest in time also emerged with the development of modernism that would add to the latter effect. Philosophical considerations played a part—owing to the analytical conclusions put forth by such influential thinkers and writers as William Gilbert, Pierre Gassandi, Gottfried Wilhelm Leibniz, Isaac Newton, and Immanuel Kant, among others—as did some practical considerations—such as the invention of the marine chronometer to determine longitude by means of celestial navigation, and the wide availability of the mechanical clock toward the end of the eighteenth century.[30] By the end of the eighteenth century, it was already clear that time had come to be conceived of as the fundamental viable parameter in physical processes. As theologian John Inge notes, everything else was "made subservient to it, beginning with place and ending with space."[31] Still, even with the gravitation toward this kind of "temporocentrism" in the modern era, space remained in the picture. Place was put on the back burner. In philosophy, physics, theology, academia more generally, and in our daily lives, time and space became the dominant categories in discussions of reality.

29. Casey, *The Fate of Place*, 77.
30. For a treatment of the thought of these modern thinkers in relation to the concept of place, see Casey, *The Fate of Place*, esp. 103–79.
31. Inge, *A Christian Theology of Place*, 9.

This space-time obsession is so deeply rooted in our society's dominant culture now that it shows up in many aspects of our common way of life, including popular Hollywood movies and television shows. For example, eight major motion picture productions centering on a space theme were released in 2018 alone.[32] Likewise, films and television shows about time travel have also been popular.[33] This suggests that the space-time motif has captured the attention of Hollywood. Since many of these movies and television shows have enjoyed either box office or ratings-related success, this motif has taken the fancy of the American public more broadly as well.

The space-time infatuation shows up in our advertisements, feature writing, and common speech forms. For example, recently, while searching for a guitar-effects pedal online, I ran across an interesting advertisement for a reverb-effect unit called "The Omni Reverb." After heralding how much reverb contributes to the feel of music, the advertisement declared in the third and fourth sentences: "Space . . . time. The most central elements of reality!" Similarly, in an article meant to gauge the market value of baseball player Marwin Gonzalez in the 2018–2019 position-player free-agent

---

32. *Maze Runner: The Death Cure, The Beyond, Annihilation, Cloverfield 3, Avengers: Infinity War, Black Panther, Solo: A Star Wars Story*, and *Predator*. If we extended our scope by only twenty years, the list would be seemingly endless and include such titles as *Avatar* (2009), *SGU Stargate Universe* (2009), *Transformers: Dark of the Moon* (2011), *Prometheus* (2012), *Starship Troopers: Invasion* (2012), *Total Recall I* (2012), *Lockout* (2012), *Ender's Game* (2013), *Oblivion* (2013), *Elysium* (2013), *Gravity* (2013), *Star Trek: Into Darkness* (2013), *Space Station 76* (2014), *Interstellar* (2014), *Guardians of the Galaxy* (2014), *The Martian* (2015), *Star Wars: The Force Awakens* (2015), *Rogue One: A Star Wars Story* (2016), *10 Cloverfield Lane* (2016), *Hidden Figures* (2016), *Star Trek Beyond* (2016), *Salyut-7* (2017), *Geostorm* (2017), and *Life* (2017). Popular space-themed television shows in a similar time frame include *Nightflyers* (2018), *Lost in Space* (2018), *Final Space* (2018), *The Orville* (2017), *Star Trek: Discovery* (2017), *Voltron: Legendary Defender* (2016), *Cosmos: A Space-Time Odyssey* (2014), *The 100* (2014), *Extant* (2014), *Rick and Morty* (2013), *Defying Gravity* (2009), *Flash Gordon* (2007), and *Eureka* (2006).

33. Film titles include *A Wrinkle in Time* (2018), *Doctor Strange* (2016), *Arrival* (2016), *Project Almanac* (2015), *Edge of Tomorrow* (2014), *X-Men: Days of Future Past* (2014), *Predestination* (2014), *About Time* (2013), *Looper* (2012), *Men in Black III* (2012), *Safety Not Guaranteed* (2012), *Midnight in Paris* (2011), *Source Code* (2011), *Hot Tube Machine* (2010), and *The Time Traveler's Wife* (2009). Television shows include *Future Man* (2017), *DC's Legends of Tomorrow* (2016), *Frequency* (2016), *Travelers* (2016), *Timeless* (2016), *11.22.63* (2016), *12 Monkeys* (2015), *Outlander* (2014), *The Flash* (2014), *Continuum* (2012), *Terra Nova* (2011), *Flash Forward* (2009), and *Terminator: The Sarah Connor Chronicles* (2008).

class, sportswriter Mike Petriello ended a syndicated column with these words: "Gonzalez couldn't be hitting free agency at a better time. He might just be the perfect free agent for this particular time and space in the baseball universe."[34] Even in baseball reporting, space and time reign supreme. Finally, common parlance examples abound. We frequently hear, "We live in space," which is a rather curious or imprecise statement given that we don't actually live in space but in places.[35] We speak of "time frames," "timelines," and "Father Time." "Time will tell" and "time after time" are other common refrains.[36] Statements like "I have no time for this," "I have time on my mind," and "I have all the time in the world" demonstrate an imagined possession of time. On occasion, we use expressions like "my time with him/her was too short," associating time with life.

These are all well-known, commonly used expressions that revolve around the notions of time and space. And, yes, it is true that the term "place" finds its way into some of our colloquialisms, but this doesn't happen anywhere near as frequently as in the case of "space" and, especially, "time." Furthermore, our lives are often grasped and ordered in terms of time. "Scheduled and overscheduled, we look to the clock or the calendar for guidance and solace, even judgment!"[37] But, as Edward Casey notes, "such time-telling offers precious little guidance, no solace whatsoever, and a predominantly negative judgment ('it's too late now')."[38] These examples show that in our prevailing Western intellectual traditions and in our wider cultural perceptions, the idea of place has tended to take a back seat to the concepts of space and time. This predilection has taken root in the field of theological studies.

The more recent move toward the linguistic and discursive emphases of post-structuralism and constructivism in theology, in which theologians have turned their attention to linguistic analyses and to social constructionist models all in an attempt to examine the role of culture, discourse, and

---

34. Mike Petriello, "This Free Agent Is Perfect for Today's Game: Gonzalez Plays Five Spots, Hit like Machado in 2017–2018," MLB.com, October 24, 2018.

35. Depending on one's definition of space, it might be more precise to say that we don't "only" live in space but in particular and meaningful places as well. For more on the matter of life in places rather than in space, see James J. Gibson, *The Ecological Approach to Visual Perception* (New York: Taylor & Francis, 2014), esp. 28–38, and Casey, *Getting Back into Place*, esp. ix–xvii.

36. I am referring to the popular song sung by singer-songwriter Cyndi Lauper, "Time after Time," from her debut studio album titled *She's So Unusual* (1983).

37. Casey, *Getting Back into Place*, 7.

38. Casey, *Getting Back into Place*, 7.

language in the constitution of social reality, could also be at work in the evasion of place. This linguistic and constructivist trend has been productive for theology, yet the privileging of textuality and cultural interpretation has distracted us from a deeper intellectual engagement with the substantiality of the material world.

In some cases, the issue seems to be that the materiality of the world is overlooked by reason of an exclusive focus on the textual, the linguistic, and the discursive. Occasionally, however, we can encounter writings that seem to imply that the real (i.e., the material) is entirely constituted by language. They suggest that "what we call the real is a product of language and has its reality only in language."[39] In these cases, the materiality of the world is not being overlooked so much as being reduced in analytical importance, at least in the sense that what is being implied is that our concern shouldn't be with the kinds of things that exist but with how these things can be known by an observer. Here, epistemology is winning out over ontology, abstraction over attention to lived experience, corporal practices, and physical substance. It suggests that we should step away from ontological concerns to focus upon how knowledge of the social world may be gained.

In other cases, the problem isn't one of oversight or slight but one of unnecessary dichotomous insinuation. In these cases, the issue is that material reality is spoken of as if it were a realm entirely separate from that of language, discourse, and culture. The work being done by new materialist scholars is helping to correct some of these oversights and inadvertent binaries, but there is still much work to be done in these areas, especially within the field of theology. It is time for a deeper consideration of the raw material, material landscapes, and the tangible relations of structure and agency that are a part of place.

I note two other factors. First, things like land, water, and the environment haven't been prioritized in Western thinking and practice. We give importance to the natural and land-based aspects of place when ownership of land, or a home, or some real estate is being considered. Consequently, our relationship to land is all too often reduced to economics, one of an owner to property; we frequently treat natural materials as external objects of labor to be worked up as commodities. We also treat them as external objects to be consumed with abandon, and we often display little or hesitant concern over the razing, ruining, and polluting of land, water, and the environment.

Second, we have a false sense of human independence and separation

---

39. Stacy Alaimo and Susan Hekman, *Material Feminisms*, ed. Stacy Alaimo and Susan Hekman (Bloomington: Indiana University Press, 2008), 2.

from nature. Consequently, we have an objectifying and reductionist view of nature; we value profits and earnings above all else, no matter what's at stake; and we tend to disregard the natural and land-based aspects of place. It is true that places are made up of and are constituted by more than just these sorts of natural, physical features. Places also have to do with experiences, histories, memories, stories, reiterative social practices, and dynamics of cultural, political, and economic power relations carried out at the local, national, and even global levels. But places almost always have a concrete form that incorporates a physical, land-based, and environmental dimension. Perhaps our deprioritizing of these kinds of things or entities has contributed to the obfuscation of place.

Furthermore, we have a tendency to view places as passive or inert entities rather than as agents. As Allan Pred rightly notes, they then become "little more than frozen scenes for human activity."[40] Or to put it in slightly different terms, they become static backdrops for personal and social life. This view, however, misses out on all of the ways in which places manifest agentic capacities. Places are one of several parties operating in the complex set of interactions out of which knowledge; ways of thinking, being, and living; and identities are constructed. Places act as quasi agents or as forces with affective and life-shaping power; as actants, not as neutral backdrops.

Finally, many current processes are making it more difficult for people to feel connected to the world through place. A combination of trends toward globalization, cyber and virtual-reality technologies, mass communication, increased mobility, and a consumer society has, at times, been blamed for an increasing homogenization or "flattening" of the world and for the erosion of a sense of place in many of our current societies in parts of the world.[41] Additionally, more of our lives are taking place in "spaces that could be anywhere—that look, feel, sound, and smell the same wherever in the globe we may be."[42] For instance, fast food outlets, supermarkets, shopping malls, airports, highways, multiplex cinemas, and big-chain hotels frequently tend to

---

40. Pred, "Place as Historically Contingent Process," 279–97.

41. For more on this topic, see the work of Marc Augé, *Non-Places: Introduction to an Anthropology of Supermodernity* (London: Verso, 1996); Edward Relph, *Place and Placelessness* (London: Pion, 1996); Jean Baudrillard, *America*, trans. C. Turner (London: Verso, 1988); Jean Baudrillard, *The System of Objects*, trans. J. Benedict (London: Verso, 1996); Zygmunt Bauman, *Globalization: The Human Consequences* (New York: Columbia University Press, 1998); and Zygmunt Bauman, *Liquid Modernities* (Cambridge, UK: Polity Press, 2000).

42. Cresswell, *Place: An Introduction*, 75.

look and feel the same wherever we go. Local place, it might seem, is being obliterated by global space.

Local ways of life and place identities are being undermined by the processes of globalization and by a standardized repertoire of architectural ambiance, consumer goods, images, and lifestyles worldwide. And this says nothing yet of the increasing experience of migration, whether forced or chosen, due to economic restructuring, labor market dynamics, the changing nature of work in advanced capitalist economies, the loss of jobs, poverty, war, political unrest, and ecological or environmental devastation, among other things. Trends like these may make it seem as if real-world places are under threat and as if they are becoming less important than they used to be. And they could make it seem as if a sense of place is becoming irrelevant, obsolete, or less important. Nothing could be further from the truth, however. Place remains as important as ever; in some ways, it is an even more important issue than ever before.

Some disciplines and realms of business and conversation have rightfully recognized this. Since the 1970s, place has increased in prominence in cultural and/or humanistic geography, architectural theory, history, sociology, spirituality, literary theory, cultural studies, race and ethnic studies, Indigenous and decolonizing scholarship, legal theory, political science, anthropology, feminist and women's studies, urban studies and the study of cities more generally, environmental studies, and psychology, among other fields or disciplines. The topic has even made inroads in Continental philosophy and in discussions of epistemology. In fact, some academics use the term placial/spatial studies to speak of the increasing awareness of place that has been emerging across the different academic disciplines in the last few decades.

Not only academics have been giving more attention to the salience of place. Artists, creative writers, activists, and grassroots organizers have been grappling with place too. Tim Cresswell points out some other ways in which place and the theme of place are being engaged, noting that place has entered the lexicon of businesses that use geographic information systems (GIS); that politicians often want to know about place to finely target their funds at swing voters; that supermarkets and online vendors and companies want to know the places we turn up in to determine potential shopping habits so they can push us to buy both more items and more expensive items; that police forces, security services, and insurance agencies want to know about the links between crime and place so that they can more effectively discipline, survey, and determine insurance rates; and that phone and computer applications like Google Maps purport to tell us about places around us in objective ways but, in fact, are always filtering place for us—directing us toward businesses that have engineered their appearance on the first page of a Google search.[43] More attention + greater visibility = greater profits.

So, why has theology been rather lukewarm toward the topic of place? Why is it missing, or not making the most of, the opportunity to engage with one of the most pressing topics of our time?

Place Matters

Place does matter—a great deal actually, and in a whole host of ways. I have already hinted at some of the ways in which it matters, but we are better positioned now to explore this point more in depth and with further detail, to explore why and how place, places, and place experiences matter. By now, it should be clear that my interest lies mostly with particular places and, therefore, with the experiential features of place and with the lived aspects of place. In other words, my focus on place verges on a concern with actual places in the world and with the significance of these palpable places in human life more so than on a concern with place as a philosophical idea or concept. Still, even though they can be distinguished for analytical purposes, we should not be confronted with an either/or choice between these two different approaches to place. Maybe they can be seen as different but interrelated dimensions of place or as different but interrelated approaches to place, with the first granting us an example of a concern with how place matters in everyday experience and the second a concern with how place matters more abstractly or comprehensively in philosophical analysis and in relation to questions regarding the nature of existence or being as such.

In fact, even though the places I am interested in are the immediate, palpable, sensed, and constantly changing locales of everyday life, I am going to begin my inventory of why and how place matters with a word about the significance of place as an ontological phenomenon—with a word about the significance of the idea or concept of place more generally. I follow that with a brief consideration of five other reasons for why place matters. My selective list is anything but comprehensive. It isn't meant to be. My aim here is simply to highlight some of the vital ways in which place, places, and place experiences matter.

---

43. See Cresswell, *Place: An Introduction*, esp. 2–3.

Place as Ontological Phenomenon

Any declaration of the importance of place should begin with an acknowledgment of how place is integral to the very structure and possibility of experience and of existence itself. Beginning this listing with an asseveration that has received much accentuation among philosophers of place—that is, with recognition of the fact that place matters as an ontological phenomenon—is fitting. After all, place is important as a central and meaningful component in human life and as a primary basis for existence. In fact, human life is impossible without place inasmuch as life always requires emplacement in the world. Philosopher Martin Heidegger underscored this fact of existence by means of the term *Dasein*, meaning "being-there" or existence more broadly.[44] His basic point was that being (i.e., existence/life) is always fashioned, produced, experienced, and expressed in and through particular places. We don't simply exist. We always exist *some-where*. As embodied beings, we require places in which to exist.

Place is a primary existential basis, a fundamental structure, and a necessary material condition for human life. This is true of all things that exist in the world, be they objects or events. There cannot be such a thing as a non-placial or non-placed entity or event. Everything that exists or transpires requires a place in which to be, a place that situates it and that allows it to come into being, to happen, to appear, to occur, to materialize, to become, or to unfold. To be is to be in place, quite literally and inescapably. As Edward Casey notes, this means that, "far from being merely locatory or situational, place belongs to the very concept of existence."[45] This *placial* business is serious business, then, involving a crucial—and maybe even an essential—element or characteristic of the human condition and, over and above that, the fundamental or primary basis of existence for anything that exists.

Place and Senses of Identity

As noted before, I believe that any declaration of the importance of place should begin with an acknowledgment of how place is integral to the very structure and possibility not only of experience but of existence itself. But since I have mentioned experience, a good second point to underline now is that places provide us with a sense of who we are. Much of our sense of iden-

---

44. See Martin Heidegger, *Being and Time*, trans. John Macquarrie and Edward Robinson (New York: Harper & Row, 1962).

45. Casey, *Getting Back into Place*, 15.

tity is derived from or mediated through the actual places we inhabit—their locations, their topography or natural landscapes, their patterns of weather, their associated histories, meanings, and practices, their demographics, and so forth. This placial particularity shapes our sense of self—our idiosyncratic characteristics or personality traits; our likes and dislikes; our preferences; our sensibilities, values, and ideals; our attitudes and/or behavioral dispositions; the way we look at ourselves; and our relationship to the world. These are the factors associated with self-identity, and they are the ones I quickly wish to consider in relation to places.

The correlation between self-identity and place is clearly revealed in the common conversational patterns of getting to know new people. We often ask one another on first meeting, "Where are you from?" or "Where do you come from?" "From Hopkinsville, Kentucky"; "from the Upper East Side [of Manhattan]"; "from El Paso, Texas"; or "from the Midwest," we might say, revealing something about how our self-identity is tied to a place and to our active engagement in and with that place. And whether the place we name is a town, a city, a neighborhood, a state, or a region more generally, the point remains that our self-identity is routinely worked out in relation to the places in which we live.

The places from which we hail or where we were born, raised, and first socialized tend to be especially consequential, and for good reason, too. Usually, in these places, we first learn how to be members of society more generally. We learn a certain set of traits and behaviors in the places from which we hail, from how to speak, walk, dress, and eat, to whom we should trust. Our cultural roots and sensibilities ordinarily begin to form or take shape in the places from which we come originally, but these aren't the only places that can leave a mark on us. Our self-identity and self-conceptualization can be worked out in places in which we lived for an extended period of time, or places where we lived through a salient experience, whether good or bad. Our being and development are also tied to and shaped by places of different scale: a building, the corner of a favorite room, a garden with particular plants and soil, a ship. These sorts of places, and other kinds of places, can shape our sense of self, which, to various degrees, is always fluid, open, and developing.

To be sure, it is important not to reduce self-identity to a simple identification of person with place. Places are part of a relationship of identity-informing and identity-forming factors that also include race/ethnicity, family heritage, cultural inheritance, gender, sexuality, social or economic class, religion, physical ability, nationality, citizen or immigrant status, age, and historical context, among other things. Moreover, places influence but do not determine our identity formation. Within certain bounds, we humans are free to operate with a considerable degree of autonomy, and we can, therefore, choose to make and remake our identities in many possible ways and in the light of the input of a whole host of experiences, social locations, and cultural and physical environments. Yet places undeniably exert an influence over our sense of self and not just incidentally or neutrally so. The distinct sensory stimuli, experiences, practices, values, and meanings to which we are exposed in particular places work their way into our sense of identity, attaching to us and becoming a part of who we are, whether subtly so or deliberately embraced.

The very physical environments of the places in which we dwell shape us. Whether we grew up in or spent some time placed in or in close proximity to glacial outwash plains, arid hillsides and valleys peopled with creekside cottonwood trees, steep slopes and green or brownish mountains, oceans and beach areas, swamps and mangroves, or the concrete- and asphalt-covered jungle in a city or metropolitan area so much part of my childhood and youth: these kinds of things, these material aspects of place, are likely to make a difference in who we are or become. They afford distinctive physical challenges and opportunities, provide distinctive experiences, and have some sort of identity-shaping significance. Add to this the consequence or power of the cultural and social features of place—the histories, narratives, practices, norms, and meanings associated with places—and you have the makings of a cogent force capable of shaping our identities.[46]

There are many illustrations I could use to highlight this point, but I lean on one from bell hooks, known to many of us as one of the most influential creative writers and cultural critics of our time. In *Belonging*, hooks reflects both on her decision to return to Kentucky to live and on the imprint that her hometown and native place of Hopkinsville, Kentucky, left on her identity.[47] She notes that the motivation to write on the subject of place and the influence of place came from the many times she had been asked to explain, when interviewed, how she became the writer she was. All of the writing

---

46. Cultural geographer David Sack suggests that places work in a complex fashion to draw together social processes, cultural practices and meanings, and physical/environmental features. Moreover, he suggests that it is the very fact that places combine these three realms that allows them to be so consequential and influential with regard to the process of identity construction. See Sack, *Homo Geographicus: A Framework for Action, Awareness, and Moral Concern* (Baltimore, MD: Johns Hopkins University Press, 1997), esp. 127–52.

47. See bell hooks, *Belonging: A Culture of Place* (New York: Routledge, 2008).

she had previously done carried and conveyed the particular flavor of the environment in which she grew up in the rural hills of Kentucky. hooks thought so, at least. And yet, for some reason or another, the vital connection between the region of her upbringing and the character of her writings had gone mostly unnoticed. Hoping to make it more obvious, hooks undertook the task of reflecting on the relation between these, the result being this wonderful work of self-discovery that uncovers the potency of place especially with regard to the matter of self-conception and self-identity.

Her discoveries regarding the connections that exist between her experiences in and with place growing up in the Kentucky backwoods and her self-conception and self-identity are considerable and instructive. She determined that all her identity-defining personality traits could be traced back to her place beginnings—her eccentric sensibility; her appreciation for nature and sense of humility in relation to nature's power; her sense of community and valuing of fellowship; her preference to live in places where she can walk, talk, and interact with others on a daily basis, and where neighbors are more likely to want to do the same; her high regard for truth-telling and the oppositional value system she has observed in order to develop a survivalist will and to abet strategies of resistance that can be life enhancing in the face of such things as white supremacy, segregationalist policies, and racism. The physical, cultural, and social features of her hometown of Hopkinsville were in the group of several parties operating in the complex set of interactions out of which her self-conception and self-identity were formed. Particular place-based entities worked on her perception and sensibility, on her sense of awe and wonder, helping to shape her appreciation for and respect for nature: the lushness of the landscape; the waterfall at Blue Lake; the caves and the trails left by the displaced Cherokee peoples; the huge fields of tobacco; the horses that make the Kentucky bluegrass a field of enchantment; the snakes, wildcats, and hazardous plants she came to know in her childhood. Even the architecture of her home place—like the porches of the homes in her hometown neighborhood—contributed something to her appreciation for and valuing of cordiality and fraternization.

For hooks, the cultural ethos of the Kentucky backwoods, particularly of the country folk who were her ancestors and kin, played a role in her gravitation toward a truth valuing and anarchist mindset. "Truth was central to their resisting anarchist mindset, their rebellion against established norms," hooks recalls.[48] Moreover, "they prided themselves on their ability to cut

---

48. hooks, *Belonging*, 171.

through the false and the fake to find the real authentic treasure," she says.[49] This mindset and ability were indispensable for such Black folk given the dysfunctional social aspect of the Southern world, particularly with regard to institutionalized racism and the internalization of this racism by many of those forced to endure it.

In the process of reflecting on the matter of place beginnings and place connections, hooks discovers that much of her sense of identity has derived from her Kentucky hometown. Hopkinsville constitutes an important part of who she is, and the discovery brings hooks to a weighty conclusion. "Geography more so than any other factor shaped my destiny," she declares toward the end of her book.[50]

Place and Products of the Mind

It is entirely possible that some of us may not be willing to go that far, that we may not be ready to announce that the places from which we come or the places we inhabit are the most influential factor or power in our lives and identities. Still, we cannot deny that the places where we were born and grew up, where we live now, and the places where we have had particularly moving experiences are a vital source of our sense of identity. Philosopher Jeff Malpas rightly notes that "the stuff of our inner lives is to be found in the outer places in which we dwell" and that those places without are always incorporated within us one way or another.[51]

On this matter of the stuff of our inner lives, it should be noted that the whole character of our mental life is tied to ideas and images of particular places. Our perceptions, thoughts, memories, and judgments all build on notions of the places we inhabit. Reflecting on our memories, for instance, we will find that it is difficult, if not impossible, to remember something or some event without remembering it in a place. As Malpas notes, we often think of memory only in connection to the dimension of time, but memory is as tied to the topological and the spatial as it is to the temporal.

> Memory requires a grasp of successiveness of events, but it also
> requires a grasp of the spatial and topographic ordering of events
> and objects (since events are "in" space no less than objects), includ-

---

49. hooks, *Belonging*, 171.
50. hooks, *Belonging*, 170.
51. Jeff Malpas, *Place and Experience: A Philosophical Topography* (New York: Routledge, 2018), 6.

ing relations not only of proximity and distance, but also of the spatial nesting of events and objects in relation to other events and objects.[52]

In short, memory depends on a process of placial nesting in our minds, a process that allows us to remember and to understand an event, object, or action in relation to the context of certain places. Indeed, it could be said that events, objects, and actions are significant only in the context of places.

Already in 55 BCE, Cicero was taking note of the placial character of memories. In *De oratore*, he writes and recommends that "persons desiring to train this faculty (of memory) must select localities and form mental images of the things they wish to remember and store those images in the localities, so that the arrangement of the localities will preserve the order of the things."[53] Today, we have access to technology, including photographs, and evidence from carefully controlled studies that help to substantiate this relationship between memories and places. Edward Relph gives the example of neuroscientists using MRI devices to find where one's sense of place is located in the brain as part of the ongoing process to study the onset of Alzheimer's and its effects.[54] He mentions that, when John O'Keefe discovered the neurons, he named them "place cells" in 1971. He didn't call them "space cells" because he saw them specifically as the neural basis for distinguishing places from their surroundings.

O'Keefe found that "place cells, which are situated in the hippocampus, a part of the brain that plays an important role in the formation and maintenance of memories, react to sensory inputs from particular places; in effect they store memories of places."[55] Relph cites John Zeisel, a neuroscientist who works with Alzheimer's patients in New York: "To remember something you need to know where it happened as well as when it happened. Place is essential to memory; without a memory of place, people lose their sense of self."[56] Yet, by themselves, "place cells" are not enough for us to find our way around. Neurons located in the nearby entorhinal cortex—called

52. Malpas, *Place and Experience*, 113.

53. Cicero, *De oratore* 2.86.354, trans. E. W. Sutton and H. Rackham; Loeb Classical Library (Cambridge, MA: Harvard University Press, 1942), 466–67.

54. See Edward Relph, "Place and Connection," in *The Intelligence of Place: Topographies and Poetics*, ed. Jeff Malpas (New York: Bloomsbury Academic, 2017), 177–204.

55. Relph, "Place and Connection," 177.

56. John Zeisel, as cited in Relph, "Place and Connection," 177.

"grid cells" since their discovery in 2004 by Edvard and Britt Moser—are necessary as well. "It is the combined neural processes of place and grid cells that compose sense of place, and it appears to be the failure of these processes that leads to Alzheimer's."[57] For our purposes, what is important is the way in which memory requires a grasp of place, and not merely of place in some general or abstract sense, but place as a consequence and manifestation of particular places in all of their specificity.

Place and Social Life

To this point, I have focused on considerations of place related to the self, indicating that place matters as an ontological phenomenon, that places provide us with a sense of identity, and that places have an impact on the products of the mind. These indications have to do with the life of the individual. But place and place experience matter in a social and more widespread manner as well. Places shape our destinies, influencing the fates of individuals and groups.

A number of individual and social factors determine or influence a people's life chances. But increasingly we are finding that one of these factors is where we live. The places in which we live affect our material well-being, our security, and our prospective success in society because they commonly determine the access or the lack of access we will have to educational, social, economic, and environmental resources. The quality of one's educational opportunities; the types of jobs available in an area; the quality of public amenities like parks, libraries, and cultural and recreational centers; the availability of reliable or first-rate medical services; the effectiveness of public servants; and the degree of exposure to violence, gangs, toxic hazards, and clean air all depend on where one lives. In fact, much of a person's success or suffering can be explained by the place in which they live.

The writers of *The Introduction to Cities* rightly note that this process begins at our beginnings:

> *Where* you are born determines, in large part, *how* you were born.
> Did your mother have access to prenatal care? Were you born in a
> well-equipped hospital? Did you first come home to a dwelling free
> of toxic hazards, violence, or other threats to your family's safety?
> What was the quality of the school you first attended? Was your

---

57. Relph, "Place and Connection," 178.

journey to school an opportunity for friendly play or fraught with danger? Even by the age of five or six, qualities of place have left their mark on children.[58]

But it is not as if the process of place's effect on the quality of our lives and the opportunities open to us ceases at the point of our beginnings. Place continues to have this kind of relevance and influence all through the different stages of our lives.

This nexus between physical environment and the quality of life and opportunities is one of the many places where the issues of justice and of place intersect, and there are two ways in which they intersect here. To begin with, it is important to recognize that different people can experience a place very differently. Factors like race, ethnicity, socioeconomic class, gender, sexuality, physical ability, and nationality affect people's access to, mobility across, experiences of, and memories of places. For example, women and men often experience the same place differently. In many cases, men can enjoy the ability to move freely about public places with little regard for the time of day or whether the places are secluded or not, while women's movements unfortunately have to be more confined and guarded and aware of place and of the possible unwanted attention and injury their presence could attract. Racial and ethnic minorities also often endure such limitations. They are regarded as "suspicious outsiders," profiled by police authorities and security guards, or explicitly told that they are not welcome. These two examples, and others like them, show that members of different social groups can and often do have different experiences of the very same places.

This is a form of placial inequality. Some people cannot enjoy certain places in the same way as others. It is also true that forms of inequality can be organized or clustered in places like neighborhoods and that these places can become sites in which inequality is generated, maintained, and reinforced. This is why it is important to consider the ways in which inequality is organized in place when one is attempting to analyze relations of injustice and when one is seeking to frame the meaning and consequences of fairness and justice. In doing so, we discover that the status of certain places could create additional disadvantages for certain individuals

---

58. Xiangming Chen, Anthony M. Orum, and Krista E. Paulsen, *Introduction to Cities: How Place and Space Shape Human Experience* (Hoboken, NJ: Wiley-Blackwell, 2018), 22–23.

and groups in society and that it could contribute to enduring, inherited inequality.

This is precisely what sociologist Patrick Sharkey discovered when studying the intersection of race and class in U.S. urban neighborhoods and when trying to decipher the ghetto's hold on Black Americans across generations. He found that, for Black families living in ghettos, the challenges and risks associated with life in the poorest neighborhoods represent a continuation of a family history of disadvantage. Sharkey discovered that "over 70 percent of African Americans who live in today's poorest, most racially segregated neighborhoods are from the same families that lived in the ghettos of the 1970s."[59] The study is not suggesting that African American family members remain in the same, exact physical space but that they remain in the same type of environment for generations: segregated, high-poverty neighborhoods. Despite the high hopes of the civil rights era, and, despite the optimism that surrounded the passing of civil rights bills and the 1968 Fair Housing Act, most African Americans remain trapped in place. The stark conditions of multifaceted inequality that existed in U.S. neighborhoods during the seventies have been passed on, with little change, to the current generation of African Americans. As Sharkey puts it,

> The current generation of African American adults has made virtually no advancement in residential America—the children who were raised in the most disadvantaged areas during the civil rights period are overwhelmingly likely to now raise their children in remarkably similar environments.[60]

Sharkey provides figures that compare the social and residential status of Black families to that of white families. He notes that, when white families live in a poor neighborhood, they typically do so for only a single generation. In the case of African American families, however, neighborhood poverty is most commonly multigenerational. Over the past two generations, 48 percent of all African American families have lived in the poorest quarter of neighborhoods in each generation. Only 7 percent of white families have experienced similar poverty in their neighborhood environments for consecutive generations.[61] Turning his attention to the overall degree of racial

---

59. Patrick Sharkey, *Stuck in Place: Urban Neighborhoods and the End of Progress toward Racial Equality* (Chicago: University of Chicago Press, 2013), 9.

60. Sharkey, *Stuck in Place*, 9.

61. Sharkey, *Stuck in Place*, 39–40.

and economic inequality in children's neighborhood environments, Sharkey indicates that, among children born between 1955 and 1970, only 4 percent of whites were raised in neighborhoods with at least 20 percent poverty, compared to 62 percent of African Americans. Seventy-five percent of white children were raised in neighborhoods with less than 10 percent poverty, compared to just 9 percent of African Americans. Only 1 percent of white children were raised in neighborhoods with at least 30 percent poverty, but 30 percent of African Americans were.[62]

The consequences of life in such poor neighborhoods are striking. In education, children from families that have lived in poor neighborhoods for consecutive generations score markedly lower than children from families that never lived in poor neighborhoods, with an average score of 94 on the broad reading test as compared to an average score of 110 in the case of their peers in the other group. Sharkey points out that the sixteen-point difference represents a cognitive deficit that is comparable to missing somewhere between four and eight years of schooling.

In health, 22 percent of children who have always lived in poor neighborhoods report having poor health. Only 10 percent of those who have never lived in poor neighborhoods do.[63] The cumulative experience of life in neighborhoods of high poverty also seems to wear on people's aspirations and expectations. Fifty-three percent of children who have always lived in a poor neighborhood do not expect to graduate from a four-year college. While still rather high in the other group, this number drops to 32 percent among children who haven't lived in a poor neighborhood. The attenuated aspirations and expectations afflict parents from impoverished neighborhoods as well, with a whopping 65 percent reporting that they don't expect their child to graduate from a four-year college and 29 percent doing so in the group of parents who haven't lived in a poor neighborhood.[64]

In terms of household wealth and home ownership, the median household wealth of whites is thirteen to fifteen *times* higher than that of Black households; times, not percent![65] A big factor in this dramatic wealth disparity is the matter of home equity and ownership. And there is still a sig-

---

62. Sharkey, *Stuck in Place*, 26–27.
63. Sharkey, *Stuck in Place*, 121.
64. Sharkey, *Stuck in Place*, 123.
65. See Rakesh Kochar and Richard Fry, "Wealth Inequality Has Widened along Racial, Ethnic Lines since End of Great Recession," Pew Research Center online, December 12, 2014, https://www.pewresearch.org.

nificant difference in white and Black ownership rates: 73 percent versus 45 percent.[66]

Of course, the reasons for such disparities are multiple, but neighborhood (or place) is implicated in this ongoing stratification between Blacks and whites in the United States. Ghetto neighborhoods deserve scrutiny, but that scrutiny should be aimed at a plethora of factors, including informal discriminatory customs carried out among the populace, institutionalized discrimination achieved through laws and regionalist planning, and even the flawed operations and adverse consequences of the emergent global economy. Think of the efforts of rural, small-town whites to preserve the racial homogeneity of their places in the 1920s, 1930s, and 1940s, when more African Americans were making their way north from the southern states during the so-called Great Migration due to limiting economic opportunities for them in the South. "Sundown towns" proliferated—small towns that prohibited African Americans from residing within their municipal limits.[67] There were laws and customs that buttressed and sustained these sundown towns. There was inherent racism in the Federal Housing Administration's practice of "redlining,"[68] together with the use of restrictive covenants or deed restrictions by private developers and homeowners' associations to bar African Americans and members of other racial/ethnic groups from purchasing homes in the newly developing suburbs during the 1930s and 1940s. The combination of these factors effectively confined Blacks to relatively small areas of northern and upper Midwest cities.

---

66. See Amy Traub and Catherine Ruetschlin, "The Racial Wealth Gap: Why Policy Matters," *Demos*, March 10, 2015, https://www.demos.org.

67. The term "sundown towns" is tied to the use of laws and customs that permitted Blacks to work in town but required that they be gone by sundown. For a work that documents the rise and proliferation of sundown towns in the United States, see James Loewen, *Sundown Towns: A Hidden Dimension of American Racism* (New York: Simon & Schuster, 2006).

68. The term "redlining" is used to describe the systematic denial of mortgages and other forms of credit in minority neighborhoods. The practice was first linked to the Federal Housing Administration's (FHA) and the Home Owners' Loan Corporation's (HOLC) policies, which included outlining Black and minority neighborhoods in red on geographic maps used by both of these federally run organizations. The practice was later adopted by the private banking industry. For more on the practice of redlining, see Richard Rothstein, *The Color of Law: A Forgotten History of How Our Government Segregated America* (New York: W. W. Norton, 2017).

Once there, the Black population quickly endured the effects of deindustrialization in these older industrial cities, seeing firms and factories close in large numbers during the 1950s and 1960s in order to move their plants and production operations abroad to increase profits by using cheaper labor.[69] The resulting loss of tens of thousands of industrial jobs in these cities affected many people across different racial and ethnic lines, but the situation was much worse for these newer residents of the northern and upper Midwest cities. African Americans were not simply "the victims of a declining economy but also continued to be the victims of an entrenched system of racial segregation."[70]

Add to all of this the behavior of ghetto landlords, who regularly invested little in residential upkeep; the persistent practice of redlining even after the passing of the Fair Housing Act in 1968, although this time by banks and other big lenders who did not make private investment capital available in Black neighborhoods; the decisions made across policy arenas at the state and city levels that have resulted in the abandonment of poor and nonwhite communities within urban settings, leading to the deterioration of public housing projects and inner-city public schools; and even the kind of snob zoning to which local politicians have been known to give the green light, allowing affluent residents and neighborhoods to prevent the construction of new affordable housing in their areas. This noxious stew of broad social forces and practices produced the highly segregated ghetto neighborhoods and is still encountered in many metropolitan areas of the United States today.

These neighborhoods have since turned into a detriment or a deterrent for the success and well-being of countless numbers of African American families living in them, becoming a mechanism of inequality in their own right. Of course, much beauty, creativity, and good continues to come out of these neighborhoods. And many individuals and families in these neighborhoods lead dignified and admirable lives filled with cheer, achievement, and fulfillment. I know this intimately because I grew up in and am a product of such a place myself, although, in my case, it was a predominantly Latino/a inner-city ghetto neighborhood. But, even with the grace and fruition achieved at times

69. William Julius Wilson has written extensively on the relation between deindustrialization and joblessness in our racially segregated inner city ghettos during the 1950s, '60s, and '70s. See especially Wilson, *The Truly Disadvantaged: The Inner City, the Underclass, and Public Policy* (Chicago: University of Chicago Press, 1987); and *When Work Disappears: The World of the New Urban Poor* (New York: Alfred A. Knopf, 1996).

70. Chen et al., *Introduction to Cities*, 208.

by those living in them, these high-poverty, highly segregated neighborhoods are dangerous places with the potential to depress life outcomes and to entrap successive generations of family members in a closed loop of systemic disadvantage "such that failure is common and success aberrational."[71] Ghetto neighborhoods have become places where inequalities, scarcities, and disadvantages have clustered over time. In the United States, racial segregation and high rates of persistent poverty characterize these neighborhoods. In turn, these neighborhoods have been deprived of many public services that are commonly available in other neighborhoods, contributing to higher crime rates, distressed and devalued housing, and under-resourced schools. The lack of social agencies and networks is also reflected by disinvestment from the private sector, including limited employment, mentors, and opportunities for workforce and higher education participation. These are the kinds of inequalities, scarcities, and disadvantages that have been passed down for generations of African American families.

I have focused here on the case of Black Americans in the United States, but there are other social groups that have similarly experienced reduced opportunities and additional existential and social hardships across many generations by reason of the low-opportunity places in which they have often been forced to live. Most Native Americans and Latino/as, for instance, tend to know that place—where one lives—powerfully structures opportunity. Individuals and families in other social groups experience the constraints of placial inequality as well. This is why Sharkey has proposed two shifts of thinking in the study of inequality and mobility in the United States. The first is a shift from a pure focus on social or economic status within the family or the individual to a broader focus on the placial environments surrounding families. The second shift involves moving from a static view of neighborhood disadvantage and advantage at a given point in time to a dynamic view of neighborhood stratification that considers mobility across the distribution of neighborhoods over individual lifetimes and across generations of family members. In other words, Sharkey argues for "the need to fully incorporate both *place* and *time* into the literature on racial inequality in America."[72]

Legal theorist Sheryll Cashin has similarly noted the relationship between places and the transmission of inequality over time and across gen-

---

71. Sheryll Cashin, *Place, Not Race: A New Vision of Opportunity in America* (Boston: Beacon Press, 2014), 24.

72. Sharkey, *Stuck in Place*, 19.

erations, recently calling on universities to reform both affirmative action and the entire admissions process by considering how residential geography plays a role in the structuring of educational opportunity and life outcomes. Taking into account and offering both data and examples that bring to light the ways in which place reinforces advantages and disadvantages over time, Cashin argues for a revamped admissions process that affords a holistic, individualized review of a variety of factors and gives extra weight to the circumstances of living in a low-opportunity neighborhood (i.e., a neighborhood with a poverty rate of over 20 percent) or attending a high-poverty school.[73] And it is important to note that Cashin is a progressive thinker and a civil rights activist who is trying to provide a blueprint for a new, stronger, and more inclusive form of affirmative action and not some conservative ideologue bent on circumventing race-based affirmative action. After analyzing five decades worth of social science research, she is convinced that the key to this and to the achievement of a new framework for true inclusion for millions of children who live separate and unequal lives is a place-based policy that tracks actual placial disadvantage and rewards those who show the ability and readiness to thrive in spite of the additional hazards and obstacles. "Those who suffer the deprivations of high-poverty neighborhoods and schools are deserving of special consideration," Cashin argues.[74]

Place and Displacement

Both Sharkey and Cashin are clear that some emplacements foster progress and well-being while others exacerbate disadvantage and distress. They lend credence to my point that places possess power to shape the fates of those who live in them, but there is another way in which place matters in a broader social manner. Place matters on account of the grievous experience of forced displacement that has been and continues to be endured by many individuals and groups. One of the most egregious exemplifications of this in the context of U.S. history is the place-based tragedy that befell and continues to befall the Indigenous peoples of North America following the arrival of the Europeans in the Americas. The tragic violence committed against Indigenous peoples from the colonial period through the founding of the United States and continuing in the twenty-first century has taken many forms: terror, torture, sexual abuse, massacres, military occupations,

---

73. See Cashin, *Place, Not Race*, esp. 63–87.
74. Cashin, *Place, Not Race*, xv.

enslavement, and the removal of Indigenous children to military-like board-ing schools in an unseemly and opprobrious attempt to assimilate them into white society. A fundamental aspect of the trauma has been place-based inasmuch it has involved the removals of Indigenous peoples from their ancestral territories and their forced placement in or displacement to frag-mented reservations in many cases.

The latter place-based part of the tragic tale is traceable to the forms of colonialism that the Indigenous peoples of North America have experienced. During the early stages of the European invasion, the Indigenous peoples experienced a colonizing venture known as "exploitation colonialism" as the Spanish, French, and Dutch Empires came to the Americas seeking to expand their colonial borders and strengthen their home economies with natural resources from these lands. The respective colonizers came looking for nutmeg, pepper, cinnamon, cloves, and silk, and they rejoiced when they found gold and silver and furs that could help to supply the surging demand for fur to make clothing and fancy hats in Europe. They took whatever natu-ral resources they wanted, but, through coercion and enslavement, they also took people's labor and physical strength.

The second form of colonialism is now known as "settler colonialism." In settler colonialism, land is the primary commodity. The colonialists' goal was and is the elimination of Indigenous populations in order to make land available to settlers.[75] Eve Tuck and Marcia McKenzie identify important differences between this latter form of colonialism and the previous one, observing that exploitation colonizers and settler colonizers want very dif-ferent things. "The exploitation colonizer says to the Indigenous person 'you, work for me,' whereas the settler colonizer—because land is the pri-mary pursuit—says to the Indigenous person 'you go away.'"[76] Tuck and McKenzie note that, in reality, settler colonizers communicate a mixture or variety of these sorts of messages to Indigenous peoples. But, no matter how it may be expressed, a central intention prevails in the case of this mode of colonialism: make Indigenous peoples disappear from the land in order to make it available for settlement.

The villainous impetus of this colonizing venture continued through the

---

75. For a noted description of settler colonialism, see Patrick Wolfe, "Settler Colonialism and the Elimination of the Native," *Journal of Genocide Research* 8, no. 4 (December 2006): 387–409.

76. Eve Tuck and Marcia McKenzie, *Place in Research: Theory, Methodology, and Methods* (New York: Routledge, 2015), 59.

colonial period, informing U.S. policies and actions related to Indigenous peoples to this day. Through repression; military campaigns; broken treaties; federal land seizures, allotments, and sales; and governmental failures to meet obligations to protect Indigenous lands—as required under supposedly protective laws—the United States has continued forcing Indigenous communities from their ancestral territories in the name of territorial expansion. A grievous saga of systematic, serial forced displacement accompanies such land theft.

The result of this continuous history of settler colonialism and involuntary displacement from ancestral homelands has been disastrous for the different Indigenous peoples and continues to be felt by today's Indigenous nations and communities. That the native peoples of North America have survived this centuries-long and continuing history of varied colonization, dispossession, and indiscriminate killing is nothing short of breathtaking. Yet, as Roxanne Dunbar-Ortiz notes, "it is breathtaking, but no miracle."[77] Their survival as peoples is due to "centuries of resistance and storytelling passed through the generations."[78] This survival is active, not passive, but it shouldn't be forgotten that the centuries-long and continuing history of settler colonialism and forced displacement has taken a toll on the various native peoples and nations.

As a group, the Indigenous peoples of North America are among the most disadvantaged in our society. Forty percent of the nearly three million people who are descendants of the fifteen million native peoples who once inhabited this land continue to live on or near federally recognized reservations that vary in size. Some 310 federally recognized reservations exist in the United States, with a land base that covers roughly fifty-five million acres of land, representing about 2 percent of the country's overall landmass. As Stephen Pevar notes, "the unemployment rate on some of these reservations is 80 percent, nearly a quarter of all Indians live in poverty, 14 percent of all reservation homes do not have electricity, and 12 percent of homes do not have access to a safe water supply."[79] The Indigenous community also falls well below the national average in education, with half of

77. Roxanne Dunbar-Ortiz, *An Indigenous Peoples' History of the United States* (Boston: Beacon Press), xiii.

78. Dunbar-Ortiz, *Indigenous Peoples' History*, xiii.

79. Stephen L. Pevar, *The Rights of Indians and Tribes* (New York: Oxford University Press, 2012), 2. Pevar uses the terms "Indians" and "tribes" in his book. Except in material that is quoted, I prefer to use the term Indigenous peoples, nations, or communities.

the population lacking a high school diploma and only 14 percent of it earning undergraduate or professional degrees compared with 24 percent for the nation as a whole. Some of the reservations have managed to improve their economic and material conditions through the construction of casinos, but the vast majority of reservations "remain impoverished, and tribal members continue to suffer from health, housing, and unemployment problems; alcoholism; and lack of economic opportunities."[80] Adding to the problem is the fact that many of these reservations are located far from industrial centers and have few of the kinds of natural resources that can be developed, if this were even to be desired by the groups. Substantial improvement in their economic situation is not, therefore, likely, at least not in this manner. Here, again, place and/or geography matters.

Forced displacement from land and place plays a huge role in all of this. The statements, actions, and forms of resistance of many of the different native nations and communities make clear that the loss of land was the primary loss in this circumstance. Coercive displacement and forced relocation are bound to be particularly traumatic when a system of sacred places has been established and deeply internalized over time and when traditions, celebrations, teachings, and forms of knowledge have been rooted in honored and cherished relationships to land, as has been the case in many of these nations and communities. In this case, land means more than a mere commodity (i.e., "real estate") to be bought and sold on the market. Land has historical, ancestral, spiritual, emotional, and intellectual significance. Land becomes an integral part of place in this case—an integral part of space that is invested with meaning in the context of power—and its loss turns out to be particularly traumatic as a result. Indeed, "no monetary amount can compensate for lands illegally seized, particularly those sacred lands necessary for Indigenous peoples to regain social coherence."[81] This is why Indigenous peoples ordinarily do not use the term "reparations" in reference to their land claims and treaty rights. Rather, as Dunbar-Ortiz notes, "they demand restoration, restitution, or repatriation of lands acquired by the United States outside valid treaties."[82]

The relationship between the Lakota-speaking peoples and U.S. claims to the Black Hills illustrates the point. On July 23, 1980, the Supreme Court of the United States ruled that Paha Sapa—the Lakota name for the

---

80. Pevar, *Rights of Indians*, 2.
81. Pevar, *Rights of Indians*, 206.
82. Dubar-Ortiz, *Indigenous Peoples' History*, 206.

Black Hills, the location of Mount Rushmore—had been taken in 1877 by the United States "in exercise of Congress' power of eminent domain over Indian property" and that "the Sioux were entitled to an award of interest on the principal sum of $17.1 million (the fair market value of the Black Hills as of 1877), dating from 1877."[83] The remuneration has been refused, and Indigenous People continue to demand return of the Black Hills because, as a *PBS NewsHour* reporter put it on August 24, 2011, "the land was never for sale."[84] Remaining in an interest-accruing account, the money had reached a figure of $757 million by 2010, but it remained untouched. In short, "the Sioux believe that accepting the money would validate the U.S. theft of their most sacred land."[85]

The decision to forgo the money and hold out for justice in the shape of the return of the land is particularly noteworthy given that, as the reporter noted,

> Few people in the Western Hemisphere have shorter life expectancies (than those on a Sioux reservation). Males, on average, live to just 48 years old, females to 52. Almost half of all people above the age of 40 have diabetes. And the economic realities are even worse. Unemployment rates are consistently above 80 percent. In Shannon County, inside the Pine Ridge Reservation, half the children live in poverty, and the average income is $8,000 a year.[86]

And yet, despite these hardships, the Lakota have steadfastly refused to touch available funds from the federal pot that are now worth close to a billion dollars. As Dunbar-Ortiz notes, "that one of the most impoverished communities in the Americas would refuse a billion dollars demonstrates the relevance and significance of the land to the Sioux, not as an economic resource but as a relationship between people and place."[87]

The case of the Indigenous peoples of North America is one of the most egregious ongoing cases of forced displacement and relocation in these parts of the world, but there are others, of course, here and abroad. There are many individuals and groups of individuals around the world who have experi-

83. United States v. Sioux Nation of Indians, 448 U.S. 371 (1980).

84. See "For Great Sioux Nation, Black Hills Can't Be Bought for $1.3 Billion," *PBS NewsHour*, August 24, 2011.

85. Dunbar-Ortiz, *Indigenous Peoples' History*, 207.

86. "For Great Sioux Nation, Black Hills Can't be Bought for $1.3 Billion."

87. Dubar-Ortiz, *Indigenous Peoples' History*, 208.

enced or who are presently experiencing forms of forced or involuntary displacement and separation from their homes, home regions, communities, means of subsistence, and, often, even from their families. The reasons and causes vary. Civil wars, generalized violence, and persecution on the grounds of nationality, race/ethnicity, religion, or political opinion are common causes. Just as natural characteristics inform place, natural disasters—earthquakes and volcanic activity—and environmental changes related to anthropogenic climate change and biodiversity loss—floods, droughts, deforestation, and desertification—are significant factors that contribute to involuntary displacement. Other reasons include disease outbreaks, human trafficking and smuggling, and upheaval occasioned by the negative effects of policies and projects implemented to advance development efforts. The numbers of the displaced are only increasing..

According to the Office of the United Nations High Commissioner for Refugees (UNHCR), the number of forcibly displaced people within countries and across borders grew by over 50 percent between 2007 and 2017. In 2007, there were approximately 42.7 million forcibly displaced people, and, by the end of 2017, the figure was 68.5 million. Noteworthy, too, is the fact that, of the 68.5 million forcibly displaced, 16.2 million people were newly displaced in 2017. The number is growing and quickly in other words. It is estimated that, today, 1 out of every 110 people in the world is displaced.[88]

In the United States, 1.7 million people experienced new internal displacement in 2017. This category and figure refer to persons or groups of persons who have been forced to leave their homes or places of habitual residence and remain displaced within the country, mostly due to natural disasters. The category and figure do not account for the untold and undeterminable number of people who have either experienced displacement or are experiencing the threat of displacement as a result of the kind of upscale development and urban-renewal agenda that has become all the rage in most of our cities: gentrification, the process in which capital is invested or reinvested in an urban neighborhood and in which poorer residents and their cultural products are displaced and replaced by more affluent and usually white and younger people and their preferred aesthetics and amenities.[89]

In many cases, the process of gentrification begins with artists and creative

88. For these figures, see the 2018 Report of the United Nations High Commissioner for Refugees (i.e., UNHCR, 2018).

89. This is a slightly revised version of a definition of gentrification given by

types opting to transform old factory lofts and warehouse spaces into studios and performance spaces in city neighborhoods. In other cases, the first stage of the process occurs when more affluent, middle-class or upper-middle-class whites opt to buy or rent in a traditionally lower-income neighborhood, motivated often by the desire to move back into the urban core and by the longing at once to "reduce their commutes, locate near high-paying economic opportunities, and gain privileged access to the better amenities that come from urban living."[90] Then, after a few years, corporations such as real estate companies and chain retail stores, seeing an opportunity to profit from the arrival of the new urban neighborhood settlers, start targeting the neighborhood and appearing within it. Soon after, large-scale developers enter the picture, now willing and able to put up the millions that investors and developers need to get a major project off the ground in the neighborhood. Machinations of local politicians and city planners, whose desire it is to attract the wealthy, the corporations, and the big businesses in order to stoke land markets, raise property values, and secure an influx of wealth through a richer tax base, spur this on by offering enticing zoning laws, tax breaks, and branding power that are, of course, not offered to the less wealthy.

The end result is usually the appearance of cafés, fine restaurants, boutique shops, higher-end supermarkets, loft-style apartments and elegant townhomes, luxurious office towers, trendy hotels, and, sometimes, even improved public services, including additional transit lines and bicycle lanes that appear when residents with deeper pockets start to move in. The process brings some benefits. Neighborhoods may become cleaner, better looking, and possibly safer in some respects, at least for some, and have more amenities; but it all comes at a steep price, and not everyone will have the chance to enjoy the neighborhood or to live in the neighborhood after it has been touched by the gentrification-industrial complex. On the whole, the process of gentrification generally brings about three distinct forms of placial or neighborhood traumas: the loss of housing affordability, the displacement of lower-income tenants, and the loss of local cultures and/or distinctive neighborhood characters.

It has been taking place since the late sixties and seventies, just more

Samuel Stein in *Capital City: Gentrification and the Real Estate State* (New York: Verso, 2019), 41.

90. Richard Florida, *The New Urban Crisis: How Our Cities are Increasing Inequality, Deepening Segregation, and Failing the Middle Class—And What We Can Do about It* (New York: Basic Books, 2017), 64.

slowly. The process has accelerated and spread rapidly and widely since the year 2000, and it can be witnessed today in many cities around the globe, even in many of the inner-ring suburbs of cities. By now, it has drawn much attention and been widely studied and debated. Not surprisingly, different appraisals of and conclusions about the process have been expressed. Especially debated has been the matter of the displacement that gentrification causes. Though more recent literature suggests that gentrification displaces far fewer people than commonly thought, the impression one gets is that many people have experienced displacement from their old or long-term neighborhoods or are at the least experiencing the threat of displacement from them due to the rising rents and housing costs that result from gentrification.[91] Because much of the gentrification occurs in cities, the number of people affected by it cannot possibly be insignificant.

Gentrification is a particular problem in magnet cities and in leading technology and knowledge hubs such as New York, Boston, and Washington, D.C., on the East Coast, and Los Angeles, San Francisco, Portland, and Seattle on the West Coast. The pricing out of poor, working-class, and now even middle-class residents from certain urban neighborhoods, however, is no longer a story only heard in cities like these. It is also being heard in gentrifying neighborhoods of cities like Houston, Austin, Denver, Cincinnati, Pittsburgh, Nashville, Raleigh, Philadelphia, Baltimore, and Miami. Even poorer or recently distressed cities like New Orleans and Detroit, and tiny ones like Portland, Maine (population sixty-six thousand), are experiencing gentrification. And with the spread of gentrification to more and more cities, and to more neighborhoods within them, comes the growing threat of further displacement of peoples.

Consider first that, even if indirectly, gentrification contributes to a trend of decline and disinvestment in other city neighborhoods. Capital investment tends to flow in and out of places. That is why, while planners, city officials, investors, developers, and landlords are busy marshaling investment, making improvements to infrastructure, boosting land and property values, and trying to attract big-box stores, retail entrepreneurs, and affluent residents into highly bounded gentrifying neighborhoods, many other neighborhoods are falling prey to inattention, disinvestment, and neglect. Poorer or less affluent residents in all of these other non-gentrifying neighborhoods

91. For example, see Lance Freeman, "Five Myths about Gentrification," *Washington Post*, June 3, 2016, https://www.washingtonpost.com/opinions/five-myths-about-gentrification/2016/06/03b6c80e56-1ba5-11e6-8c7b-6931e66333e7_story.html.

are required to do without the community improvements; the decent housing; the safer, cleaner streets; and the credit markets available to those in
gentrifying neighborhoods due to the lower exchange value of land and
properties in their neighborhoods. All of this leads to an urban landscape
marked by uneven development and increasing economic and place-based
inequality.[92]

Second, gentrification exacerbates one of our country's most pressing
social problems: the problem of unaffordable housing. Even though gentrification is limited to particular areas of cities and inner-ring suburbs, it tends
to have a trickle-down or ripple effect on housing markets in surrounding
neighborhoods, resulting in rising rents and home prices even in neighborhoods outside of but near gentrifying neighborhoods. With this comes an
affordability crisis that compromises the economic standing of working and
middle-class residents all across the country. In New York City, for example,
the share of rent-burdened households spending 30 percent or more of their
pretax income on rent rose from 42 percent in 2000 to 53 percent in 2014. It
grew even more in non-gentrifying neighborhoods, however, going from 46
percent to nearly 60 percent of households over the same period.[93] This is a
possible indication of gentrification's trickle-down effect on housing prices.

The problem of housing affordability transcends New York City, however.
Average move-in rents in the United States have more than doubled over the
last two decades.[94] With the rise in rental prices and the general stagnation
and even decline of real wages, many tenants are in a bind. Samuel Stein
notes, "There is not a single county in the country where a full-time mini-
mum wage worker can afford the average two-bedroom apartment."[95] Rent
burdens are becoming onerous even for people on typical working-class and
lower-middle-class salaries. The problem, of course, afflicts people of color in
segregated neighborhoods all the more. Around the country, "rent burdens
in Black neighborhoods average 44 percent; in Latino neighborhoods, it's 48
percent."[96] Rising housing costs and the problem of insufficient affordable

---

92. For more on the topic and idea of uneven development, see Neil Smith, *Uneven
Development: Nature, Capital, and the Production of Space,* 3rd ed. (Athens: University
of Georgia Press, 2008). See also David Harvey, *Spaces of Global Capitalism: A Theory
of Uneven Geographical Development* (New York: Verso, 2019).

93. Florida, *The New Urban Crisis,* 74.

94. U.S. Census Bureau, *Housing Vacancies and Homeownership* (CPS/HVS),
online, First Quarter 2019.

95. Stein, *Capital City,* 4.

96. Stein, *Capital City,* 4.

housing are further reasons to fret about the process and spread of gentrification.

Third, city governments have become dependent on the revenue stream and growth rhetoric tied to gentrification. Early gentrification proved to be a boon to city officials who were looking for ways to counter shrinking municipal budgets and to reshape metropolitan spaces and places following both the flight of manufacturing from urban centers to suburbs and abroad and the loss of industries, jobs, and wealth in cities due to manufacturing decline after World War II. Because the model proved effective in some cities, it became all the rage in other cities here and abroad. Along the way, urban real estate has become central to capital's global growth strategy. In most cities today, real estate is becoming the primary commodity, revenue stream, and political priority. As Stein observes, "global real estate is now worth $217 trillion, thirty-six times the value of all the gold ever mined."[97] It makes up "60 percent of the world's assets, and the vast majority of that wealth—roughly 75 percent—is in housing."[98]

With all of this in play, with municipalities, developers, financiers, real estate agencies, construction companies, landlords, and big businesses all standing to gain great profits from the upscale development of the metropolis, gentrification is likely to continue to spread like wildfire across cities here and around the world. Consequently, the loss of affordable housing, the displacement of lower-income tenants from city neighborhoods, and the flattening of neighborhood character are likely to continue—a continuation and an extension of a political system that focuses more on the accretion of business opportunity and profits than on the well-being of the majority of its citizens.

The violence of forced displacement, whatever its forms and origins, is a serious matter that deserves our attention. It has affected and continues to affect the lives of many people in the United States and around the world, usually leaving much trauma and disruption in its wake. Conscientious persons need to know more about these experiences of displacement. The promotion of programs that can contribute to reparations, restitution, and a more just reordering of society insists and depends on an awareness of these unresolved issues of involuntary displacement from lands, homes, neighborhoods, and communities—another way in which place matters.

In all, I have described five ways in which place is important:

---

97. Stein, *Capital City*, 2.
98. Stein, *Capital City*, 2.

place matters as a necessary condition for life;

place provides us with a sense of who we are;

place has an impact on the products of the mind;

places shape our destinies, influencing the fates of individuals and groups; and

place matters by reason of the grievous experience of displacement endured by numerous individuals and groups.

Place also matters by reason of the many challenges that places are facing and the many changes that they are undergoing here and abroad, including enduring homelessness, environmental deterioration, growing urbanization, and resource wars. These are among the most portentous dynamics that are reshaping places and the experiences of millions of people around the world, presenting other reasons why place matters.

In sum, it can be said that few topics and actualities are as crucial, multi-faceted, wide-ranging, or all-encompassing as place. Everything from the experiential fact of our existence and human subjectivity to the nature and well-being of community and much else in between depends on, passes through, and is touched by the quiddity of place. Given that there is no current social, political, justice, global, environmental, land-related, or nature-related issue that doesn't intersect with place in some way or another, we have all the more reason to question theology's tepid, patchy, and episodic consideration of the issues of place until now. Crucially and multifariously, place matters.

But Where Is This Place You Speak Of?

Taking all of this into consideration, we need more works on place. And there is room for different approaches to this multifaceted topic. But I am interested in a particular kind of place writing, in a practice of place writing that includes commentary on such things as the unique attributes of, the kinds of social and nonhuman forces that are involved in the construction of, and the sort of vicissitudes and achievements experienced in a particular place. I fancy place writing that attends to the particularity of *a* place, immersing itself in the feelings, stories, and materials of a place in order to narrate how particularities and distinctions of place influence and are influenced by the people emplaced there.

Many thinkers with and interpreters of place tend to use imagined examples and thought experiments when talking about place, or they may resort to talking about place in a generalized, abstract sort of way. We could stand to lavish more attention on the specificity and materiality of place, I believe.[99] In our discourses about place, we could stand to incorporate more material and tangible specificity drawn from particular places and from our experiences in and with particular places. We could stand a syncretistic or coalescing form of place writing, incorporating elements of a phenomeno-logical, sociological, reflective, and descriptive approach to place that isn't afraid to grapple with and point up the distinctiveness and particularity of places in the world.

The recent place writing practices of Patricia Price, Laura Ogden, and Sharon Zukin are inspiring and instructive in this case. They draw from and interweave different theoretical frameworks, branches of knowledge, and writing styles even through their incorporation of narrative and analytical commentary. They present micro- and macro-level views of places. In this way, they manage to shed light on the locations, the hallmarks, the mean-ings and practices, and the particular travails associated with individual places. While doing so, they also call attention to the ways in which these places are always constructed in relation to wider physical processes and social-structural conditions that prevail beyond them. Hence, Price, Ogden, and Zukin are able to bridge the discursive/experiential and the local/global divides. What's more, they show that these divides are artificial, unneces-sary, and avoidable.[100]

Following their bridging example, I do not envision attempts to pay court to the issue of human subjectivity and to the affective agency of physical environments (both natural and constructed) as an either/or matter. At times, we writers and intellectuals are made to feel as if we have to choose to draw attention to one or the other of these factors, realms, or elements. When it comes to the topic of place, however, it is helpful to consider the

---

99. A rare example of a work in theology that does manage to delve into and to immerse itself in the particularity of a particular place in a substantive or sustained manner is the volume edited by Leonard Hjalmarson, *The Soul of the City: Mapping the Spiritual Geography of Eleven Canadian Cities* (Skyforest, CA: Urban Loft Publishers, 2018).

100. See Patricia L. Price, *Dry Place: Landscapes of Belonging and Exclusion* (Min-neapolis: University of Minnesota Press, 2004); Laura A. Ogden, *Swamplife: People, Gators, and Mangroves Entangled in the Everglades* (Minneapolis: University of Min-nesota Press, 2011); and Sharon Zukin, *Naked City: The Death and Life of Authentic Urban Places* (New York: Oxford University Press, 2010).

deep connections that exist between the different physical environments we inhabit and the character of our thoughts and beliefs. The back stories of our intellectual work and the stories of our lives could be more fully gleaned, grasped, and discussed when we reflect on and learn more about the stories of the places from which we come—as Ada María Isasi-Díaz seems to have known when she asked me about place and the ideas articulated in my doctoral dissertation. In my case, these stories take me to a place known as East Harlem, Spanish Harlem, or "El Barrio" in New York City.

· 2 ·

A Place Called Spanish Harlem: Spanish Harlem Remembered

There is a rose in Spanish Harlem. A red rose in Spanish Harlem. It is a special one, it's never seen the sun. It only comes out when the moon is on the run and all the stars are gleaming. It's growing in the street right up through the concrete. But soft and sweet and dreaming.

—Ben E. King[1]

By examining a place, we come to know its people—we feel their sorrows and are exalted by their dreams.

—Judith Noemi Freidenberg[2]

Since I am writing about place connections and the epistemic significance of place experiences in particular places and communities, it is appropriate for me to say something about the place from which I come and in which I grew up. I will return to the question of the influence that Spanish Harlem has had on my knowledge claims in the next chapter in an effort to present myself as a case in point. Here, however, I focus on and throw light upon Spanish Harlem itself because, although my interest could be said to revolve around questions of thought and belief in relation to place (i.e., epistemology), I want to make sure to lavish attention on the distinctiveness

---

1. Ben E. King, "Spanish Harlem," on *Spanish Harlem,* Atlantic Records, 1961.
2. Judith Noemi Freidenberg, *Growing Old in El Barrio* (New York: NYU Press, 2000), 1.

and particularity of actual geographical places in order to then highlight the roles they play in structuring the ways we think and the ways we view and experience the world. In other words, I don't want place to get cheated.

The whole point of grappling with the complex history and multifaceted materiality of the place I called home for twenty-seven years of life is to high-light the agentic contributions of the places from which we come. I want to do this before attempting to decipher the ways in which that place echoes through my subconscious and informs my understandings of thought and belief. For me, this involves the effort to give thought to the geographical location, the historical processes, the wider and more local social forces, the physical features, the associated meanings and practices, and the memories and narratives that have played a part in the construction of a place known variously as East Harlem, Spanish Harlem, or El Barrio.

The place of which I speak is an extended neighborhood located on the upper northeastern corner of Manhattan in New York City. Cutting rea-sonably deep into Manhattan, across two square miles of landscape, the neighborhood runs from Fifth Avenue to the East and Harlem Rivers and, roughly, from Ninety-Seventh to 135th Street on Manhattan's East Side. It lies within Manhattan Community District 11 and includes two zip codes—10029, which covers the southern section of the neighborhood, and 10035 to the north. Given the area that the neighborhood encompasses, and the fact that two zip codes are used for it, it is fair to ask whether we are truly speaking about one neighborhood or about various neighborhoods instead.

City Planning Commission reports mention subareas in some cases, and East Harlemites themselves acknowledge that areas of the community have had their own identity historically. Locals may even talk of neighborhood subsections at times—the midsection of East Harlem, the small section in the northeastern part of the neighborhood that hints of a time when the neighborhood incorporated the original Little Italy, and the so-called Triangle at the northern end of East Harlem that brings the neighborhood into contact with Black Harlem or Central Harlem. Still, this doesn't stop East Harlemites from referring to these environs as "the neighborhood" more generally. In short, their perspective ordinarily leans toward a more comprehensive understanding of the area.

New Yorkers from other parts of the city also tend to speak of the area as "a neighborhood." Those in the know associate the area with a regional and a communal identity, allowing for talk of an extended neighborhood. And it is unquestionable that since at least the late 1940s, the neighborhood has largely been defined in relation to its Puerto Rican history and semblance. This is a big reason why, for more than seven decades, East Harlem has also been known as Spanish Harlem or El Barrio, the designation serving as an alternative place name for the region.[3] Becoming home to the largest Puerto Rican community in the continental United States, the neighborhood also served as the de facto center of Puerto Rican life in New York City and, arguably, the cultural heart of the Puerto Rican community in the entire United States. Add this to the strong presence and the influence of other Spanish-speaking Latino/a groups in the neighborhood, and you can begin to understand the Spanish Harlem and El Barrio monikers. Simply put, the neighborhood has been recognized as a Puerto Rican and Latino/a settlement.

Many changes have occurred in the neighborhood more recently, enough to put all of this into question—to a certain extent at least. Still, it is unquestionable that the neighborhood symbolized this and was regarded in this way by many people and for many decades. In fact, many people continue to see it in this light despite the many changes the neighborhood has been experiencing recently due to gentrification pressures and population shifts. Hence, there is a fair amount of truth in Arlene Davila's asseveration that the meaning of Spanish Harlem to Latino/as, and especially to Puerto Ricans living in the United States, is "similar to African American perceptions of Harlem, the Black capital of the world."[4]

It is also true, however, that this meaning isn't as widely known as Black Harlem's. It's not that Spanish Harlem hasn't received its fair share of attention: it has. It has featured in expressions of popular culture, as in the case of the lyrics of Ben E. King's 1961 hit single "A Rose in Spanish Harlem," which speaks about a rose struggling to take root in the cracked pavement of Spanish Harlem. The song was popularized even further when Aretha Franklin released her cover version of it in 1971. Carlos Santana's love song titled "Smooth," featuring the alluring, raspy voice of Matchbox Twenty

---

3. East Harlem is the official name for the district. The neighborhood, however, is commonly referred to as Spanish Harlem and as El Barrio. Hence, the terms can be used synonymously. I will employ them interchangeably in this way. My preference or tendency, however, is to use the terms Spanish Harlem and El Barrio specifically when referring to the period of time in which the neighborhood has been marked by a Puerto Rican and Latino/a identity. This span stretches roughly from the late 1940s to the present.

4. Arlene Dávila, *Barrio Dreams: Puerto Ricans, Latinos, and the Neoliberal City* (Berkeley: University of California, 2004), 5.

vocalist Rob Thomas, makes reference to the place when it speaks of a Barrio-based "muñequita"—a beautiful woman so dazzling as to be called a "Spanish Harlem Mona Lisa."[5] Because it is Spanish Harlem and a Puerto Rican town we are talking about here, we should imagine this Mona Lisa with unmistakable brown skin or a wheaten or yellowish brown complexion at the least. "Trigueña" we would call her in everyday Puerto Rican parlance. It is also known that Puerto Rican and other Latino/a musicians who lived in the neighborhood played a big part in the creation and evolution of Latin freestyle, salsa music, and the boogaloo sound of the 1960s and 1970s. Additionally, it is home to the Grammy-nominated Spanish Harlem Orchestra, and is where shows like BET's *106th and Park* and *The Chappelle Show* have been set or produced.

While the well-known and stereotype-filled 1961 movie musical *West Side Story* was based across the Upper West Side of Manhattan, those in the know, and certainly many native New Yorkers, know that famous sequences of the movie were filmed on location in El Barrio of Spanish Harlem. The lot where the famous "dance fight" opening sequence was filmed was located on 110th Street and Third Avenue, just ten city blocks away from the street on which I grew up. Moreover, the neighborhood is often mentioned in connection to the development of street art, especially in its mural forms. It has also been featured or mentioned in a host of popular novels, and it has served as a focal site of inspiration for the writing of the Puerto Rican diaspora (i.e., Boricua literature) and for what is known as Nuyorican literature.

The wider East Harlem area is, likewise, associated with an impressive list of prominent figures who were either born there, grew up there, or spent a significant part of their lives there, including Fiorello LaGuardia, Norman Thomas, Rafael Hernández Marín, Pura Teresa Belpré, Langston Hughes, Vito Marcantonio, Burt Lancaster, Vince McMahon Sr., Dr. Jonas Salk, Julia de Burgos, Antonia Pantoja, Tito Puente, Frank Bonilla, Piri Thomas, Al Pacino, Ray Barreto, Aida Perez, Joan Hackett, Eddie Palmieri, Nicholasa Mohr, Johnny Colon, Angelo Del Torro, Marta Morena Vega, Juan D. González, Iris Morales, Jesús Abraham "Tato" Laviera, DJ Kay Slay, Marc Anthony, Walter Berry, Tupac Shakur, Frankie Cutlass, Melissa Mark-Viverito, Monifah, James De La Vega, and Destiny Frasqueri. Finally I will note that the neighborhood lamentably served as the setting for a host of sociological and anthropological studies during the 1950s and '60s that suf-

---

5. Carlos Santana, vocal performance of "Smooth," on *Supernatural*, Arista Records, 1999.

fered from the psychological-reductionist culture and personality school of thought that dominated U.S. sociology and anthropology at the time, fueling conservative "blame-the-victim individualistic interpretations" of the persistence of poverty, while also casting the neighborhood almost exclusively in a gloomy light.[6] These people, movements, and events have brought the place a fair amount of attention through the years.

Still, the neighborhood isn't nearly as known or renowned as its more fabled geographical borderer to the north and west—Black Harlem. East/ Spanish Harlem is also defined to some extent in relation to the more upscale and mostly white neighborhood to its immediate south: Yorkville, or the Upper East Side, one of New York City's most affluent neighborhoods and home of some of the world's richest and most celebrated people. George and "Weezie"—George and Louise Jefferson—wanted to move to the Upper East Side in the popular and long-running television sitcom *The Jeffersons*. That was and still is the neighborhood to which one wanted to move in New York City if one wanted to be able to say and even to sing, "we're moving on up to the East Side, to a deee-luxe apartment in the sky."[7] Is the same sung about East Harlem, Spanish Harlem, or El Barrio, located just slightly to the north, in that same East Side of Manhattan? Not so much. In fact, the neighborhood I'm from is still slighted by the bus tours that take tourists to see the city's most famous landmarks and attractions. You can explore Downtown, Yorkville uptown, or Harlem even farther uptown— Black Harlem that is—and you can even explore parts of Hell's Kitchen in Manhattan or Brooklyn if you want to. East Harlem/Spanish Harlem is not to be found on any of these bus-tour routes nor on most tourist maps, for that matter; but it should be.

Despite its being mostly a lower-income urban enclave and a relatively modest neighborhood for more than a century now, East Harlem/Spanish Harlem is a special place. It is a place with much history and with an important story, or two, to tell. Indeed, the locale should be of interest to many people for many reasons. Those interested in exploring the development of immigrant and/or migrant neighborhoods, or the development of neighborhoods in which one racial or ethnic group becomes widespread in the context of central U.S. cities, would do well to explore East Harlem/Spanish

---

6. For more on this point, see Philippe Bourgois, *In Search of Respect: Selling Crack in El Barrio* (New York: Cambridge University Press, 2003), esp. 64–66.

7. Ja'net DuBois and Oren Waters, vocal performance of "Moving On Up," by Jeff Barry and Ja'net DuBois, *The Jeffersons*, 1975–1985.

Harlem. Those wanting to inquire into the significance of urban diversity and inequality should check into it as well. Those wanting to see how cities can be markedly different places for different people should go through my hometown in New York City. Those wanting to attend to the conflict between the need for more affordable housing and the expanding interest in urban upscale redevelopment and gentrification would do well to keep tabs on what is happening there. Those wanting to know more about Puerto Rican history and Puerto Rican life in New York City should check out El Barrio. Those who care enough, as informed and conscientious U.S. citizens, to want to learn more about Puerto Rico's relationship with the United States and about the trials of the oldest colony in the modern world—one of the few remaining colonies in the world—should consider the history of the neighborhood. Those interested in exploring the notion of citizenship and the possibility of a citizenship of an inferior order would do well to look into the history of Spanish Harlem, for we, the Puerto Ricans who have made up the majority of its population since the middle of the twentieth century, can tell tales not in the abstract but in and through places there about what it is like to be treated as a foreigner despite having U.S. citizenship. Those interested in the effects of race, imperialism, and colonization, including what the U.S. practices of imperialism and colonization result in and look like on the ground and in the formation and development of diasporic communities within the United States must pay attention to *mi barrio*.[8]

I could mention still other reasons why the neighborhood deserves more attention than it has received, but the ones I have mentioned should suffice to make my point. East Harlem/Spanish Harlem is a noteworthy place with wide-ranging significance. I trace El Barrio's history, character, and identity over the last century or so to highlight its hold on my knowledge claims, but Spanish Harlem is a key site to examine various important dynamics beyond this book, a site that is germane to much larger stories.

It should already be clear by now that any telling of the story of East Harlem needs to take into account its particular Puerto Rican history and identity since the late 1940s.[9] So how exactly, one may ask, did this neigh-

8. In the case of East Harlem, the term "barrio" isn't used in a general sense to delineate a working-class Latino/a neighborhood. El Barrio in New York City refers specifically to East Harlem. It functions as a proper or personal name for the neighborhood, in other words.

9. Puerto Ricans finally ceased being the largest subpopulation in East Harlem in 2012, their predominance in the neighborhood lasting roughly from 1940 to 2012. Latino/as still make up the largest segment of East Harlem's population collectively.

borhood become a predominantly and recognizably Puerto Rican town? And what did this imply on the ground with regard to this neighborhood's character, fortunes, and saga? These questions call for a good origins story, I believe.

Un sitío nos es nacido / For unto Us a Place Is Born

N ow, bear in mind that origins, beginnings, or genesises are often best spoken about in terms of historical processes rather than as instant or sudden occurrences. And, oh yes, they can be messy. They can be chaotic even.

The creation story in the first chapter of Genesis in the Hebrew Bible has always intrigued me because of its allusion to an emergence or formation that emanates from a series of occurrences and metamorphoses over time and from chaos.[10] The intimation fits here.

In the case of Spanish Harlem, the turns of events, factors, and chaos includes Puerto Rico's more than half a millennium of recorded colonial history; the concessions Pope Alexander VI granted Catholic Spain in 1493, giving it exclusive jurisdiction, authority, and absolute rights over the discovered lands and those still to be discovered in the New World of the Americas; and Spain's occupation of Puerto Rico in 1508. Its emergence also includes the rise of New York City as a magnet destination for Puerto Rican merchants, artisans, agricultural workers, and cigar makers as a result of the Spanish government's encouragement of commercial agriculture and the growing trade between Puerto Rico and a burgeoning U.S. nation during the 1800s; the emergence of liberation movements and independence parties in Puerto Rico and Cuba that fought for independence from Spain and found New York City to be an excellent haven for expatriation; and the U.S. invasion and seizure of Puerto Rico at the end of the Spanish-Cuban-American War in 1898, owing to expansionist feelings, commercial interests, and a desire to establish U.S. hegemony over the Caribbean.

---

10. Various other creation stories found in other religious traditions embrace a similar theme of gradual formation out of chaos, including Sumerian creation myths (written in the Sumerian languages and dated to around 1600 BCE), the *Enuma Elis* (a Babylonian creation myth), *Cheonjiwang Bonpuri* (a Korean creation myth), the Mandé creation myth, the creation stories found in the Raven Tales (known among the Indigenous peoples of the Pacific Northwest), and the Navajo myth of emergence (known among the Diné of the Southwest).

Further events and circumstances of significance amid the chaos include the forced attempt by the United States to incorporate Puerto Rico into U.S. trade circuits and to foster U.S. investment in Puerto Rico through passage of the Foraker Act in 1900; the granting of U.S. citizenship to Puerto Ricans in the island through passage of the Jones Act in 1917, partly to abate Puerto Rican dissatisfaction with the colonial regime, partly to quiet political agitation for independence, and partly to facilitate compulsory service in light of the pressures of World War I; the limitation of European immigration from Southern, Central, and Eastern Europe following the Immigration Act of 1924; the recruitment of Puerto Ricans as a source of low-wage labor by U.S. employers from the early 1900s to the late 1950s; the industrialization of Puerto Rico and the reorientation of the island's economy from an agricultural economy to an industrial economy with U.S. capital from the 1940s to 1970; and the displacement of large numbers of workers who lost their jobs in the island during the interval of this economic transformation. The hardships caused by intense hurricanes that pummeled Puerto Rico in 1928, 1932, 1956, and 1960; a booming postwar economy in the United States after World War II; and the emergence of East Harlem as an ideal locale for migrant Puerto Ricans by virtue of its cheap tenement apartments, its proximity to factories, restaurants, hotels, and manufacturing and service industry jobs in downtown Manhattan, and its accessible public transportation all contribute to the origins of El Barrio.

The long list of contributive events and circumstances brings me to the following conclusion: a lot goes into and is involved in creating or forming a place. That is certainly the case here, for these are just some of the pivotal factors that created the conditions that prompted the migration of waves of Puerto Ricans to the eastern section of Harlem, allowing for the transformation of a good portion of that region into Spanish Harlem/El Barrio. Of course, Puerto Ricans were neither the first nor the only ethnic group to populate and to make a place for themselves in the area. It's believed that the region had human occupants as far back as seventeen thousand years ago. Taken to be a first generation of nomadic hunters, these residents would have left the area some nine thousand years ago, when the effects of continued climatic warming drove away the big beasts on which they depended.

A more favorable environment made it possible for a second generation of human residents to settle in the area about sixty-five hundred years ago. This assemblage mostly comprised the Wiechquaesgecks, one of a dozen or so groups that formed the Lenape people of northeastern Algonquin culture.

The most numerous of the Lenape groups, the Wiechquaesgecks lived in what we know today as northern Manhattan, the Bronx, and Westchester County. We don't know how many of them lived in the area, probably because it wasn't a year-round residence for them. Consequently, they left behind few clues of their numbers. It is likely that these Wiechquaesgecks, a band of small-game hunters and foragers, moved to the area for fishing in the spring; stayed over to plant some crops, hunt, gather, and fish some more in the summer; and then pulled their things in the fall, bringing in the crops and smoking and drying the meat before retreating to more protected winter quarters inland in the Bronx. But, even if in such a three-season residential pattern, they were nonetheless long-term residents of the area, living a productive life in today's East Harlem for more than four hundred generations before the Dutch arrived on the scene in the early 1600s.[11]

The Dutch made their way to the area in 1638, about twenty-eight years after arriving in Manhattan. That same year, Andries Hudde received a patent giving him the right to "possess, inhabit, cultivate, occupy and use, and also therewith and thereof to do, bargain, and dispose" of a tract of land lying north of the initial Dutch settlement dubbed New Amsterdam in the Lower East Side of Manhattan.[12] This tract of land to the north covered what is now Harlem and included the subsection of East Harlem.

The general area of Harlem became a new Dutch settlement rather quickly. It was named Nieuw Haarlem after the Dutch city of Haarlem and then formally incorporated into the New Netherland Company's charter in 1658. With the arrival of Hudde and, soon after, the arrival of other Dutch settlers, the whole of the area of Harlem, including the East Harlem area, began to take on the shape of a farming village. This would remain a central feature of the area for the next two centuries, with the clearing of land for farming becoming a common practice of newly arriving European settlers.

During those centuries, the area became a site of repeated bloody battles between the encroaching Dutch colonists and the Wiechquaesgecks who lived there. Looking to establish a line of defense against the Indigenous group, the Dutch took to building homes more closely together with garden plots and planting fields between them, advising against the erection of iso-

---

11. For more on the Wiechquaesgecks and the Lenape, see Eric W. Sanderson, *Mannahatta: A Natural History of New York City* (New York: Harry N. Abrams, 2009), esp. 104–35; and Edwin G. Burrows and Mike Wallace, *Gotham: A History of New York City to 1898* (New York: Oxford University Press, 2000), esp. 3–13.

12. Burrows and Wallace, *Gotham*, 35.

lated farms. Additionally, with enslaved labor, they constructed a stockade as a defensive outpost in the general area of 125th Street for protection from future attacks. These measures, along with the effects of the constant barrage of war, epidemics, and other calamities, played a role in driving away a substantial part of the Indigenous population. The land clearing, the home and farm construction, and the added safety measures combined to make the area more attractive to other European newcomers.

The area came under the control of the English in 1664, when they seized the New Netherland colony. Soon after, its name was anglicized, changed from Nieuw Haarlem to Harlem. George Washington used the western section of Harlem as a strategic post from which to oppose the British in the American Revolution a little more than a century later, in 1776. Washington's modest victory there came at a great cost to the southwestern parts of lower Manhattan and to New York City's developing infrastructure, however, as sympathizers either of the British or the American side started a fire, hoping to eliminate any profit that could be gained from the capture of the city by one side or the other. The fire ravaged a considerable stretch of land, consuming as much as a third of the city's homes, farms, businesses, churches, and schools. Although the fire affected mostly the southwestern end of lower Manhattan, from Broadway to the Hudson River, it carried consequences for other areas of Manhattan, including the East Harlem area, inasmuch as it forced residents who had lost their homes and possessions to find refuge in other parts of the city.

In the wake of all of this, and by means of all of this, East Harlem emerged in the 1800s as a diverse sort of place. It became the dwelling place of prosperous white settlers who hailed from different parts of Europe. It became a countryside haven of sorts for prominent families of the colonial era that yearned for a retreat from congested downtown Manhattan, which was a full hour and a half away by stagecoach. These families built plantations and estates in the area. As Philippe Bourgois notes, "even Franklin Delano Roosevelt's great-grandfather owned property in the patchwork of bucolic stream valleys and small farms that crisscrossed the district."[13] However, a sizable group of settlers of more modest means resided alongside these prosperous settlers. Unable to find work in the more congested downtown area of the city and mostly poor, these straitened settlers looked uptown to the Harlem area, where land had been cleared and soil was ripe for farming. They settled on the outskirts of the region and built little cottages from

13. Bourgois, *In Search of Respect*, 56.

fieldstone, wood, and shingles. Freed Africans and slaves lived alongside both of these groups of mostly white settlers. Hence, in the early and mid-1800s, East Harlem was a rural farming hamlet or village with two economic communities, complete with large estates for the wealthy and huts for the poverty stricken.

The demographics of the area changed considerably in the late 1800s, mostly due to population pressures and housing scarcity in lower Manhattan and incipient industrialization and urbanization in the district. All three factors played a role in the arrival of a new wave of European migrants and immigrants to the area during the 1860s, 1870s, and 1880s, setting in motion a steady increase in the area's population. To begin with, a good number of German Jews moved from downtown Manhattan to East and West Harlem during the first two of these decades, owing to population density, diverse forms of ethnic tension, the intolerable condition of older tenements, and the loss of apartment houses that were razed and replaced by factories, parks, and the Brooklyn and Williamsburg Bridges in the Lower East Side of Manhattan. Shortly thereafter, Eastern European Jews, who came directly from Europe and also from other parts of the city, joined these transplanted German Jews. Residential settlements had developed in East Harlem in the 1860s and were still readily available and affordable, making the area an attractive location. Upon their arrival, some began to open stores and to push for the founding of communal aid societies and synagogues in the area. The greater number of them had to find work in the garment industry, in food production, and in retail sales, many as peddlers at first and, later on, as owners of shops and even department stores in the area and in other parts of the city.

Irish immigrants joined the mix in the mid-to-late 1870s. Many of them were hired as construction workers, laying trolley tracks, elevating transit lines that were starting to appear in the area, and digging the subway tunnels that eventually crisscrossed much of Manhattan. The Harlem River Railroad along Park Avenue, the elevated rails of the New York Central Railroad along Second and Third Avenues, the First Avenue Trolley, and the Lexington Avenue subway line were all part of a massive infrastructural construction project funded by privately owned transportation companies and the municipal government of the City of New York, making transportation more convenient, accessible, and affordable throughout the growing city. All of these transit lines went through East Harlem, making the neighborhood more accessible to other parts of the city and more attractive to future newcomers looking for an affordable place to live with convenient access to factories, sweatshops, and other places of employment downtown.

This is also where and when a wave of Italian immigrants entered the picture. Many Italian immigrants were brought to the area in the late 1870s and early 1880s by J. D. Crimmons, a wealthy Irishman and contractor, and by management of the First Avenue Trolley, replacing Irish track layers who had gone on strike over shoddy pay and treatment. Italian laborers from lower Manhattan were brought in at first, but, when more men were needed, Crimmons and the operation's administration requested and hired more Italian laborers from Italy, mostly from southwest Italy. This group was joined by tens of thousands of other Italians who were looking to escape poverty and the hardships caused by droughts that had destroyed the farmlands and occasioned cholera, malaria, and other plagues in southern Italy in the early 1890s.[14]

Once here, the gathering began to replicate life in southern Italy, reproducing its regional divisions and villages. By the 1920s, it was possible to observe a pattern of Italian residency in East Harlem: there was a settlement from Bari on 112th Street; people from Sarno, near Naples, lived on 107th Street; Sicilians from Santiago lived on 100th Street; and a large group of Calabrians, from the southern tip of Italy, were on 109th Street. The colony eventually stretched from Ninety-Sixth Street to 125th Street, although mostly along Second Avenue, First Avenue, and Paladino Avenue—the avenues closest to the East River. This was New York's original Little Italy, and its overall habitancy was substantial.[15] By the 1930s, over 110,000 Italian-Americans lived in East Harlem. Not surprisingly, the community influenced the fabric of the neighborhood. Italians had their own restaurants, bakeries, candy stores, ice cream shops, banks, social clubs, and funeral parlors in the area. They even had local youth street gangs and organized Italian gangs that formed the Italian-American Mafia.

This, too, is part of the neighborhood's history and ongoing narrative. After all, East Harlem was the founding location of the Genovese crime family, one of the Five Families that dominated organized crime in New

---

14. Nazzareno Diodato and Gianni Bellocchi, "Historical Perspective of Drought Response in Central-Southern Italy," *Climate Research* 49, no. 3 (October 2011): 189–200, and Oliver Staley, "How a Severe Drought in Sicily in 1893 Created the Mafia," *Quartz* (December 20, 2017), https://qz.com.

15. Matthew Small, "Harlem's Hidden History: The Real Little Italy Was Uptown," *Harlem Focus*, July 17, 2016, https://medium.com.

York City and the crime family that controlled East Harlem under the leadership of Michael "Trigger Mike" Coppola and, then, the infamous mobster Anthony "Fat Tony" Salerno. Older residents living in the neighborhood still speak in whispered tones about the sway and deeds of the Genovese crime family. Long-time residents of the neighborhood, especially Puerto Rican residents who have lived in the neighborhood for a long stretch of time, can also tell of the skirmishes they either witnessed or in which they willingly or unwillingly became embroiled with Italian-American youth gangs that were looking to protect their home turf from newcomers.

Today, only remnants of the former Italian community remain, mostly in a small section of the neighborhood between 114th and 118th Street and from First Avenue to Paladino Avenue, a four block and one avenue stretch. Italians began to move out of the area in the late 1930s, around the end of the Great Depression and the time when Puerto Ricans and African Americans began to move into the neighborhood in increasing numbers. Presumably, they did so to leave the small and crowded apartment buildings of the neighborhood. They also left to avoid getting mixed up with the darker-skinned newcomers to the area, especially because Italians had suffered from discrimination themselves at the hands of the area's previous Irish and Jewish residents when they arrived in large numbers from Italy. By this point, they had struggled for decades to assert their whiteness.

World War II played a big role in the decline of the Italian community in East Harlem as well. A good number of young Italian men joined the military for the war and were removed from the community. With the help of VA benefits, many of these young men decided to take up residence in the outer boroughs and suburbs of New York City and in certain towns of New Jersey after completing their service time. Consequently, large Italian communities developed in areas of Brooklyn, Staten Island, eastern Long Island, and New Jersey. In East Harlem, however, the community dwindled. Even so, the Italians managed to leave traces of their once thriving community in the neighborhood.

Remnants of the neighborhood's Italian heritage are kept alive by the handful of octogenarian and nonagenarian Italian residents who continue to live in the neighborhood along Pleasant Avenue, from 114th to 118th Street, and by the few Italian restaurants that remain in the area, like Patsy's Pizzeria—where one can still get one of the best slices of pizza and pizza pies in the city—and the famous Rao's—one of the most exclusive restaurants in New York City with a reservation waiting list that is at least a year long.

Our Lady of Mt. Carmel Church, on 115th Street and Pleasant Avenue, a Roman Catholic church, continues the cultural heritage of Italian Harlem by holding an annual feast every July 16 in honor of the Virgin Mary and another festival in the first week of August known as the Dance of the Giglio in honor of St. Anthony.[16] Both of these cherished traditions bring thousands of Italian pilgrims and other visitors to the neighborhood annually. Remembrance of the Italian community remains alive in these parts, of course, through the memories that are held and the stories that are told by long-time residents of the neighborhood. Many of them remember interacting with the community back in the day. Puerto Rican residents still living in the area, including many in my own family, remember the interactions well. Some are of pleasant memories, and others are not; but they exist and endure, indicating that the Italian history of East Harlem remains a part of the narrative of the place.

Though more traces of the Italian settlement and inhabitation of the neighborhood can still be stumbled upon because of its more recent vintage, each of the migrant and immigrant ethnic groups that lived there managed to leave a mark on the place. The Wiechquaesgecks can be remembered for being among the first group of peoples to discover the geographical appeal and bestowal of this particular patch of land. The Dutch and the British had a hand in the naming and in the residential development of the place. There are buildings still being used for religious worship and instruction in the neighborhood that harken back to the time when German and Eastern European Jews populated the area. They may be banks or Pentecostal churches today, but once they were synagogues; and the physical appearance of these buildings, including carvings on the outside walls, make this known. Plenty of storefronts in East Harlem still call to mind the Jews who once lived and worked in the area. The elevated Park Avenue viaduct and railroad line built in the late nineteenth century by Irish and Italian men from the area still cross the neighborhood in its entirety. The Richie Riches, living south of Ninety-Seventh Street along Park Avenue, have not had to deal with the noise, vibrations, pollution, unsightliness, and other inconveniences caused throughout all these years by what is now the Metro-North Railroad Harlem Line, but residents of East Harlem have had to and still do. The neighborhood still continues to bear witness to its diversified ethnic past in these and other ways.

---

16. Robert A. Orsi, *The Madonna of 115th Street: Faith and Community in Italian Harlem, 1880–1950* (New Haven, CT: Yale University Press, 2010).

Furthermore, we should note that, because the ethnic groups that moved to the area in the late 1800s and early 1900s were predominantly poor, the neighborhood took on both the physical appearance and the social reputation of a low-income ethnic urban enclave. The cheap and now-shabby four-, five-, and six-story railroad flats that still extend throughout the area were once built to accommodate the mass influx of mostly fortuneless and low-paid Jewish, Irish, and Italian workers and families who began arriving in the late nineteenth century looking for affordable apartments and for jobs either in the large-scale infrastructural construction projects taking place in the district or in other sectors of the economy in other parts of the city. The rough-hewn, unpolished, and gritty look that has long characterized the neighborhood is traceable to the poor ethnic groups it was designed to harbor from the late nineteenth century on. This, too, is part of the neighborhood's inheritance from this European ethnic period and past.

Discussing the rich ethnic diversity of the neighborhood's history emphasizes that Puerto Ricans weren't the first to make a place for themselves in nor the first to leave marks on East Harlem. Each of the groups I have mentioned established a presence in the neighborhood for a considerable length of time, and each ended up playing a role in establishing its infrastructure, character, cultural patrimony, and reputation. What's more, even during the extended time of their predominance within it, Puerto Ricans have always had to share the neighborhood with others.

Puerto Ricans have certainly shared it with African Americans, who have maintained a strong presence in the neighborhood since the 1940s. African Americans have generally registered as and been regarded as the second-most-prevalent group in the neighborhood. On the whole, Latino/as have been in the top population spot, with Puerto Ricans being the majority in that category, and, then, African Americans the runners-up.[17] I remember that, in all the years I lived there, from 1967 to 1992, and then again from 1998 to 2000, most of my friends were either Puerto Rican or African American. And I am certain that most people who grew up in East Harlem after the late forties can say the same thing because, with reference to skin

---

17. New York region census data through the years bears this out. See also the portraits and the reporting presented in the published oral histories of the neighborhood's residents. For example, see Christopher Bell, *East Harlem Remembered: Oral Histories of Community and Diversity* (Jefferson, NC: McFarland, 2013); Russell Leigh Sharman, *The Tenants of East Harlem* (Berkeley: University of California Press, 2006); and Freidenberg, *Growing Old in El Barrio*.

tone, this part of town has generally been decked out in hues of brown and Black ever since. The cumulative effect of successive waves of Puerto Rican in-migrations to these parts over many decades, and the entry of thousands of African Americans into the neighborhood following the Great Northward Migration, ensured that.[18]

Neighborhood sharing involved other groups of people as well. People from other countries in the West Indies, especially from Jamaica, Bermuda, Barbados, Antigua, Trinidad, and the Virgin Islands have called East Harlem home during its Puerto Rican incorporation. Latino/as from other parts of Latin America and the Caribbean, notably from the Dominican Republic, Cuba, and, more recently, Mexico, have certainly done the same. And even though Spanish Harlem has never been a Chinese enclave, people from China have made their presence felt there all the same, especially since the 1980s, and particularly through small restaurants dotted around the neighborhood, serving takeout food from the other side of plexiglass panes at all hours of the day.

Amid the neighborhood sharing and its resulting cultural, architectural, and culinary legacies, there can be no denying that this part of town has sported a Puerto Rican semblance since the 1940s. The semblance has faded a bit in the 2000s, following a marked decrease in the number of the neighborhood's Puerto Rican residents; but it was nice and strong and in place for all to see, hear, smell, and talk about from the 1940s to the early 2000s. It remains in existence and effect today even after some fading, so it is not a thing of the past—not yet at least. We are talking about seven decades of inhabitance and influence here—no small thing in the history of the neighborhood and in the history of the Puerto Rican diaspora more generally.

The Puerto Rican presence and influence has been measurable and palpable. The population numbers tell part of the story: 20,000 in 1935, 63,000 in 1950, and 75,400 at its peak in 1960.[19] The look, feel, sounds, and even

---

18. For more on the topic of the Great Northward Migration, see James N. Gregory, *The Southern Diaspora: How the Great Migrations of Black and White Southerners Transformed America* (Chapel Hill: University of North Carolina Press, 2005); Nicholas Lemann, *The Promised Land: The Great Black Migration and How It Changed America* (New York: Vintage Books, 1991); and Isabel Wilkerson, *The Warmth of Other Suns: The Epic Story of America's Great Migration* (New York: Vintage Books, 2011).

19. For these figures, see Freidenberg, *Growing Old in El Barrio*, esp. 15–19, and "An Economic Snapshot of the East Harlem Neighborhood," published by Office of the New York State Comptroller (December 3, 2017), www.osc.state.ny.us.

the smells of East Harlem are more significant and convincing even than the population numbers since 1935. The ubiquitous flags of Puerto Rico are posted all over the neighborhood. Spanish is spoken practically everywhere in the neighborhood, and the murals on the side of tenement buildings pay homage to Puerto Rican entertainers and to other Puerto Rican icons. The salsa music and boleros blaring from windows above and from cars and stores below fill the neighborhood. The many cuchifrito establishments, other restaurants serving up Puerto Rican comfort food to locals and the general public, and the bodegas at almost every street corner sell all kinds of Puerto Rican food items and copies of Puerto Rico–based and Spanish-language daily newspapers: *El Vocero*, *El Mundo*, *El Nuevo Dia*, and *El Diario La Prensa*. The piragua pushcarts sell delicious Puerto Rican shaved ice desserts shaped like a pyramid and covered with sweet, fruit-flavored syrup. Lively sidewalk groups would usually form after 5:00 p.m. on certain streets during the spring, summer, and fall seasons, composed mostly of men playing dominoes or listening to a baseball game or boxing match.

The neighborhood is full of Puerto Rican–owned barbershops, music stores, and travel agencies with easily recognizable Puerto Rican names. The Banco de Ponce branches mark the place with their locations on 106th Street and Third Avenue and on 116th Street between Third and Lexington Avenues. Unmistakably Puerto Rican merchandise is sold by Puerto Ricans all through the famous La Marqueta, an enclosed marketplace that used to exist under the elevated Metro North railway tracks between 111th Street and 116th Street on Park Avenue. Together with the figurines of the *santos* of Puerto Rican towns that are openly displayed in retail store counters, storefront windows, and on car dashboards, these cultural markers clearly communicate to any and all persons: "Not only are you in a predominantly Latino/a neighborhood, you are in a predominantly Puerto Rican neighborhood." I used to tell non–Puerto Rican friends or Puerto Rican family members who were visiting from out of town, "You are in the Puerto Rican part of town now." More often than not, they responded, "Yeah, I can see that." They could just as easily have said, "Yeah, I can hear that, smell that, and sense that," for the distinctive character and pervading tone and mood of the place were unmistakably Puerto Rican. This was the case in the decades that I lived in the neighborhood, and people who lived in East Harlem before me, in the forties and fifties, can paint a similar picture.

So, how exactly did East Harlem's transfiguration into a colonia, or settlement of the Puerto Rican diaspora, come about and *take place*? Well, I will say this: It occurred gradually over a long stretch of time and by virtue of various extended migration cycles. Many writings on the history of the Puerto Rican community in the United States, in New York City, and in East Harlem tend to focus on what has come to be known as the Great Migration of the late 1940s and 1950s. Some begin the story at the point of the Puerto Rican migrations around the time of World War I, but there are much earlier Puerto Rican roots in the United States, in the city, and in East Harlem. Even while Puerto Rico was under Spanish rule, Puerto Ricans were making their way to the United States, especially to the East Coast of the United States.

Reforms were introduced in the Spanish colonies in the late 1800s to foster economic development and commerce throughout the colonial empire. The loosening of what once had been significantly restrictive Spanish mercantile policies opened the way to growing trade between Puerto Rican and Anglo-American colonists all along the Eastern seaboard. This flourishing trade, based mostly on the buying and selling of Puerto Rican sugar and molasses, tied the ports of Puerto Rico with port cities in New York, New England, and Pennsylvania, and brought Puerto Rican merchants to these parts on a more consistent basis. Some of these merchants settled with their families in cities along the East Coast, becoming the first Puerto Rican residents in New York City and in other cities like Philadelphia, New Haven, and Boston. New York City, already a magnet city for transplants from all over the globe, attracted the larger number of these early Puerto Rican émigrés, although the numbers remained small in this initial phase of settlement.

These merchants were joined soon thereafter by Puerto Rican political émigrés, who were forced to leave Puerto Rico to escape political persecution as a consequence of their fight against Spanish colonialism, and by tabaqueros (cigar makers) looking to ply their trade in the principal centers of cigar manufacturing, which included New York City, New Orleans, Tampa, and Philadelphia. Along with others who came as students, as adventurers, and as seamen in connection with the thriving waterborne transport industry, these emigrants proceeded to establish footholds in several cities, providing a basis for the more extensive Puerto Rican migrations that would follow. In New York City, clusters of Puerto Rican emigrants began to form in the Borough Hall and Red Hook sections of Brooklyn, along the Navy Yard and waterfront area, and also in Chelsea, the Lower East Side, Central Harlem, and East Harlem in Manhattan.

Once settled, these newly arrived Puerto Rican New Yorkers quickly began to make their mark in the New York area through various organizational, entrepreneurial, and political activities. As far back as 1830, there were Puerto Ricans among those who joined to form a Spanish Benevolent Society in New York City, hoping to promote commercial interactions between the Caribbean islands and the United States and to provide help to immigrants coming from Puerto Rico, Cuba, and Spain to the United States. By 1874, the first Puerto Rican newspaper had already been published in New York City—*La Voz de Puerto Rico*. In 1895, a branch of the Cuban Revolutionary Party was formed by Puerto Rican political activists involved in the island's separatist or independence movement against Spain.[20] And, before the end of the nineteenth century, a few boardinghouses and some small businesses catering specifically to newcomers from Puerto Rico began to appear. Moreover, a host of notable Puerto Ricans either became part of the life of the city or spent some years of struggle in the city before Puerto Rico became a possession of the United States in 1898, including Julio L. Vizcarrondo, Ramón Emeterio Betances, Lola Rodriguez de Tío, Eugenio María de Hostos, Sotero Figueroa, Inocencia Martinez de Santaella, and Arturo Alfonso Schomburg. These small clusters of immigrants and immigrant families, living in different neighborhoods throughout the city, gave witness then and serves as evidence now of a blossoming and active Puerto Rican community well before the 1940s.

These early clusters remained small through the nineteenth century and into the 1920s, even in the case of the East Harlem community, which would soon become the largest and most significant of all the Puerto Rican colonias. Bernardo Vega indicates its small size in his memoirs. Vega was one of the many politically active cigar workers to immigrate to New York City in the early part of the twentieth century. His memoirs are one of the few surviving testimonies of Puerto Rican life in the city during the early twentieth century. And in a section of his *Memorias de Bernardo Vega* (Memoirs of Bernardo Vega), when recalling the year he moved to the city, Vega says this:

> When I took up residence in New York in 1916 the apartment buildings and stores in what came to be known as El Barrio, "our" Barrio,

---

20. For more, see Virginia E. Sánchez Korrol, *From Colonia to Community: The History of Puerto Ricans in New York City* (Berkeley: University of California Press, 1983), esp. 211–40; and Clara E. Rodríguez, "Forging a New, New York: The Puerto Rican Community, Post-1945," in *Boricuas in Gotham: Puerto Ricans in the Making of Modern New York City*, ed. Gabriel Haslip-Viera, Angelo Falcón, and Félix Matos Rodríguez (Princeton, NJ: Markus Wiener Publishers, 2004), 195–218.

or the Barrio Latino, all belonged to Jews. Seventh, St. Nicholas, and Manhattan Avenues and the streets in between were all inhabited by Jewish people of means, if not great wealth. 110th Street was the professional center of the district. The classy, expensive stores were on Lenox Avenue, while the more modest ones were located east of Fifth Avenue. The ghetto of poor Jews extended along Park Avenue between 110th and 117th and on the streets east of Madison. It was in this lower-class Jewish neighborhood that some Puerto Rican and Cuban families, up to about fifty of them, were living at that time.[21]

Those last two sentences are of particular interest to me since they are the ones that apply to East Harlem specifically.

Because the Puerto Rican community was sprinkled about the entire Harlem area at that time, Vega makes allusion to two neighborhoods that are now differentiated: Central Harlem and East Harlem. In due course, but without haste, the East Harlem neighborhood would become the cradle of the largest Puerto Rican settlement in the city and in the States. Besides the mention of the ghetto status of the neighborhood even then, what is interesting here is that he sets the number of Puerto Rican and Cuban families living there at fifty. Since he is including Puerto Rican *and* Cuban families in this count, we can imagine the Puerto Rican figure being something like twenty-five or thirty families in 1916. In other words, it isn't a large number of East Harlemite Puerto Ricans; but they were in the district, and they were starting to make a place for themselves and for other Puerto Ricans in the neighborhood already by the first part of the twentieth century. Their numbers would grow significantly during the World War I years and in the interwar period as a result of a second migration phase.

This second extended phase of in-migration from Puerto Rico to the States and to New York City and East Harlem was prompted by a number of events that transpired roughly between 1898 and 1938. First and foremost, the United States took control over Puerto Rico from Spain in 1898, and the United States subsequently attempted to incorporate Puerto Rico into U.S. trade circuits, fostering U.S. investment in Puerto Rico. The United States' interest in the annexation of Puerto Rico contained an economic motive

---

21. Bernardo Vega, "Memorias de Bernardo Vega," in *Puerto Rican Arrival in New York: Narratives of the Migration, 1920–1950*, ed. Juan Flores (Princeton, NJ: Markus Wiener Publishers, 2005), 55.

from the start. The principal motivation was of course a military one. By reason of its geographical location in the middle of the Caribbean, Puerto Rico figured prominently in the United States' strategic plans for stability in the Caribbean and for a military outpost from which to protect the Panama Canal, the Southern Atlantic and Gulf States, and the trade routes of the Caribbean. The idea was to build a defense triangle that included Puerto Rico, MacDill Field near Tampa, Florida, and Panama.[22]

We can imagine, too, that the United States saw the Spanish-Cuban-American War (1898) as a splendid and well-timed opportunity finally to kick Spain out of the hemisphere and to establish hegemony over the Caribbean. This is the way of industrial empires, but it is clear that the United States' interest in this territorial prize of war was also commercially driven. Statements made by President William McKinley right around the time that the United States was negotiating terms of the compensation for the Spanish-Cuban-American war with Spain seem to make this plain. "We have good money, we have ample revenues, we have unquestionable national credit," he said, "but what we need is new markets, and as trade follows the flag, it looks very much as if we are going to have new markets."[23] Once the Treaty of Paris was signed on December 10, 1898, those new markets officially became Puerto Rico, Guam, and the Philippine Islands, all annexed by the United States as war booty.

In the case of Puerto Rico, trade had already proven to be profitable for the United States. In terms of export, Puerto Rico was already "the tenth market for American goods in the hemisphere, with a favorable trade balance of nearly $2.5 million."[24] Imports from Puerto Rico—mostly based on sugar, coffee, tobacco, and other island agricultural products—totaled less than those of Brazil, Cuba, Mexico, and Venezuela and ahead of imports from the rest of the Caribbean and Latin America, including Colombia, Uruguay, Chile, and Peru. The annexation of Puerto Rico afforded the United States the opportunity to further its economic interests in the island and by way of the island. It did this by removing obstacles that could hinder U.S. investment in Puerto Rico, by prohibiting Puerto Rico from negotiating treaties with other countries or determining its own tariffs, by making

---

22. For more on this point, see Arturo Morales Carrión, *Puerto Rico: A Political and Cultural History* (New York: W. W. Norton, 1983), esp. 129–51 and 242–55.

23. See José Trías Monge, *Puerto Rico: The Trials of the Oldest Colony in the World* (New Haven, CT: Yale University Press, 1997), 27.

24. Carrión, *Puerto Rico*, 133.

Puerto Rico part of the U.S. monetary system, by requiring that all goods be transported in U.S.-owned shipping containers, and by promoting the interests of the sugar industry, which had been the basis of the commercial connections between Puerto Rico and the United States before the takeover. The Passenger Vessel Services Act of 1886, the Foraker Act of 1900, and the Jones-Shafroth Act of 1917 enabled these changes and demands.

The result of this imperialistic economic involvement could be foreseen. Obviously, many of these policies were not on the side of Puerto Rico, disproportionately benefitting U.S. corporations and investors. History shows that this legislated imperialism disadvantaged most in this "unincorporated territory" of the United States. The harmful effects that these policies prompted were considerable, and, for many of the agricultural laborers in Puerto Rico, they proved to be crippling and life altering. Restricted to trading almost exclusively with the United States, Puerto Rico's economy became tied to and dependent on the United States. Moreover, U.S. companies took control of Puerto Rico's economic production and shifted its focus toward sugar production. Puerto Rico became a monoculture colony, producing a single crop for export to a single market.

Furthermore, because the U.S. companies that came in were starting to rely on mechanization for their business, less of a local workforce was needed to produce that sugar. With the coffee and tobacco industries forced into a decline, hordes of agricultural workers were left facing underemployment or unemployment. Long-term unemployment rose to alarming levels on the island, contributing to greater poverty. The problem of chronic unemployment and of worsening poverty grew to such an extent that it forced policymakers and government officials on the island and in the metropole (i.e., the United States) to pay attention. Labor was a second factor that prompted increased migration from Puerto Rico to the States, and to New York City and East Harlem in particular, during World War I and the interwar period.

To ease the problem of chronic unemployment and the dreadful poverty to which it was contributing, policymakers took to promoting contract-labor programs, opening the way for corporations to recruit Puerto Ricans as a source of low-wage labor in the States and elsewhere. The idea was initiated in the early 1900s. The implementation of contract-labor recruitment continued into the early 1970s, at first through private agencies and then through government-sponsored contract-labor programs.

The first major migration prompted by its implementation under U.S. rule was to Hawaii. Between 1900 and 1901, U.S.-owned corporations recruited more than five thousand Puerto Rican men, women, and children to work on sugar plantations there.[25] Those U.S.-owned corporations likewise recruited Puerto Ricans to work in the Dominican Republic, Cuba, Ecuador, Venezuela, Mexico, and St. Croix after the United States purchased the Virgin Islands from Denmark in 1917. Here in the States, they were recruited to work in areas of California, Arizona, Wisconsin, Missouri, Illinois, Ohio, Pennsylvania, and on the farms of Long Island, the Connecticut River Valley, and the southwestern agricultural regions of New Jersey. The last four of these locations brought Puerto Rican emigrants closer to East Harlem in Manhattan, setting the stage for their prospective immigration into the neighborhood.

Three recurring patterns tended to occur in cases when Puerto Rican workers elected not to return to Puerto Rico at the end of their contracts. First, sometimes, contracted workers stayed where they had been recruited, sending for their family and friends. Second, in some cases, workers opted not to continue long journeys to faraway places like Hawaii, which involved travel by ship from Puerto Rico to New Orleans, by train to California, and then by ship to Hawaii. They elected instead to remain at other points along the journey. Often, a third scene would take place. Puerto Rican workers encountered ill treatment, exploitation, lack of or partial pay, and poor working and living conditions at their worksites. At times, this occasioned the difficult and daring decision to back out of a work contract and to flee an encampment or workplace. In these cases, contracted workers returned to Puerto Rico if they could, or they would enlist the help of a friend, acquaintance, or family member living in relative proximity or somewhere else within the United States as a means to establishing a residence in a given location.

Either way, these contract labor initiatives generated increased migration from Puerto Rico to the United States and prompted the growth of the diasporic Puerto Rican communities settled in the United States, including the one that was sprouting in East Harlem. The passage of the 1921 and 1924 immigration laws, restricting immigration from Southern and Eastern Europe and Asia until 1965, were significant events that served as a third factor that contributed to this second cycle of Puerto Rico in-migration

---

25. For more on this point, see Carmen Teresa Whalen, "Colonialism, Citizenship, and the Making of the Puerto Rican Diaspora: An Introduction," in *The Puerto Rican Diaspora: Historical Perspectives* (Philadelphia: Temple University Press, 2005), esp. 3–12.

into the States, New York City, and East Harlem. With these statutes in effect and given the curtailment of potential laborers they occasioned, more employment opportunities became available in the United States, especially for semi-skilled and manual laborers. In combination, these factors created the conditions for an understandable emigration outcome. Displaced by economic change at home, recruited as a source of low-wage labor, and presented with ample work opportunities, rural and working-class Puerto Ricans boarded steamships and aircraft, coming to the States in larger numbers. A few of the ships were even given familiar Puerto Rican names, including those of island towns—Borinquen, San Juan, Ponce, Coamo, etc. And with each ship's manifest came the prospect of further growth in the stateside Puerto Rican population. The U.S. Puerto Rican population grew from approximately 2,000 people in 1900 to 11,811 by 1920 and 52,774 by 1930.[26]

New York City received the majority of these newer entrants from the island, and, within the city, East Harlem, the inevitable magnet for working-class settlements, welcomed them. New York City's pull was considerable and foreseeable. As the nation's financial and industrial hub, the port city had traditionally been the site of immigrant disembarkation. As Virginia Sánchez Korrol notes, "the shipping lines connecting the island and the mainland had their terminus in New York City," and the sea routes between the island and the city "offered several different class fares, were more efficient, and boasted the best facilities."[27] Moreover, while destinations in other states could offer a warmer climate and less travel time, their ports were often unequipped to receive larger passenger ships from Puerto Rico. By contrast, passenger ships from Puerto Rico to New York could dock in the city without any difficulty. In addition, the developing Puerto Rican colonias in the city were reasonably established by this point, and it simply made sense for newer migrants to live in areas with other Puerto Ricans and where their language, customs, attitudes, and interests could be encountered and indulged at least from time to time.

In addition to these attractive characteristics, East Harlem was on the margins of the New York City real-estate market, having already developed a reputation and a following as a lower-income immigrant neighborhood that offered low-cost housing with relative proximity to jobs in downtown

---

26. See Edna Acosta-Belén and Carlos E. Santiago, *Puerto Ricans in the United States: A Contemporary Portrait* (London: Lynne Rienner Publishers, 2006), 47.

27. Sánchez Korrol, *From Colonia to Community*, 44–45.

Manhattan and accessible transportation close by to get to them. It is little wonder, then, that, after disembarking in the ports of Brooklyn and Staten Island, so many Puerto Ricans headed for East Harlem. They proceeded much in the same way as the straitened Jewish, Irish, and Italian immigrants had done previously.

Of course, it is important to bear in mind that, for a good stretch of this second-cycle migration period, Puerto Ricans were arriving as U.S. citizens by means of the Jones-Shafroth Act, signed into effect by President Woodrow Wilson in 1917. Nevertheless, considering the harsh treatment, racial antagonism, cultural misrepresentation, and the social, economic, and political marginalization they were to confront in the neighborhood, by the media, and by many of their fellow U.S. citizens, their citizenship amounted to a citizenship of an inferior order. For all intents and purposes, "they were foreigners with U.S. citizenship, immigrant-citizens but not Americans."[28] But here they were, East Harlemites now and in increasing numbers—about twenty thousand by the mid-thirties. El Barrio of East Harlem, Spanish Harlem, was on its way and would arrive fully with the influx of a third extended cycle of in-migration from the island during and after World War II.

Called the "Great Migration," the third cycle stretched across three decades and incorporated an extensive outflow of people relative to the size of the island's population base—a yearly average of 32,000 individuals in net migration from Puerto Rico between 1947 and 1949 and approximately 470,000 people out of an island population of about 2.2 million during the decade of the 1950s.[29] The dynamics of this migratory phase brought the U.S. Puerto Rican population to 1,391,463 by 1970; 860,584 of those people took up residence in New York City.

The transformation of Puerto Rico's economy from an agricultural economy to an industrial economy using U.S. capital was the main push factor during this period, spanning the World War II years and the postwar years from 1945 to 1970. Spoiling for a new developmental model that could modernize Puerto Rico's economy, create more jobs, promote social mobility, and expand the business and entrepreneurial base of the economy, island officials and policymakers endorsed a rapid industrial development

---

28. Lorrin Thomas, *Puerto Rican Citizen: History and Identity in Twentieth-Century New York City* (Chicago: University of Chicago Press, 2010), 3.

29. See Sánchez Korrol, *From Colonia to Community*, esp. 35–36, and Acosta-Belén and Santiago, *Puerto Ricans in the United States*, esp. 80–83.

plan known as Operacíon Manos a la Obra or Operation Bootstrap. The plan's goal was to increase U.S. investment in Puerto Rico, seeking to attract more U.S. investors to Puerto Rico through the provision of tax exemptions, freedom from import duties, advisory and technical assistance, rental subsidies on buildings, and, of course, the lure of lower wages than in the United States.

The plan worked to a certain extent. It did increase U.S. investment in the island. It also advanced modernization in the island through industrialization and further urbanization. It even boosted the construction industry and allowed more productive wealth to reach the middle sectors and certain lower sectors of the economy. Troubling aspects and outcomes, however, waited underneath this economic headway.

Primarily, the industrialization program failed to replace the jobs lost in agriculture and in agricultural processing. Moreover, it created other forms of worker displacement as it favored certain industries while disfavoring others, aiding mostly the developing urban areas and not the larger rural areas of the island. Consequently, migration to the United States continued unabated, primarily due to harsh economic conditions on the island.

In the meantime, on the U.S. side of the migration, urban economies were experiencing a boom in the aftermath of World War II. Jobs in the garment industry, in light manufacturing, and in the services sector became readily available in the United States, especially since white Euro-American World War II veterans were able to take advantage of new programs established by the federal government to promote upward economic and social mobility. With the help of this backing, they started to leave the congested inner city for the greener, more open spaces of the suburbs, creating a momentary vacuum in the manufacturing and service sectors of the urban economy.

Most of these jobs were at the bottom rungs of the economic ladder—in textile, garment, and munitions factories; in soldering and metal plating; and in restaurants, grocery stores, hotels, and office buildings. The jobs were often unpleasant, low paying, and unglamorous, but they provided work and income nonetheless. Because of all of this, Puerto Ricans came to the cities of the United States, especially to New York City. They came in droves, especially during the 1940s and 1950s, transitioning from the steamship to the low-fare flights made available at first by smaller wildcat lines using Army surplus planes purchased by former G.I. pilots and then by such commercial airlines as Eastern Airlines, Pan American Airways, American Airlines, and

Trans World Airlines.[30] East Harlem's Puerto Rican population numbers make the dynamism of this third cycle clear, growing to 63,000 people by 1950 and 75,400 by 1960.

As could be expected, their considerable number enabled the Puertorriqueños to put their mark on the neighborhood, and this mark was and continues to be a visible, unmistakable reality, obvious in the neighborhood's sights, feel, sounds, smells, and cultural and emotional associations or meanings. It is equally true that the Puerto Rican connection has played a role in the forms of disrespect, neglect, misgovernance, inequity, disadvantage, hardship, and misfortune the neighborhood has had to endure since the late 1940s. The effects of an ongoing colonial story and of a massive migration occasioned by unemployment and economic distress were bound to emerge. Old and deep-seated maladies of racism and economic inequality have only been exacerbated by major economic restructuring that led to a decrease in blue-collar manufacturing jobs in the late twentieth century in the United States. Rampant suburbanization of industries and people contributed to urban blight. In response, many property owners and developers in the city practiced tactics of abandonment and disinvestment, contributing to further weathering and deterioration of tenement-based housing stocks that were considered substandard soon after they were built between the 1860s and 1890s. Densely populated public housing projects were constructed in the decades following World War II and have since become associated with residential segregation, urban blight, crime, grime, and poverty. In this multifaceted context, the lure of illegal forms of entrepreneurship responding to chronic unemployment, reduced prospects, and the weakening of dignity become vital ingredients of a placial hardship tale. You have the makings of some mean streets.

The dramatic placial story I tell unfolded in the streets of El Barrio, of East Harlem, touching the lives and memories of the Puerto Ricans who lived there and also the lives and memories of everyone who has ever lived

---

30. For more on the complex history of the unique, troubled, but much beloved *isla del encanto* (Puerto Rico), see Olga Jiménez de Wagenheim, *Puerto Rico: An Interpretive History from Pre-Columbian Times to 1900* (Princeton, NJ: Markus Wiener Publishers, 1998); César J. Ayala and Rafael Bernabe, *Puerto Rico in the American Century: A History since 1898* (Chapel Hill: University of North Carolina Press, 2007); Jorge Duany, *Puerto Rico: What Everyone Needs to Know* (New York: Oxford University Press, 2017); and Ed Morales, *Fantasy Island: Colonialism, Exploitation, and the Betrayal of Puerto Rico* (New York: Bold Type Books, 2019).

there since the 1940s. It has become part of the neighborhood's legend and continuing narrative.

From Mean Streets to Streets
of Perseverance and Resistance

The foibles and difficulties of the neighborhood have attracted the most attention in these legends and narratives. And I get it—to a certain extent. First off, drama, tragedy, and plight captivate audiences, tending to sell well in literature and the popular imagination. But there is also adequate cause to focus on the difficulties, problems, and challenges that El Barrio of East Harlem has faced. The truth is that these have been all too apparent. The problem, of course, emerges when the pathologizing slant gives way to narrow characterizations and to stigmatizing tropes.

In short, if we focus on the problems and roughness of the neighborhood exclusively or too one-sidedly, we can end up ignoring its beauty, artistry, splendid tenacity, and vibrant agency. We could neglect, overlook, or downplay how the great majority of its residents went to work, cared for their families, attended festivals, parties, and churches, and created art, music, and culture all while also leading lives of meaning, dignity, and achievement despite whatever structural and place-based obstacles they may have faced. At times, even those who have attempted to speak or write from an insider's perspective and on behalf of the neighborhood's community have inadvertently detracted from the importance of these triumphs. I know well that life in Spanish Harlem was difficult, was grim even. I did not learn about this via books. I lived it.

Walking down the streets of *mi barrio* when I was growing up, I used to think to myself that even the landscape of East Harlem could test one's resolve. East Harlem retains some hilliness, unlike the rest of the East Side of Manhattan, which is quite flat. The street on which I grew up, 100th Street between Third and Lexington Avenue, is a hill—a hill street with a good amount of steepness to it. Ninety-Eighth Street, 99th Street, 101st Street, and 102nd Street are just as precipitous. Then there is the legendary Duffy's Hill, located on Lexington Avenue between 102nd and 103rd Streets. It is the steepest hill in Manhattan, dropping twenty-eight feet across two hundred feet. It is so steep that, at one time, Lexington Avenue buses would detour onto Park Avenue to avoid the hill. Still today, one will find vehicles getting stuck on the hill while trying to scale it, especially in snowy conditions. Even the topography or terrain of the neighborhood requires one to be strong, one could say.

But there is more about the neighborhood's built environment that has loomed grim and forbidding over the years. The noticeability of its hardship is made all the more obvious by the neighborhood's proximity to Yorkville, the more affluent and ritzy neighborhood on its southern border. Nowhere in New York City and in few other places around the world are power, wealth, economic, residential, and placial inequalities more self-evident than on the border of these two neighborhoods. This inequality is in full view at Ninety-Seventh Street and Park Avenue. There, one can look to the south and see the Park Avenue made famous in movies and pictures, owing to the manicured wide boulevard lined with trees and greenery, the iconic Met Life Building, the Helmsley Building, the Waldorf Astoria, Grand Central Terminal, and, now, 432 Park Avenue, which sits on Billionaire's Row and is currently the tallest residential building in the world. And there too are all of the door-person-attended luxury apartment houses that line both sides of the avenue from Forty-Seventh Street to Ninety-Sixth Street.

But look north, and you will see a quite different Park Avenue, the one that cuts right through Spanish Harlem. This one isn't as featured in movies and tourism pictures and for good reason. This side of Park Avenue isn't as spruced up and well dressed. It has no iconic structures and luxury buildings. It is lined, instead, with old and poorly maintained tenement houses and several public-housing-project complexes. This side of Park Avenue is marked by the massive granite and steel viaduct that serves as the foundation for the elevated railway tracks of the Metro North Line. These tracks aren't seen south of Ninety-Seventh Street, of course. The architects and planners who designed the city and the Harlem/Metro North Line made sure that the tracks would be out of sight and out of mind for all of the inhabitants of Park Avenue south of that street. But the tracks, and the trains they carry, burst from underneath the streets of the Upper East Side at Ninety-Seventh Street for all to see, hear, and feel all through East Harlem, with rumbling noise and persistent vibrations from the passing trains and the unsightly inconveniences of the viaduct itself forced upon the neighborhood. As you might expect, the neighborhood's residents and the neighborhood's property values have been detrimentally shaped by those elevated railway tracks.

The ugly stone and steel viaduct has caused other neighborhood troubles through the years. I remember the elevated railway's pedestrian underpasses being vaulted, dark, damp, and downright dangerous. Water (or whatever liquid it was) dripped perpetually from the viaduct's stone ceiling, forcing pedestrians to dodge the drops in those murky underpasses. Dodging was only necessary, though, if one absolutely had to risk walking through one of them, since they were dark, usually smelled of urine, and could be dangerous because of crime at night. Even when one made it through one of these passageways unscathed, one still had to watch out for vehicles zooming down the avenue at either end of them.

The hill streets, especially on the southern part of the neighborhood, and the chunky granite railway viaduct are but two of the features that give the neighborhood's built environment a rough look. The housing stock has contributed much to that rugged look as well. The old tenement buildings and the public-housing projects spread throughout the neighborhood are among the first things one will notice when encountering the neighborhood, whether it be from the south, the north, or the west side.

And it all stems from those largely undifferentiated, low-slung tenements built back in the mid-to-late 1800s. That was a long time ago; yet, to this day, these old four-, five-, and six-story tenements form the basis of housing for most of the residents of East Harlem. The long, old-law tenements that I have in mind, often called "railroad flats" because their rooms are organized like cars on a train, can, of course, be seen scattered throughout other neighborhoods of New York City. They are a familiar housing type for the urban poor more generally. So it's not as if El Barrio of East Harlem has held a monopoly over the tenement. But it is certainly a poster child for this housing type. After all, in East Harlem, the tenement has been the main dish with respect to housing.

It is something of a miracle that the lion's share of these old tenements remains in existence in the neighborhood after all these years. They are neither a paragon of good design nor good construction. They never were. Built rather hurriedly and cheaply, the tenements were intended as low-cost housing for the urban poor. Most have four dwellings on each floor, with a central core containing a stairway. A few have only two dwellings per floor. No matter the number of the dwellings, there is nothing fancy about the design of these tenements. The walls of the apartments were constructed of plaster, and, through the ubiquitous cracks in the walls, one could see surprisingly thin strips of wood. If a rodent died inside the wall, which happened quite frequently as I remember, a vile stink permeated the apartment for many days until the corpse dried out. The rooms of these railroad flats are small and oddly shaped. They were rarely fitted with doors for privacy. The hallways of the buildings are mostly dark with few if any windows, having, therefore, limited lighting. Outside, the buildings are mostly unadorned, with metal fire escapes traversing the fronts and backs of the structures.

I remember that maintaining these buildings and the apartments within them was always a difficult task for residents and their landlords. One couldn't keep up with plastering the cracks and holes in the walls, repairing apartment ceilings because of broken water pipes, and tending to flooded basements because of heavy rains. The mice and roaches took delight in the impossibility. It is little wonder that they were ever present.

Something to bear in mind is that many of East Harlem's tenements have not been well maintained by their landlords over the years. In addition, abandonment, disinvestment, and arson were carried out in the neighborhood at times, especially in the 1960s and 1970s, resulting in abandoned buildings, vacant lots, and dilapidated tenements over stretches of time in the neighborhood's history. The abandoned buildings and empty lots have been infrequent since the late 1980s or early 1990s, but they were there for all to see in preceding decades. For many Puerto Ricans and other residents of the neighborhood, the battered tenements are more than just a matter of sight, for they have to live in them, as I did and as my parents still do.

The dilapidated tenements were already a problem in the late 1930s, contributing to East Harlem becoming a target for slum clearance and so-called urban renewal under the Federal Housing Act of 1937. Sometimes called the Wagner-Steagall Act, the legislation was part of Franklin D. Roosevelt's Third New Deal program. Through a public corporation that was formed to supervise housing programs—the United States Housing Authority (USHA)—it provided for bonds and subsidies to be paid by the U.S. government to local authorities to improve living conditions for low- and moderate-income families. For East Harlem and for other urban neighborhoods in U.S. cities, that meant the construction of housing projects, and a whole lot of them. In the case of East Harlem, these projects were complexes of mid-rise and high-rise buildings, neither isolated nor smaller-scale six-story buildings that comprised housing projects elsewhere.

Indeed, the first high-rise tower-project in the history of New York housing philanthropy was constructed in East Harlem: the East River Houses, a sprawling housing-project complex with ten mid-rise and high-rise buildings located between 102nd and 105th Streets, next to the East River and completed in 1941 as the city's fifth USHA-financed development. The first USHA-funded project in New York City was Red Hook Houses in Brooklyn, completed in 1939. These were of the six-story variety, however, which was the more normal and suggested height at the time. East Harlem was "blessed" with the high-rise projects.

The first series of East River Houses display a mixed height design of six-, ten-, and eleven-story buildings. The tower projects that followed took the concept to another level, eventually going as high as twenty stories. Other complexes contain buildings of nineteen, sixteen, and fourteen stories. Thirteen additional sites would go up in our neighborhood, many of these emerging in the late 1940s, followed by others in the late 1950s and early 1960s. These housing decisions and constructions were not something to which we aspired. They were thrust upon us. As a result, today, approximately one-third of East Harlem is covered with postwar subsidized housing, and almost all of it is designed in the vein of the mid- or high-rise tower project. Actually, East Harlem has the second largest concentration of public housing projects in the city and in the United States more generally. It is second only to the Brownsville section of Brooklyn.[31]

There was some merit to the construction of these public housing projects of course. The idea was to erase some of the urban blight that existed in East Harlem largely due to a housing stock made up mostly of aged tenements that needed rehabilitation. The hope behind their construction was also to relieve some of the overcrowding taking place in the neighborhood's inadequate tenements, lessening the shortage of decent housing for eligible low- and moderate-income families. This is all quite understandable. In hindsight, however, the construction of these large tower complexes brought much harm to the district.

First, the projects were not originally intended for everyone but for those

---

31. For more on the history of public housing projects in New York City, see Richard Plunz, *A History of Housing in New York City* (New York: Columbia University Press, 2016), esp. 243–45. For more on the history of public housing projects in East Harlem, see Samuel Zipp, *Manhattan Projects: The Rise and Fall of Urban Renewal in Cold War New York* (New York: Oxford University Press, 2010), esp. 253–99. For more on the history of public housing in the United States more generally, see Edward G. Goetz, *New Deal Ruins: Race, Economic Justice, and Public Housing Policy* (New York: Cornell University Press, 2013); R. Allen Hays, *The Federal Government and Urban Housing* (Albany, NY: SUNY Press, 2012), esp. 87–138; Richard Rothstein, *The Color of Law: A Forgotten History of How Our Government Segregated America* (New York: W. W. Norton, 2017), esp. 17–58; Gwendolyn Wright, *Building the Dream: A Social History of Housing in America* (Cambridge, MA: MIT Press, 1983), esp. 220–39; and Lawrence J. Vale, *After the Projects: Public Housing Redevelopment and the Governance of the Poorest Americans* (New York: Oxford University Press, 2019), esp. 3–40.

deemed "worthy of help." Members of minority groups, the unemployed, pregnant women who were not married, and large extended families were regularly denied access to these through housing policies that included "interviews for tenant suitability, apartment inspections for hygiene, wait lists for apartments and other forms of tenant surveillance."[32] In fact, at first and for a while, the new housing did not aid many of those actually living in the neighborhood! Instead, it dislodged a good number of them from their homes and forced them to find residence in other areas of the city, including Brooklyn, Queens, and the Bronx. As José Ramon Sanchez and Arlene Davila have noted, in the case of Puerto Ricans living in the district, it wasn't until civil strife and protest took place in the late 1960s and 1970s that they began to gain parity in their entrance to public housing because policies tended to favor low- and middle-income whites at first and, then, African Americans beginning in the mid-1960s, when their basic rights began to be recognized.[33] Until the late 1960s and early '70s, the Puerto Rican community was seen as a "transient and vulnerable population not worthy of permanent welfare aid."[34]

Second, the giant public-housing complexes wiped out a fair amount of East Harlem's local entrepreneurship early on, in so doing, razing micro-communities and worsening the profile or structural visibility of the neighborhood for the long haul. As Christopher Bell notes, up to 1,573 local businesses and stores, employing over 4,500 people, were eliminated in a relatively short period of time as block after block of tenements and other buildings were torn down by bulldozers to make room for the tower projects.[35] The lost institutions were the kinds of mom-and-pop stores and small businesses that brought a local character and a communal spirit to the district, including bakeries and pastry shops, grocery stores, barbershops, beauty shops, candy stores, bars, restaurants, cleaners, laundry stores, music stores, hardware stores, TV repair shops, law offices, travel agencies, and the social clubs that allowed neighbors to interact and develop support systems. These provided for a sense of cohesiveness and camaraderie in the neighbor-

---

32. Dávila, *Barrio Dreams,* 31.

33. See José Ramon Sanchez, "Housing Puerto Ricans in New York City, 1945–1984: A Study in Class Powerlessness," PhD diss., New York University, 1990; and Dávila, *Barrio Dreams*, esp. 30–38.

34. Dávila, *Barrio Dreams,* 32.

35. Christopher Bell, *East Harlem Remembered: Oral Histories of Community and Diversity* (Jefferson, NC: McFarland, 2013), 117.

hood as well as a livelihood. The projects did not kill off all of East Harlem's entrepreneurship and street life, but they significantly reduced it.

They also adversely affected the look and feel of the neighborhood. The projects' drab slab block and muddy-brick color have done East Harlem no favors in the looks department. Their construction also required the elimination of many cross streets throughout El Barrio, disrupting the orderly grid that characterizes much of Manhattan, cutting off pedestrian flows, eliminating potential parking spaces for cars, and creating odd-looking superblocks. In addition, the architects of some of the large public-housing complexes skewed their buildings forty-five degrees in relation to the Manhattan gridiron. The chosen angle may have been an aesthetic decision, or it could have intended to allow for a longer side with a river view for the complexes located closer to the East River.[36] Whatever the reason, although no functional explanation was ever given by the architects and city planners, the angular orientation has wreaked havoc on the topography of El Barrio of East Harlem. Not only does it disrupt the orderly grid that much of Manhattan has fought so hard to maintain, producing an abrupt schism between the projects and their surrounding built environment, it is also the cause of some wicked winter wind tunnels through the pedestrian walkways between the buildings of these large complexes.

I remember them well. Whenever I had to walk home through the walkways of Washington Houses during the winters, going from Second Avenue to Third Avenue on 100th Street, I knew I had to brace for some fierce winds. At times, the air blasts were so strong that they could hold me in place even when I wanted to move forward. The tower projects were hostile in their design, and the complexes designed an equally inhospitable geography for the residents and neighbors.

On top of all of this, the projects have contributed to increased crime in the neighborhood over the years partly because they cram so many people into a residential zone. The scale of the buildings prevents normal exercise of family territoriality, and their poor design often prevents some of the units' rooms from having visual contact with open space, blocking proper public surveillance.[37] Management staffs at these projects have frequently been reduced in size by local public authorities, and the projects have not always been well patrolled by the city's police department. As a result of all

---

36. For more on the choice of this odd angular building orientation, see Plunz, *A History of Housing in New York City*, esp. 243–46.

37. See Plunz, *A History of Housing in New York City*, esp. 247–79.

of these factors, the projects have experienced decay and high crime through the years. There is an element of irony in this. Originally intended to reduce the urban blight, grime, and crime that existed in East Harlem, the tower projects have only added to them.

There's no doubt that the grim look of the neighborhood's housing stock has contributed to its poor reputation through the years. A load of old tenements and tower housing projects in a bounded area will do that. In the case of the housing stock's effect on the physical appearance of East Harlem, however, it is important to consider not only what is there but also what isn't. For instance, El Barrio of East Harlem has none of the luxury high-rise buildings that populate the Upper East Side, Central Park West, and West End Avenue in Manhattan. Outside of a couple of blocks, the neighborhood also goes mostly without the more elegant brownstones that can be found throughout Central Harlem. East Harlem does not have the charming single-family row houses and the "garden apartments" of the outer boroughs of New York City either. I remember being gnawed with envy whenever I visited someone living in the garden apartments in The Grand Concourse and Pelham Parkway neighborhoods of the Bronx and in the Kew Gardens of Queens. Spanish Harlem even lacks the nicer philanthropic tenements that were built in Yorkville, the Lower East Side, Washington Heights, and parts of Brooklyn. Those were "model tenements" complete with open stairs, iron and glass awnings and roof structures, stairs onto internal courtyards, and small window seats integrated into the ironwork of each stair landing.[38] None of these in East Harlem.

The Puerto Ricans and other residents of East Harlem were snubbed in the very construction of those public-housing projects. The projects they received were of inferior physical and amenities design. East Harlem's projects cannot compare with some of the ones that went up on the Lower East Side and in areas of Brooklyn, for instance. Those, at times, contained courtyards that were well furnished, planted, and paved in brick. Sometimes, they even included murals and sculptures in the buildings or in the landscape design, along with interior courtyards containing swimming pools and gardens and large roof playgrounds. Knickerbocker Village on the Lower East Side and Flagg Court on Bay Ridge Boulevard, between Seventy-Second

38. For more on the array of designs that can be found in tenement architecture in New York City and in Boston, see Zachary J. Violette, *The Decorated Tenement: How Immigrant Builders and Architects Transformed the Slum in the Gilded Age* (Minneapolis: University of Minnesota Press, 2019).

and Seventy-Third Streets in Brooklyn, are examples of some of the fancier projects found in other neighborhoods.[39] We did not have these in East Harlem. Ours were bare and unadorned. Even in government philanthropy in public housing, then, we in East Harlem were unlucky. Consequentially, we have been left to manage with a second-rate and undistinguished housing stock over the years.

East Harlem has had other housing options. New "plaza" social-housing projects emerged in the mid-1970s. These combined medium-rise housing with limited commercial space or parking garages.[40] There are also the Taino Towers a little bit farther uptown, and the few private homes constructed on public lands in the late 1990s by Puerto Rican housing advocates and developers, who, already back then, were hoping to ward off gentrification and the displacement of Puerto Rican residents from the neighborhood. Their efforts led to the construction of the Cacique and the Nueva Esperanza Houses along 110th and 112th Streets. In line with the earlier discussion of gentrification and forced displacement, the neighborhood has seen the arrival of some "classy" looking buildings that contain pricey condos and apartments in more recent years. These were designed to attract a new "class" of citizen to Spanish Harlem; but, even with the arrival of these more recent housing types, it is quite clear that East Harlem's housing lot still lies with the tenements and projects. Together with non-residential buildings that comprise Metropolitan Hospital, Mount Sinai Hospital, the Museum of New York City, and El Museo del Barrio, these newer residences only serve to break up the monotony of the tenements and projects. I am certain that, if a visitor were asked to comment on the housing type of Spanish Harlem, they would say "old tenements and projects are largely what I see."

Add to the punctuated regularity of tenements and projects the absence of public statues, monuments, and sculptures, and you have the makings of a drab structural and physical appearance. We do have beautiful murals on the outside walls of some tenement buildings and the graffiti-style writing "Hall/Wall of Fame" along Park Avenue, between East 106th and 107th

---

39. For more on the varieties of public housing projects design in the different neighborhoods of New York City, see Plunz, *A History of Housing in New York City*, esp. 207–46.

40. Both 1199 Plaza, located between 107th and 111th Streets, along the FDR Drive, and Metro North Plaza, which is now called River Crossings, come to mind. The latter is located between 100th and 102nd Streets on First Avenue. Likewise, Franklin Plaza is a big complex of co-op apartments stretching from 106th to 109th Streets and from First to Third Avenues.

Streets, but the structural and physical character of the neighborhood is still defined by the old tenements and projects. The hindrances, deficiencies, nuisances, and affronts caused by this are part of the placial hardship through which Puerto Ricans and other residents of Spanish Harlem have endured and live through.

East Harlem has historically suffered from other social issues that include high crime, joblessness, and poverty; long stretches of drug trafficking and activity; and an asthma rate that has, at times, registered at five times the national average.[41] These are all noteworthy; but here I briefly want to say something about crime and drugs, especially since these have drawn much attention and have been tied to the reputed "mean streets" of Spanish Harlem through the years.[42] I begin with the problem of crime.

Concern about crime has been a part of the narrative of East Harlem and something that residents of the neighborhood have had to contend with in terms of inner perception, external reputation, and everyday life. The crime-ridden charge and reputation go back to when there were many Italian crime syndicates in the district. From the Italian extortion racket that was known as Black Hand to the more organized Italian gangs that formed the Italian-American mafia and the local Italian youth street gangs that engaged in turf wars, the area saw more than its fair share of criminality during the decades in which it was known as Italian Harlem (ca. 1890 to the late 1930s). In one way or another, the issue has persisted through the years. In the 1950s and 1960s, Puerto Rican youngsters formed their own gangs to protect themselves from Italian youth gangs, giving rise to gangs like the Viceroys and Dragons. More recently, Black youths have formed gangs, known as Air It Out, True Money Gang, and Whoadey, especially inside the areas of housing projects.

The district has had to grapple with more than just gang-related crimes. Every category of crime has tended to rate high in East Harlem when compared to other neighborhoods in the city, including violent crime, property crime, public-order crime, and others. Even with a precipitous decline in reported crimes over the last two decades, the neighborhood still tends to

---

41. For more on these issues, see Community Health Profiles 2015—Manhattan Community District 11: East Harlem, www1.nyc.gov; NYC—Manhattan Community District 11, 2018—East Harlem PUMA, NY, www.censusreporter.org; and An Economic Snapshot of the East Harlem Neighborhood 2018—Office of the State Comptroller (December 3, 2017), www.osc.state.ny.us.

42. This is, of course, a tongue-in-cheek reference to Piri Thomas's autobiographical novel *Down These Mean Streets* (New York: Vintage Books, 1997).

get a poor grade in the crime department.[43] In a recent survey by the website BestPlaces, the neighborhood's violent crime rate registered at 63.9 on a scale of 1 to 100. The same survey placed property crime at 66.9. In comparison, the U.S. average was listed at 22.7 in both categories. Based on this, the website accorded East Harlem the grade of C in the crimes department for the 2019 calendar year.[44] Areavibes wasn't as generous, giving East Harlem an F grade in this category on the basis of a total crime count of 3,999 in 2018. The average for communities of a similar size in other parts of New York was 2,043, it reported, and, in the nation, 2,580.[45] These surveys were conducted after a reported drop in crime estimated to be as much as 37 percent in violent crime and 64 percent in overall crime over the course of the 1990s.[46]

When it comes to crime, the perception of the neighborhood's residents themselves and the beliefs or opinions generally held by people who know about the neighborhood but don't live in it also matter. There are a number of books on the market that contain the voices of former and recent residents of El Barrio that reveal that concern for crime—fears of being robbed, knifed, attacked, or bullied, of becoming an innocent victim of a shooting or having a loved one become one—has been and still is a part of people's lives in the neighborhood.[47] This jives with my experiences in and memories of the neighborhood. Judith Freidenberg rightly says that the perception of crime in the streets is "multiplied manifold by the fear of crime instigated by the media," which brings me to the matter of outside perception and reputation.[48]

East Harlem has been known as a crime-infested neighborhood to be avoided if possible. I remember that pizza shops and restaurants located south of Ninety-Sixth Street would not deliver to my home or to my father's

43. For data on East Harlem's crime rates through the years, see "Crime Statistics, 23rd Precinct—NYPD," www.nyc.gov.

44. "East Harlem—Carnegie Hill (zip 10029), NY," *Sperling's Best Places*, www.bestplaces.net.

45. "East Harlem, New York, NY Area Guide," AreaVibes, Inc., www.areavibes.com, 2023.

46. See Sharman, *The Tenants of East Harlem*, esp. 19 and 69.

47. See Patricia Cayo Sexton, *Spanish Harlem: Anatomy of Poverty* (New York: Harper & Row, 1965), esp. 116–19; Sharman, *The Tenants of East Harlem*, esp. 38–39, 96–100, and 178–83; Freidenberg, *Growing Old in El Barrio*, esp. 208–227; and Bell, *East Harlem Remembered*, esp. 122–35.

48. Freidenberg, *Growing Old in El Barrio*, 211.

church on 100th Street whenever the youth or some other group in the
church he pastored held an event or gathering and wanted food delivered.
They would go only as far as Ninety-Sixth Street. This had nothing to do
with distance or delivery area but with the belief that East Harlem was dangerous because of crime. If we wanted pizza or food delivered from some
establishment in the Upper East Side, we had to meet the delivery person at
Ninety-Sixth Street to complete the transaction.

I was reminded of the neighborhood's bad reputation recently when a
guest in one of my classes at Yale Divinity School came up to me after a class
and confessed that his parents used to prohibit him from venturing into
the streets of Spanish Harlem from his home in adjacent Yorkville. It was
dangerous because of violence and crime, they would tell him. Truth be told,
the neighborhood is still trying to distance itself from this reputation today.

My guest's recollection brings to mind what Philippe Bourgois calls
"a racist 'common sense' that persuades whites, and middle-class outsiders of all colors, that it is too dangerous for them to venture into poor
African-American or Latino neighborhoods."[49] Such a common sense further compounds the dangerous and crime-ridden reputation of East Harlem. Moreover, as in any given inner-city neighborhood, most violent crimes
in East Harlem are often confined to "a small subgroup of individuals who
are directly involved in substance abuse and the underground economy, or
who are obviously vulnerable, such as frail elderly persons."[50]

I also remember that the danger in Spanish Harlem was significantly
worse at night. During daylight hours and even during the early evening, El
Barrio's streets usually bustled with activity. Because only 10 percent of the
nonstreet acreage of East Harlem is park, children often played tag, double
Dutch or hopscotch, stoopball, stickball, or the bottle cap game known
as skelsy or skully on the streets. In the cement schoolyards, young men
played basketball, handball, and touch football all through the day. Older
men played cards or dominoes on wobbly tables on the sidewalks. In the
summers, it wasn't uncommon to see people sitting on stoops, peering out
from tenement windows, and even lounging on fire escapes while youngsters
danced in and out of water sprayed by their friends from open fire hydrants.
Crowds of people from the neighborhood usually occupied the streets during the day and early evening hours, walking to someone's home or to one
or more of any of the many eateries, discount stores, and corner bodegas in

---

49. Bourgois, *In Search of Respect*, 32
50. Bourgois, *In Search of Respect*, 32.

the community. Obviously, crime and violence are far more limited in the streets of Spanish Harlem during these hours.

The playful activity in the streets and sidewalks isn't nearly as visible now as it was when I was growing up in East Harlem, but, even today, the streets of the neighborhood are rather populated, lively, and loud all through the daylight hours. These are nothing like the more demure streets of nearby Yorkville in the Upper East Side.

It is important to keep the difference between day and night in mind alongside Philippe Bourgois's points so as to avoid negative stereotypes and biased fears. I'm not saying that the neighborhood was safe. I'm just saying that we need to keep things in proper perspective. Of course there was crime in the neighborhood. We shouldn't expect a place that suffered from chronic unemployment, low wages, poverty, density, the lack of structured after-school activities for children, and the lack of educational opportunities to keep unemployed youth busy or to upgrade their skills to be free of violence and crime. Even with the violent and crime-ridden reputation of the district, however, it wasn't often that one actually was a victim of a criminal attack in the neighborhood. I also remember a sense of community prevailing in the neighborhood despite its poverty, struggles, and rough edges.

Those job opportunities that attracted so many Puerto Rican residents started to disappear in the latter half of the twentieth century, one of the casualties of industrial restructuring and suburbanization in the United States and of New York City's own fiscal crisis in the 1970s.[51] The result for them and for other poor and lower-skilled residents of East Harlem was extensive and long-term joblessness and all that comes with that. It is important to keep these larger structural factors and systemic forms of neglect in mind, as well as the despondency to which they can lead, when talking about the crime-ridden, mean streets of *mi barrio*.

As the son of a minister and as one who was brought into contact with a large segment of the community through the years because of this, I was always uniquely positioned to gain understanding of the neighborhood's danger due to crime. I still remember the periodic accounts of parishioners who were robbed in the elevators of the neighborhood's housing projects

---

51. For a well-known work that interprets the effect that industrial restructuring had on U.S. inner-city settings, see William Julius Wilson's *When Work Disappears: The World of the New Urban Poor* (New York: Vintage Books, 1997). For treatment of New York City's 1970s fiscal crisis, see Kim Phillips-Fein, *Fear City: New York's Fiscal Crisis and the Rise of Austerity Politics* (New York: Metropolitan Books, 2017).

or when leaving a bank or check-cashing place. I periodically heard cases of congregants who were victims of car burglars targeting car radios and items left in cars. One of my former colleagues recounts having the wedding cake stolen from his car on the day of his wedding, which was held in a Baptist church located on 102nd Street, between Third Avenue and Lexington Avenue. My best friend had his camera stolen once when visiting the neighborhood and trying to take pictures of a community center located on 104th Street, between Third and Lexington Avenues, for a class assignment in college. I remember well hearing gunshots and street skirmishes at night from time to time while trying to sleep in my parents' home all through my childhood, adolescent, and early adulthood years. In short, crime has been a concern in the neighborhood over the years, especially at night.

Things have gotten better in this regard in more recent years, but, taking everything into account, crime has to be considered among the placial or place-based jeopardies with which the Puerto Rican and other residents of East Harlem have had to contend. The significance of this shouldn't be discounted, for it means that those residing in the neighborhood have had to live with the sense of physical vulnerability and with the psychological weight that comes with a sense of everyday danger. This, too, is part of the placial hardship tale involving Spanish Harlem and the tenants of Spanish Harlem.

Drugs, specifically the illegal drug trade, are the last placial jeopardy to mention in relation to El Barrio of East Harlem. Philippe Bourgois brought much attention to the problem, focusing on the crack-cocaine epidemic of the 1980s and early 1990s. It is worth noting, however, that the problem of drug use and drug trafficking in the neighborhood predates the period of time and the particular outbreak on which he focused. In his autobiographical novel, *Down These Mean Streets*, Boricua writer Piri Thomas makes extensive reference to drugs and to street-level drug dealing in the neighborhood.[52] Thomas was reflecting on the conditions of life in El Barrio during the 1940s and early 1950s, describing a teeming drug scene even then. East Harlem is also associated with the infamous Purple Gang, an Italian-American heroin-smuggling ring that dominated heroin distribution in Harlem and the South Bronx during the 1970s and early 1980s. Though the neighborhood has dealt with drug problems for decades, it does seem as if the problem became even more pronounced and evident in the years on which Bourgois focuses. The oral accounts of residents and studies carried

---

52. See Thomas, *Down These Mean Streets*.

out by subject-matter experts point in this direction. I certainly remember the problem being noticeable.

Most major cities across the United States witnessed a surge in crack-cocaine use in those years, but New York, along with Newark and Philadelphia, held the highest crack index.[53] Spanish Harlem was among the neighborhoods that became focal points for crack-cocaine sale in New York City. The drug's affordability was part of its appeal in impoverished neighborhoods along with the intense and immediate high that smokers would get from this freebase form of cocaine that was usually mixed with baking soda or ammonia. Spanish Harlem's location in Manhattan, and the neighborhood's accessibility by practically every form of transportation, made it an ideal setting from which to sell crack cocaine. The many vacant lots and abandoned buildings that existed in the neighborhood at that point, plus the chronic unemployment and apparent lack of opportunities, combined with the transportation accessibility to make a wonderland from a crack dealer's perspective. For the overwhelming majority of law-abiding East Harlemites, it was anything but a wonderland, since the crack epidemic resulted in a number of social consequences such as increasing crime and violence as well as a resulting backlash in the form of tough-on-crime policies. For them—for me—it was a nightmare—a nightmare that lasted ten to twelve years.

Street-level crack dealing was ubiquitous in those years, especially in and around housing projects, and there were particular crack sale spots that were popular in the neighborhood. I lived right across from one, on 100th Street between Third and Lexington Avenues. Along with the corner of 110th Street and Lexington Avenue, this was one of the hot spots for the sale of crack in the neighborhood. For me and for my family, this meant getting used to seeing lines of people waiting to purchase their vials of crack on our street in broad daylight and through until the next dawn, when people from outside the neighborhood would leave, thinking it unsafe to stay around.

Drug dealers had commandeered an abandoned building almost directly across from our home, and they sold their wares all through the day and the early evening hours. I remember once asking my mother during my early teenage years why lines of people were gathering outside the tenement building across from ours. Hoping to shield me from the reality of the illegal drug trade, she responded that the government was distributing basic food-stuff for the needy. I accepted the response at the time but quickly came to

---

53. See Roland G. Freyer et al., "Measuring Crack Cocaine and Its Impact," *Economic Inquiry* 51, no. 3 (July 2013): 1651–81.

doubt its veracity because I noticed that the line would hurriedly disperse whenever a police car was spotted turning onto our street. Usually, somebody shouted "bajando" (i.e., coming down) anytime they noticed a patrol car or a potential undercover agent. These were the coded alarms that lookouts, posted on dealing corners, would use to alert "pitchers"—those who made the hand-to-hand sales—and buyers that a law-enforcing agent was approaching. When heard, everyone in the line would scatter like roaches running for cover when a light is shone on them.

For residents who lived on certain streets of Spanish Harlem, this was a daily occurrence all through the 1980s and the early 1990s. But the entire neighborhood dealt with the consequences of drug dealing, including relatives consumed by drug addiction, the constant fear of seeing a young family member cave in to the temptation of the alternative lifestyle presented by the underground economy, the increased violence and crime spawned by the illegal drug trade, the eerie sound of empty crack vials underfoot in certain blocks of the neighborhood, the bad repute suffered by the neighborhood, and the high cost in human rights and municipal operational expenses occasioned by New York's get-tough-on-crime policy. The tenants of East Harlem all had to contend with the reverberations of narcotics trafficking one way or another.

These are among the many placial hardships and jeopardies with which the Puerto Rican and other residents of East Harlem grappled over many years. Still, as in the case of our personal lives, places and the groups of people that dwell within them aren't wholly defined by their struggles and misfortunes. These may constitute a part of their stories, and they may play a role in affecting their footing in life; but they don't define all that they are. As in the example of our own lives, much can be gleaned from the way in which neighborhoods and the people who live in them respond to the vicissitudes and the placial injustices of life.

Signs of the resilience, creativity, and realization of the diasporic Puerto Rican community of El Barrio could be seen everywhere in the neighborhood: in the vibrant street life; in the play of children in the side streets; in the continuation of purposeful and meaningful life normalcy by the overwhelming majority of the community's adults; in the countless Puerto Rican restaurants, shops, and businesses populating the district; in the bustling commerce taking place in the famous "marqueta" and all along Third and Lexington Avenues and on 106th and 116th Streets; in the Catholic street processions, scores of Pentecostal churches, and La Gran Parada del Niño

Cristiano held every year in mid-June; in the notable house parties, street jams, and festivals the neighborhood was known for; in the famous Puerto Rican annual festival that spans more than twenty city blocks and brings hundreds of thousands of visitors to the neighborhood the day before the National Puerto Rican Day Parade in early June; and in the Museo del Barrio, the Harbor Conservatory for the Performing Arts, the Grammy-winning Spanish Harlem Orchestra, the Center for Puerto Rican Studies, and the Julia De Burgos Cultural Arts Center. These and other community exploits let everyone know "we are here and we are going to achieve and celebrate while being here." All this and more served as a communal shout of strength, exuberance, joy, celebration, and achievement.

Even the neighborhood's favored form of Christian expression, the Pentecostal Christianity that could be seen and heard all through Spanish Harlem, was lively. There are other kinds of churches and religious gathering places in the district, for sure, but the Pentecostal church reigns supreme in Spanish Harlem, filling more or less every other block. The churches are ubiquitous. Though most of them are small storefront churches, a few are larger, including Iglesia Pentecostal La Sinagoga on 125th Street, Macedonia Church on 106th Street, and Iglesia de Dios Pentecostal at 200 East 116th Street. No matter the size, you were and are still likely to know there's a Spanish-speaking Pentecostal church nearby, for their services are usually loud, vivacious, and enthusiastic.

"Charismatic" fittingly describes the Pentecostal movement and style. In the summertime, they often held their loud and proud services outside, in front of the storefront meetinghouse. Their effervescent character was both a part and emblematic of El Barrio's inner resilience and ebullience.

In instances of sustained hardship caused by structural injustice, such vibrancy can be vitally important for the community. Strict Marxists would likely be troubled by the theology accompanying the services in these Pentecostal congregations, thinking that its constant allusions to an afterlife in a heavenly realm free of suffering only serves to prevent people from seeing the class structure and oppression all around them here on Earth. There may be some truth to this critique, but even Marx premised his structural-functional argument with the observant admission that religion could reduce people's immediate suffering while providing them with pleasant illusions that could give them the strength to carry on. The privileged and comfortable can dismiss such things from their minds. The poor and the disadvantaged generally don't have this luxury. In the case of East Harlemite Puerto Ricans, it seems that the cheerfulness and the future-oriented aspect of Pentecostalism raised morale and inspired hope. It is another way in which this diasporic community expressed its resilience, buoyancy, and aspiration.[54]

The celebrated murals of the neighborhood yielded other expressions and indications of this resiliency, along with a healthy sense of community, artistic creativity, a celebratory spirit, and an activist impulse. One could not make one's way through the neighborhood without encountering one of these. They were all over the place, painted often on the outside walls of tenements, and, at times, on the metal security gates of storefront businesses and on the sides of stairs leading up to apartment buildings. These colorful paintings spoke loud and clear with regard to the neighborhood's spunk, offering demonstrations of art and beauty. Some, like the famous four-story mural known as "The Spirit of East Harlem," found on the corner of 104th Street and Lexington Avenue, celebrated the people of the community and highlighted elements of the neighborhood's prevailing Puerto Rican ethos. It features domino players, a man playing the Puerto Rican cuatro (the ten-string guitar-like instrument prominent in Puerto Rican folk music), and the ubiquitous Puerto Rican flag, along with well-known personalities from the community.

Other pieces were commissioned by families who lost loved ones in the neighborhood. Based around artistic representations of the deceased loved one, these "RIP" murals served as public memorials. Some murals aimed to preserve the memory of famous residents and cultural icons from the neighborhood, like poet Julia de Burgos, Nuyorican poet and playwright Pedro Pietri, musician Tito Puente, novelist Nicholasa Mohr, and even the Young Lords' legacy. Others celebrated Latino/a artists and activists more gener-

54. For more on the history and characteristics of Pentecostalism, see Harvey Cox, *Fire from Heaven: The Rise of Pentecostal Spirituality and the Reshaping of Religion in the Twenty-First Century* (Cambridge, MA: Da Capo Press, 1995); Walter J. Hollenweger, *Pentecostalism: Origins and Developments Worldwide* (Peabody, MA: Hendrickson Publishers, 1997); Donald W. Dayton, *Theological Roots of Pentecostalism* (Grand Rapids, MI: Baker Academic, 1987); Eldin Villafañe, *The Liberating Spirit: Toward an Hispanic American Pentecostal Social Ethic* (Grand Rapids, MI: Eerdmans, 1993); Daniel Ramírez, *Migrating Faith: Pentecostalism in the United States and Mexico in the Twentieth Century* (Chapel Hill: University of North Carolina Press, 2015); Gastón Espinosa, *Latino Pentecostals in America: Faith and Politics in Action* (Cambridge, MA: Harvard University Press, 2016); R. G. Robbins, *Pentecostalism in America* (Westport, CT: Praeger, 2010), Arlene Sánchez Walsh, *Latino Pentecostal Identity: Evangelical Faith, Self, and Society* (New York: Columbia University Press, 2003), and Arlene Sánchez Walsh, *Pentecostals in America* (New York: Columbia University Press, 2018).

ally, including Cuban-American singer Celia Cruz, Puerto Rican Bronx-born rapper Big Pun, Cuban independence fighter Ernesto "Che" Guevara, Puerto Rican nationalist Pedro Albizu Campos, and even the Zapatista Movement in Mexico. Some contained aphoristic messages from community artist James de la Vega, such as "Become Your Dream," "You Are More Powerful Than You Think," and an anti-gentrification missive that appeared toward the end of the 1990s and is among my favorites: "Don't think for a minute that we haven't noticed that the 96th Street boundary has moved further north." Others stood as direct calls to action, like the one demanding that Oscar López-Rivera be released from federal prison. One way or another, the colorful murals of the district displayed El Barrio's fortitude, determination, comradery, dignity, hope, and zest for life.[55]

The murals give some indication of the neighborhood's notable social awareness and activist impulse, but nothing displays this more than the many political actions and agencies to which the neighborhood has been connected through the decades. Puerto Ricans were socially and politically active in New York City from very early on. Their participation in the Spanish Benevolent Society already in 1830 is a case in point. This sort of organizational activity and sociopolitical venture has been a constant in the community and is why I could never understand the claims made by some earlier sociologists who insinuated a lack of organizational leadership and framework within the New York Puerto Rican community.[56] I don't know where they were looking or not looking, but the community has never lacked for active and activist organizations. Puerto Ricans have organized to meet the needs of the community in the city and beyond through the mutual aid societies established by pioneer migrant tobacco workers in the late nineteenth and early twentieth centuries: La Aurora, La Razon, El Ejemplo, the

---

55. For more on the history, art, and significance of street murals in New York City and more generally, see Janet Braun-Reinitz and Jane Weissman, eds., *On the Wall: Four Decades of Community Murals in New York City* (Jackson: University of Mississippi Press, 2009); Rafael Schacter and John Fekner, *The World Atlas of Street Art and Graffiti* (New Haven, CT: Yale University Press, 2013); Cher Krause Knight and Harriet F. Senie, eds., *A Companion to Public Art* (Malden, MA: Wiley-Blackwell, 2016); and Anthony W. Lee, *Painting on the Left: Diego Rivera, Radical Politics, and San Francisco's Public Murals* (Berkeley: University of California Press, 1999).

56. For two early examples of authors and works that either insinuated this or stated this, see Nathan Glazer and Daniel Patrick Moynihan, *Beyond the Melting Pot* (Cambridge, MA: MIT Press, 1968), esp. 101–7; and Sexton, *Spanish Harlem*, esp. 7–21 and 120–47.

Círculo de Tabaqueros, Club Ibero-Americano, the Porto Rican Brotherhood of America, La Liga Puertorriqueña e Hispana, the Casa de Puerto, Ateneo Obrero Hispano, the Spanish Merchants' Association, Casita Maria, Club Demócrata Puertorriqueño, Alianza Obrera Puertorriqueña, the Council of Hometown Clubs (El Congreso del Pueblo), and the National Puerto Rican Forum.[57] Presumably, Puertorriqueños from the most prominent Puerto Rican colonia in the city participated in and played a prominent role in these communal, social, and political organizations. Additionally, a number of Puerto Rican-led political and social organizations materialized and were based in El Barrio of East Harlem, including Ateneo Obrero Hispano, the Liberty Republican Club, the Real Great Society of East Harlem, the Urban Planning Studio, the East Harlem Tenants' Council, la Sociedad de Albizu Campos or SAC (Society of Albizu Campos), and Antonia Pantoja's various community organizations like the Puerto Rican Association for Community Affairs, the Puerto Rican Leadership Forum, and ASPIRA.

Finally, no telling of East Harlem's story, especially regarding its vibrant social organizing, would be complete without mention of the Young Lords Party. Inspired by the radical social movements of the late 1960s and by Puerto Rico's long-standing cultural nationalist movement, and patterned after the Black Panther Party and the Chicago Young Lords Organization, the group managed to make its mark in the life and ongoing narrative of the neighborhood through its unique form of public involvement. Comprising mostly college-aged and college-going Puerto Rican women and men, the group blended political theory with civic activism and even a little bit of gang-like strategy to bring about justice and social change in El Barrio.

The Young Lords' eleven-day takeover of the First Spanish Methodist Church on the corner of 111th Street and Lexington Avenue is now the stuff of legend and part of the neighborhood's fame in activist circles. Hoping to start a free breakfast program at the site, the group met with the church's directors to pitch the idea only to be rebuffed several times. Undeterred, the Young Lords proceeded at first to attend various Sunday church services, "testifying" to the present-day meaning and value of Jesus Christ's precept of solidarity with the poor and marginalized and staging a sit-in at the church

---

57. For more on these New York Puerto Rican organizations and the history of Puerto Rican political activism in New York City, see Sánchez Korrol, *From Colonia to Community*, esp. 131–240; Rodríguez, "Forging a New, New York," in *Boricuas in Gotham*, 195–218; and Acosta-Belén and Santiago, *Puerto Ricans in the United States*, esp. 147–67.

when their call to meaningful Christian discipleship went unheard. During the eleven-day church seizure, held from December 28, 1969, until January 7, 1970, the Lords established a free breakfast and lunch program, a free health clinic, and a clothing drive at the site while also instituting political education classes, poetry readings, and a music festival. They were able to accomplish all of this because the group managed to draw media attention to its cause and to garner the support of community merchants; celebrities like Bette Midler, Jane Fonda, and Sammy Davis Jr.; and the 1199 Union. Even Mayor John Lindsay instructed the cops to stay away. The event was just one of the group's heroics in the neighborhood. The Young Lords can also be credited for forcing the city to pass legislation to eliminate lead; for calling attention to health, sanitary, and environmental concerns in the neighborhood; for compelling the New York Sanitation Department to provide more garbage cans throughout the neighborhood and to implement more regular garbage pickups; for pressuring the city to build a new Lincoln Hospital in the district; for making the free lunch programs in public schools a reality; and for demanding that Puerto Rican and Latino/a studies programs be established at colleges and universities in the city and across the nation.[58] In short, their impact in East Harlem and beyond was considerable, and it all came from the bosom of my home neighborhood.

These and other examples of vitality, agency, creativity, and organizational activity show that El Barrio of East Harlem had more going for it than just some mean streets. We can't forget the struggles lived in and through that place, of course, for those need to remain in the picture. Doing justice to the legacy of the place and to the lives of the people who lived in the place and who shaped, formed, and comprised the place requires remembering the challenges, the struggles, and the injustices that were faced there and continue to be faced there. Justice also requires recognizing the abundant and admirable resilience, dynamism, beauty, ingenuity, activism, performance, attainment, and success in *mi barrio* as it has been visible in its many expressions of livelihood, commerce, culture, art, music, religion, and activist organizations. This, too, is part of El Barrio's character, history, and legacy.

---

58. For more on the legacy of the New York Young Lords, see Johanna Fernández, *The Young Lords: A Radical History* (Chapel Hill: University of North Carolina Press, 2020); Darrel Wanzer-Serrano, *The New York Young Lords and the Struggle for Liberation* (Philadelphia: Temple University Press, 2015); and Miguel "Mickey" Melendez, *We Took the Streets: Fighting for Latino Rights with the Young Lords* (New Brunswick, NJ: Rutgers University Press, 2005).

No sé lo que va a pasar con Spanish Harlem /
I Don't Know What's Going to Happen
to Spanish Harlem

The future of El Barrio is now in question. The city streets and avenues that contain and comprise the place are still there of course, and many of the physical structures and sights to which I've called attention can also still be found in place. The character and identity of the neighborhood, however, have been gradually changing over the last two decades, and the changes have intensified and become more noticeable in the last decade. The Puerto Rican identity and history of the district are especially in question. The ongoing placial transformation within Spanish Harlem is mostly owing to the effects of gentrification, the flight of Puerto Ricans from the district, and shifts in the population.

Regarding gentrification, people who once shunned the neighborhood began to look upon it as an "acceptable" or "livable" place in the early and mid-1990s. Whites wanting to move back into the city or relocating from other parts of the city, from other U.S. cities, or from cities abroad started to arrive in greater numbers during these years, growing from .02 percent of the population in 1990 to 7.3 percent in 2000.[59] The inflow was due to the cheaper rents that could be found in the district relative to the rest of Manhattan or, at least, most of Manhattan. This growth has continued steadily as well, as this segment of the neighborhood's population stood at 16.1 percent in 2018.[60]

As could be expected, with this growth and with thought of the possible arrival of a more upscale consumer base, new interest in the neighborhood emerged among real-estate speculators, city planners, banking institutions, private developers, and investors. Public and private investment capital started to become more readily available in and for the district. Some fancier restaurants began to appear within it. A few of the old tenements were renovated, and some were replaced with more elegant buildings, containing nicer apartments and even condos. The attempt at another neighborhood facelift was on its way, this one fueled by the tenets of the urban neoliberalism being

---

59. See Bell, *East Harlem Remembered*, 219.

60. See "East Harlem Neighborhood Profile–2019," NYU Furman Center, www.furmancenter.org; see also "An Economic Snapshot of the East Harlem Neighborhood–2018."

pursued here and in other cities around the world as part of a pattern of upscale redevelopment.

To be sure, the neighborhood is still largely characterized by the old tenements and the high-rise public-housing projects of which I spoke earlier. The neighborhood retains its rough, gritty look in other ways as well, but attempts have been made at its upscale redevelopment, and they are visible. Today, one can stumble upon the odd scene of a fancy new apartment building lodged between a row of old, rundown tenements in some of the neighborhood's streets. One will also find the occasional hip burger joint, the upscale Latino/a steakhouse, Ricardo's, between 110th and 111th Streets, on Second Avenue, and a couple of trendy-looking cafés and music bars. In other words, the neighborhood has not escaped the clutches of the gentrification craze, but it is also evident and interesting that the trend hasn't totally taken off within it.

Ironically, it may be that the numerous high-rise public housing projects and the ubiquitous old tenements covering the neighborhood have sheltered it from a more thoroughgoing and callous gentrification process—a no-win situation really. It will be fascinating to see which interests win out in the neighborhood as the avowed intent of the city's government to maintain a certain number of affordable/low-income housing units throughout the city competes with gentrifiers' appetite for more property. A large number of the city's desired affordable/low-income housing units are located in East Harlem, mostly in those high-rise public-housing projects and in some tenements that the city has refurbished. It makes sense that the city will want to preserve these, even as it seeks to create more affordable housing to deal with the affordability crisis that neighborhoods are experiencing.

Still, the gentrifiers' desires for hipster districts; luxury housing; brand-name chains; and trendy restaurants, cafés, and music bars is strong. Gentrification has captured the attention and affection of investors, developers, city officials, and consumers alike. Such gentrification will be hard to resist going forward. Already we've seen real-estate developers trying to rebrand the neighborhood, calling it "Upper Yorkville," "Upper Carnegie Hill," "Spa Ha" (aka Spanish Harlem), or "SoHa" (aka South Harlem).

Even in a diluted and patchy form, the gentrification trend has already had an effect on the neighborhood, hastening the flight of Puerto Ricans from the district on account of rising rents. The Puerto Rican community was already in decline within the district by the 1990s, a consequence of the effects of New York City's fiscal and high-crimes crisis in the 1970s, the diminution of blue-collar and service occupations in the city during the

1970s and '80s, and the desire of middle-aged workers and retirees of the pre–World War II and early post–World War II generations to resettle in their homeland or move to warmer states like Florida. The truth, too, is that the pressures of life in El Barrio have worn on many within the community.

Having to work so hard for so long, defying compounding material inequality, placial disadvantage, demeaning labels, and racist stereotypes all within a wintry weather inner-city environment, *eso no es fácil compay*. That's no easy thing, friend. There is no denying that the soaring rents on apartments and commercial properties are driving many away as well. It is the number one reason that many of my neighbors and the majority of my extended family members offered when asked why they moved from El Barrio. That many in the community elected to move to areas of the South Bronx or to locations in New England, Pennsylvania, and Florida is also telling, for these are regions known to have more affordable housing markets.

All told, these factors influence the contraction of the East Harlem Puerto Rican community. From its high mark of 75,400 in 1960, the community's numbers fell to 40,542 by 1990.[61] It was estimated at 37,878 in 2005 and at 26,724 in 2017. Even at this rate, the community maintains a considerable presence in the district, comprising approximately 27.7 percent of the population in the neighborhood's 10029 zip code area and 23.4 percent in its 10035 area, but there's no denying that it is not nearly as formidable as it once was.[62]

El Barrio of East Harlem has been changing, becoming more diverse in the last two decades by reason of gentrification pressures and population shifts. As a result the area's role as a physical and symbolic repository of diasporic Puerto Rican experiences, exploits, and traditions is now in question. Its future with regard to distinctive identity is difficult to predict at the moment. Other ethnic groups are burgeoning in East Harlem. The Mexican American community has especially expanded in the neighborhood, becoming markedly visible and strong within it in the last ten to fifteen years. The famed 116th Street, a prominent broad street that has served as a center for Puerto Rican life and commerce in the district for many decades and that has been named Luís Muñoz Marín Boulevard because of it, has Mexican flags and other Mexican-themed public display signs from one end to the

---

61. For that latter figure, see Timothy Williams and Tanzina Vega, "As East Harlem Develops, Its Accent Starts to Change," *New York Times*, January 21, 2007, https://www.nytmes.com/2007/01/21/nyregion/21east.html.

62. See 2014–2018 American Community Survey 5-Year Data Profile, U.S. Census Bureau, www.census.gov.

other. It is a clear sign of the growing Mexican presence and influence in the region.[63] While this has been happening, the Black community has also continued to grow in the district. As of 2017, it held the highest percentage of the population in the neighborhood at 30.3 percent overall. The figure is 25.3 percent in the 10029 zip code area and 35.3 percent in the 10035 area.[64] The Asian population, especially from China, has also been growing gradually, making up 8 percent of the neighborhood's total population in 2016 with 11,100 residents.[65]

I suppose that changes in both the physical landscape and the social community were to be expected. As places, neighborhoods are subject to change, shifting over time and space through interactions with flows of people and constantly evolving networks that are social, cultural, and environmental. Still, it is proper to worry about and to interrogate the changes. The matter of punishing rents, of housing's emergence as a symbol of inequality, and the displacement of low- and middle-income residents from their long-standing neighborhoods should concern everyone who has a social conscience and sense of morality. The annihilation of historic districts, whether by reason of urban renewal or gentrification, should occasion sorrow as well. In this case, there is also the matter of the social and cultural meanings of El Barrio of East Harlem as a place in and through which diasporic Puerto Ricans and other Latino/as contended against the reaches of colonialism and social inequality, amassing a vast trove of struggles, achievements, cultural traditions, stories, and cherished memories.

Much is at stake here, in other words. The possible erasure of a significant communal past and present that are deeply embedded in this place called Spanish Harlem or El Barrio is not merely a matter of nostalgia. It is about historical awareness, about ethnic or race-related respect, about recognition of cultural achievement and political action, and about the right of groups, especially of less-advantaged and marginalized groups, to put down roots and have synergies with a place.

---

63. Mexican Americans have also established a number of community organizations in East Harlem. Among them are Mexicanos Unidos en Nueva York (UNIMEX); the Mexican Community Center, or Centro Comunal Mexicano en Nueva York (CECOMEX); a local chapter of Tepeyac, a city-wide social advocacy organization; and the Mexican American Workers' Association, or Asociacion de Trabajadores Mexico Americanos (AMAT). See Davila, *Barrio Dreams*, 157.

64. 2014–2018 American Community Survey 5-Year Data Profile, U.S. Census Bureau.

65. See "An Economic Snapshot of the East Harlem Neighborhood."

Some steps have been taken to preserve Spanish Harlem's past and present. Mostly, this has consisted of renaming certain city streets. Luís Muñoz Marín Boulevard on 116th Street is named after the Puerto Rican journalist, politician, and statesman who was elected the first governor of Puerto Rico. Tito Puente Way, a five-block stretch of 110th Street is named after the beloved Puerto Rican percussionist, bandleader, and composer. I wonder if more can be done on this front, including the legal conservation and preservation of some of the district's murals, the placement and registry of plaques on historic buildings and sites, and the construction of a couple of public statues, at the least, to honor prominent Puerto Rican and Latino/a figures from the district and to acknowledge and remember the honorable causes they advanced. Maybe someday that long-discussed statue of Tito Puente will finally appear next to Duke Ellington's on Fifth Avenue and 110th Street.[66] I don't think "Sir Duke" would mind it at all. In fact, I think he'd welcome the company, especially since some people used to call Tito "the Duke Ellington of Latin music."[67] Still, none of this would replace the ideal of seeing more Puerto Ricans and Latino/as having the chance to remain in place in Spanish Harlem if they so desired, maybe even in an improved and more secure Spanish Harlem and without the forbidding, gentrified price tag of recent times. I can dream, right? We can dream, right?

Whatever happens to El Barrio of East Harlem, I am certain that it will live on in the hearts and minds of countless natives and longtime residents. The children of Spanish Harlem, I call them. Whether they continue to reside in it or have chosen or been forced to move on, I am sure that the neighborhood endures as a subtle force, acting within them and upon them in untold ways. I am convinced of this because I've discovered it to be so. I am one of the children of Spanish Harlem after all, and, by virtue of my growing interest in the centrality of place in human experience, I've arrived at a deeper understanding of its hold on me—of its hold on my understandings of thought and belief particularly. A discovery and growing awareness, I call it, and its significance is such that it has prompted me to reconsider the beginnings of my work. You'll see what I mean in our next chapter.

---

66. For more on this topic, see Davila, *Barrio Dreams*, esp. 128–52; and Sharman, *The Tenants of East Harlem*, 74–78.

67. See Tim Blangger, "Tito Puente Dips Jazz into Salsa," in *The Morning Call*, October 7, 1990, www.mcall.com.

• 3 •

Theological Writing and the Power of Place

Is the beginning of a given work its real beginning, or is there some other secret point that more authentically starts the work off?
                                                                    – Edward Said[1]

I have been thinking about intellectual beginnings for some time now, so it is not surprising that the epigraph from Edward Said would hook and inspire me. This musing kindles my curiosity and inklings regarding the placed origin of thinking. A line from T. S. Eliot's famous poem "Little Gidding" has a similar effect on me because it connects inner exploration and self-discovery with a return to a starting place.[2] "We shall not cease from exploration/And the end of all our exploring/Will be to arrive where we started/And know the place for the first time," is the line in mind. Of course, I am after a different beginning than the ones that animate Said and Eliot.

Said's reference to beginnings is tied to a longing for a willful, nonconformist, self-confident, and purpose-driven style of writing. He is affirming the possibility of a form of writing that can free us from the oppressions of past cultural, political, and psychological habits of mind or institutions while also keeping us away from the textual skepticism and indeterminacy of deconstructionist thought. In other words, Said's quest for beginnings is really about authorial intent and mindset—beginning intentions and

---

1. Edward W. Said, *Beginnings: Intention and Method* (New York: Columbia University Press, 1985), 3.

2. See T. S. Eliot, "Little Gidding," in *Four Quartets* (Boston: Mariner Books, 1943), 49.

dispositions in the creative and discursive process. If Said asks you about your beginnings, he is really asking you, "What are your inclinations and intentions as a writer?" T. S. Eliot is getting at a renewed and renewing engagement with the past and a spiritual awakening in a historical moment of doubt and despair in Britain's life as a nation during World War II. The place, or starting place, about which he is talking and to which he is trying to get us is not really a place, at least not a geographical place. It is an existential mood, disposition, or state—a state of hope, of resilience, and of willingness to resume, restart, or renew if necessary.

The three of us are not really meaning the same thing, then, with the subject of beginnings. Said's beginning intention, Eliot's action of beginning something again after a pause or interruption (i.e., resumption), and my attention to the placed origin of our thinking are different beginnings.

And yet, Said's and Eliot's words are so fitting in relation to my pursuit. I do believe that there are often secret or unacknowledged points that spark our works, and I do believe that, if we reflected on these more often and more thoroughly, we would find that the physical, geographical places from which we come are among them. Such a discovery would bring us back to the start, so to speak, back to the places from which we come, and back to a reexamination and reconsideration of the role that those places play in the provenance of our thinking and writing.

It is not often that we stop to think about the ways in which particular places and our experiences in and with them inform and give shape to our intellectual projects and compositions. If asked to identify the proper beginning of our thinking or the generative locus out of which our writing emerges and from which it gains its direction and sustenance, we are more likely to recall things such as personal interests; "pure ideas"; philosophical, political, or moral motivations; historical or life events; and our encounters with thinkers, authors, and their texts. Place? Not so much; at least not as a determining cause or first principle, nor as a motivational or psychological impetus, and, especially, not place as a factor that shapes the character of our intellectual work.

Nevertheless, I think we *should* get into the habit of thinking about places in these ways. After all, places have an impact on the products of the mind. They have form-giving influence on our thoughts and beliefs—epistemic power, I call it. The power I speak of rests on and springs from a confluence of factors.

To begin with, places can act on our psyche through the agency of various constituents. The geographic location of a place; the natural landscape of a place; the patterns of weather encountered in a place; the people and social groups one is likely to encounter in a place; the animals, fish, trees, plants, fungi, and insects inhabiting a place; the human-made structures, features, and facilities chanced upon in a place; the histories, narratives, cultural practices, norms, and meanings associated with and engaged with in a place; the opportunities, privileges, inequalities, scarcities, disadvantages, and hardships seen and experienced in a place: each of these aspects of place carry with them the potential to supply us with different experiences, to leave an indelible imprint in our innermost self, and, therefore, the potential to influence what we think and say about the world. Now, imagine the perceptual and cognitive power that is to be found when these or a number of these are combined. Such is the power of place. Places have the capacity to affect us in a variety of ways through their sheer multidimensionality.

The extraordinary, form-giving, epistemic power of places can also be attributed to the ways that places typically incorporate natural, cultural, and social features. Places are both made up of physical realities and drenched in cultural meaning. Patricia Price insightfully writes that the "landscapes shaped by narratives are as real as those sculpted by the action of the wind, waves, and glaciers."[3] Her point is that the imprints of cultural narratives and traditions can be as considerable, as durable, and as formative as those produced by natural phenomena. And surely the cultural milieus we create, inherit, actualize, and impart do hold power over us. But places don't present us with an either/or scenario. Fortunately, they combine the natural *and* the cultural.

Moreover, the places within which we live and act also incorporate a social dimension. In one way or another, places are always instances of wider social processes that influence our lives. These processes range from vast, overarching processes and structures such as imperialism, neocolonialism, capitalism, neoliberal development policies, racism, and patriarchy to smaller-scale processes and structures such as private sector development programs, local advisory boards and commissions, community-based organizations, and face-to-face social interactions and group dynamics. These social processes can take distinctive forms and can manifest themselves in particular ways in individual places, having a marked impact on their configurations and on the lives of those who live within them. Importantly, places incorporate all

---

3. Patricia L. Price, *Dry Place: Landscapes of Belonging and Exclusion* (Minneapolis: University of Minnesota Press, 2004), xxii.

of these powerful experiential dimensions—the natural, the cultural, and the social.

Places, then, are multidimensional sites of gathering. Places gather human and nonhuman materialities; animate and inanimate entities; buildings, trees, cars, roads, sidewalks, people, and signs; histories, experiences, memories, stories, and social and cultural practices. Philosophers Edward Casey, Manuel DeLanda, and Tim Creswell, along with architectural theorist Kim Dovey, have noted that places are syncretic and dynamic sites of gathering and assemblage.[4] This unique assemblage of human and nonhuman forces and of material and expressive existence grants places the power to be potent epistemic catalysts.

Finally, places have this influential nature because they influence all of our ways of knowing. Sight, sound, smell, touch, and taste can all be engaged in the course of our experience in and with a place. Places can appeal to our eyes in the spectacle of a majestic mountain, a babbling brook, an array of dilapidated and abandoned tenements, or public art. Places can appeal to our ears in the rumble of a mighty river, commuter vehicles, or an elevated train. Places can appeal to our noses through the whiff of blossoms, freshly turned earth, local fare, or roasting garbage on the street. Places can appeal to our touch with the feel or texture of wet grass, pavement cracks, flaking paint from the exterior of dowdy city buildings, and crumbling mortar. Places can appeal to our mouths through the savor of a region's drinking water, harvests, and local specialties. Places capture our interest and attention in all of these ways, imprinting themselves upon our bodies and minds. In fact, place's very same assault on all of our senses makes it a powerful source of memory.[5] Places, along with the events, people, and experiences encountered within them, can live on in our memories, exerting a subtle influence on how we know, perceive, feel, act, and believe even after we have moved away from them. We can call this the silent and lasting workings of

4. Edward S. Casey, "How to Get from Space to Place in a Fairly Short Stretch of Time," in *Senses of Place*, ed. Steven Feld and Keith Basso (Santa Fe, NM: School of American Research Press, 1996), 13–52; Manuel DeLanda, *A New Philosophy of Society: Assemblage Theory and Social Complexity* (New York: Continuum, 2006), esp. 8–25; Tim Creswell, *Place: An Introduction* (Malden, MA: Wiley Blackwell, 2015), esp. 23–61; and Kim Dovey, *Becoming Places: Urbanism/Architecture/Identity/Power* (New York: Routledge, 2015), esp. 13–32.

5. Dolores Hayden, *The Power of Place: Urban Landscapes as Public History* (Cambridge, MA: MIT Press, 1995), esp. 14–43.

the memories and of experienced places, which is why Dylan Trigg is so right when he says that "we carry places with us."[6]

We carry them in our bodies actually, for the chemical gas cocktail that we inhale in a place becomes a permanent part of who we are. Our lungs, brains, and the rest of our bodies are made of the nitrogen, oxygen, hydrogen, and the several other particular elements we inhale (and imbibe and eat) in our places of dwelling. Our lungs most certainly bear the marks of the places in which we've lived and breathed. Those marks might be non-threatening scars on the lung tissue, especially in the case of us city dwellers, or the direr scarring of miners. At times we may also carry scars in our flesh from cuts, scrapes, and burns sustained in a particular place. We carry places with us even in this way. Furthermore, the social consequences of life in the places in which we live have relevance and influence all through the different stages of our lives, whether for good or ill. Whether in the form of enduring advantages or disadvantages, places possess power to shape the fates of those who live within them. All this is part of the placial inheritance I mentioned in chapter 1 and still another way in which places are carried.

We also carry places with us psychically by way of our memories. The places from which we came and in which we grew up are commonly locked in our memories, and we continue to experience them in their particularity in that manner. Even when we pay no conscious attention to places—which is often or most of the time, I imagine—they function in our lived experience as a never-ending chain of what some social psychologists call "primes." A prime, as Sarah Goldhagen puts it, is a "nonconsciously perceived environmental stimulus that can influence a person's subsequent thoughts, feelings, and responses by activating memories, emotions, and other kinds of cognitive associations."[7] In the entirety of their complex assemblage, places function as primes, but every single detail of their composition can act as a prime in its own right. The character of the buildings, the frigid wind tunnels rushing around surrounding buildings, the revolting stench of that uncollected garbage, and the configuration of the natural landscape or cityscape are all primes. The form, pattern, light, color, and texture of small-scale features in a neighborhood, geographical area, edifice, vessel, or room, likewise, can be a prime, affecting one's thoughts, perceptions, moods, and actions. In the

---

6. Dylan Trigg, *The Memory of Place: A Phenomenology of the Uncanny* (Athens: Ohio University Press, 2013), 11.

7. Sarah W. Goldhagen, *Welcome to Your World: How the Built Environment Shapes Our Lives* (New York: HarperCollins, 2017), 59.

places that we inhabit, every building element, every sequence of voids, every surface, every construction detail, every natural feature, and every social and cultural encounter could potentially prime our cognitive processes, whether conscious or unconscious. This suggests that places and the diverse attributes of places can continue to function as primes even after we've moved away from them.

These things called memories are certainly powerful, as are our connections and associations with places, even when these live on solely in our memory. Canadian geographer Edward Relph notes that we often transfer our memories and perceptions between places. This means that, when we move on to a new dwelling place, "our sense of each new place is always informed by experiences of previous places."[8] Relph's observation shows how the touch and influence of place perpetuate.

Not surprisingly, the places from which we hail or in which we have spent a good deal of time tend to be especially memorable and cognitively influential. Places in which we have spent relatively brief periods of time can, of course, be epistemically consequential, particularly if they are places where we have lived through a salient experience, whether good or bad. Still, the places in which we have lived for long periods are particularly memorable, for not only may we have developed deeper associations with them and broader webs of meaning in relation to them, but also we may have been touched epistemically by them in a myriad of ways, perhaps even in ways that we have not allowed ourselves to recognize and comprehend. There is something to be said for this sense of place. Placial affect is likely to be layers deep when you develop deep knowledge of the local geography—when you become familiar with roads, streets, shops, and the housing stock; learn where safety, beauty, and danger may lie; gain real-life insight into the differences between this district and that district; meet people, engage with the residents, participate in the choreography of everyday life; experience the weather; take in the smell, sights, and sounds; become involved in the community's struggles and hopes. That touch of place, that affect of place, comes in different ways and reaches out to each and every one of us in a variety of ways. That touch of place should not be glossed over, least of all in present-day academic work in which identifying the range of different subjectivities that give knowledge claims their location and premise is professedly important and good.

If the past places that have formed important parts of our lives really

---

8. Edward Relph, "Place and Connection," in *The Intelligence of Place: Topographies and Poetics* (New York: Bloomsbury Academic, 2017), 192.

carry the cognitive weight and the epistemic sway I have ascribed to them, then it is likely that they have also had some kind of impact on the values we incorporate into our belief systems and on the knowledge claims we make. It is likely that they have had some kind of impact on our thought and belief. In the case of academics, that impact is also likely to be ensconced in our intellectual projects and compositions despite the academic habit to disregard the matters, dynamics, and traces of place. Theologians and religious scholars, especially those of us who see ourselves as tenants of the wide left side of the theological spectrum and who, appropriately, insist on the need to take the range of different subjectivities into account in academic work, must take heed.

On that account, I wonder, what discoveries might we chance upon if we were to ask ourselves such questions as:

- What is the true and/or entire provenance of my thinking?
- In what place or places does my thinking take place?
- What has been the role of topos or place on my thinking and writing?
- Is it possible that I have somehow internalized or absorbed the physiognomy of the places in which I have dwelled into my self-perception and into my writings, and if so, how?
- Is it possible that the experiences I have had in and with a place have shaped my thinking and my writing in some way, and, if so, how?
- What is the connection between the region of my upbringing or the places in which I have lived and the character of my thinking and writing?
- What is to be gained in an exploration of the placed origin of our thinking and writing in any case?
- What are other latent possibilities that can be explored and developed through place-oriented theological thinking and writing?

I hope it is becoming clear that these are not only interesting but also meaningful, worthwhile, and potentially revelatory questions—even though our responses to them will vary. Some of us may find deep, obvious, and, perhaps, surprising connections between the region of our upbringing or our places of dwelling and the character of our thinking and writing. For others, the connections may seem less momentous or obvious. For a number of us, such place-based questions might seem novel, unaccustomed, or untried, requiring more time to ponder. Such a response as the latter would be understandable, for dominant Western culture does not prime us to consider these questions.

Either way, I feel confident that if we reflected on the matter more regularly and more observantly we would discover that the places from which we come echo through our subconscious, informing our understandings of thought and belief some way or another. We would discover that the places in which we dwell and through which we move contribute something to the knowledge and truth claims we make. In some cases, we might even find that the places we are from have played a constitutive role in our process of thought and writing even if unbeknown to us. In this instance, we may suddenly realize that the character of our thinking and writing has been sustained and guided by something that has remained mostly unspoken—namely, the perceptual and epistemic agency of place.

In either case, the discovery should lead to an important conclusion: places are not passive or ornamental backdrops for personal and social life. Places are not mere settings for the human story. Even if they might be secret or unacknowledged points of beginning for our work, places are actors in life and agents of life with affective and life-shaping power, power influencing what we know and what we say about the world. Places are one of the primary factors of our story *if* we recognize them in this light. As such, places play an important cognitive role in our lives and must be considered in any adequate account of our knowing and of our writing.

Much of What I Think and Write I Owe to Thee

I have certainly discovered that places have such central importance in my own life and thinking. Admittedly, this realization is recent, and it came gradually as I, too, have been influenced by the aforementioned taken-for-grantedness of place. For it may seem an obvious thing to say that our knowledge claims and beliefs are inextricably bound up with the places in which we live, or that places exert an influence on how we think, what we believe, and therefore on what and even why we write. Generally or instinctively, however, most of us in the late modern Western world do not think of place in this way. Discovery of the importance of place in and on our lives often requires prompting.

Ada María Isasi-Díaz's question to me twenty years ago and a question from a colleague at the end of a public lecture more recently encouraged my intentional discovery.[9] Both colleagues wondered about the placed origin of

---

9. Nancy Pineda-Madrid asked the second question during a question-and-answer period after a public lecture I delivered at Boston College on April 28, 2017.

my thinking as expressed in my writings, and, with their prompting, I developed a better understanding of how indebted I am to Spanish Harlem for the character of my thinking and my writing. When I examine my written work, I can see vital connections between the region of my upbringing and my thinking and my writing, vital connections to which I had previously paid little attention and that I had, frankly, underestimated and underappreciated. There are various emphases, themes, and traits I could give as examples, but, here, I limit myself to three that are clearly traceable to my place beginnings in Spanish Harlem, namely: (1) a critical social-justice orientation that stays focused on matters of economic inequality; (2) a pragmatist approach to things; and (3) an unequivocal Latino identification.

A critical social-justice orientation that stays focused on matters of economic inequality has been visible in my work from the very beginning of my career. Issues of social justice have always been of prime importance to me. Indeed, every piece of writing I have produced thus far has managed to relate its subject matter with the question of social equality one way or another. Whatever religious theory, whatever historical analysis, whatever theological idea or interpretation I have tendered, examined, or supported has been linked somehow to discussions on social justice. And I have tried to be comprehensive and inclusive in my deliberation. I have striven to account for and to give recognition to the different struggles for justice currently in evidence here in the United States and throughout the world. Relations of injustice, status hierarchies, and emancipatory projects bearing upon race, ethnicity, class, gender, sexuality, and ability have all been aspects and issues that have entered the picture of my writing.

At times, I have even attempted to broaden the discussion on justice to include political ecology, the ongoing nature of colonial space-making, epistemological injustice, and, now, land claims and cultural geography.[10] In doing so, my hope has always been to make sense of my own tensions and experiential or social disconcertments, throwing light on systemic relations of dominance, subordination, exclusion, and marginalization, and promot-

---

She wanted to know what life experiences may have motivated me to emphasize the seriousness of political economy and economic inequality in my work and to seek to transcend the borders of an identity politics. In my response to her, I was reminded once again of the power of place, of the epistemic sway East Harlem has held over my thinking and writing.

10. Benjamín Valentín, *Theological Cartographies: Mapping the Encounter with God, Humanity, and Christ* (Louisville, KY: Westminster John Knox Press, 2015), esp. 127–34.

ing ways of thinking and being that could conceivably contribute to a little more social justice among us—*un poquito de justicia quizas*.[11] And yet, for all that, it should be obvious that matters relating to economic injustice and material inequality have a special place in my heart.

Actually, I have spent the better part of my career urging fellow members of the U.S. liberationist and progressive camps in theology and in religious studies to pay closer attention to the economic dimension of justice, encouraging them to devote particular attention to injustices of political economy.[12] This is mostly due to a finding or observation. Early in my career, I noticed that we were focusing most of our attention on matters of cultural or symbolic injustice, devoting most of our analytical and discursive energies on the task of addressing and contesting oppressions that have to do with cultural domination, marginalization, nonrecognition, and disrespect. Whether by design or not, we had set our sights mainly on the cultural dimension of justice. For that reason, one could notice that we had made the discovery, defense, celebration, and reconstruction of cultures and identities; the recognition of difference, whether of nationality, ethnicity, race, gender, sexuality, or ability; and the fight against assimilationist tendencies and hurtful stereotypic public representations a central aim in our theologies and religious studies discourses. This, I have noted, is a good thing and a necessary thing. These concerns and struggles are valid and have everything to do with justice, and they must continue to be part of any emancipatory project and, therefore, of U.S. liberation and progressive theology as well as of liberationist and progressive-minded religious studies scholarship.

My concern, however, was that the focus on matters of cultural or symbolic injustice may have been diverting our attention away from issues that are related to socioeconomic injustice. Whether for this reason or others, we can note that injustices corresponding to exploitation, economic mar-

---

11. I am reminded here of Ada María Isasi-Díaz's ethical aspirations as expressed in her article "Un Poquito de Justicia—A Little Bit of Justice," in *Hispanic/Latino Theology: Challenge and Promise* (Minneapolis, MN: Fortress Press, 1996), 325–39.

12. For three examples of this in my writings, see Benjamín Valentín, *Mapping Public Theology: Beyond Culture, Identity, and Difference* (New York: Bloomsbury T&T Clark, 2002), esp. xi–xxi and 97–101; "Dialogic Mediations: Reflections on the Hopeful Future of U.S. Liberation Theology," in *The Reemergence of Liberation Theologies: Models for the Twenty-First Century*, ed. Thia Cooper (New York: Palgrave Macmillan, 2013), 49–56; and "What's 'Liberation' Got to Do with It?" *Reflections* (Spring 2017): 36–38.

ginalization, and deprivation have received less attention in our theologies and religious studies discourses. Various scholarly works and plenty of statements exist that mention and denounce the mal-distributive effects of capitalism, poverty, and other such socioeconomic problems.[13] Even still, if placed on a balance or weighing scale, sustained attention to matters concerning forms of cultural injustice outweigh those relating to economic injustice in the annals of our theologies.[14] Outside of a few authors who have been consistent in their treatment of issues in socioeconomic justice, something similar could be said of progressive theology in the United States.[15] After all, it is one thing to mention and denounce these social and economic conditions in passing or vague forms and quite another to devote a good deal of attention to them by way of careful and sustained analysis of their causes, conditions, and prospects for remediation. For that reason, I have suggested that we liberationist and progressive-minded theologians and religious stud-

---

13. For some examples of works that take up issues concerning socioeconomic injustice in a more sustained manner within the context of U.S. liberation theology, see Dwight Hopkins, *Down, Up, and Over: Slave Religion and Black Theology* (Minneapolis, MN: Fortress Press, 2000), esp. 51– 95; Emilie M. Townes, *Breaking the Fine Rain of Death: African American Health Issues and a Womanist Ethic of Care* (New York: Continuum, 1998), esp. chaps. 1–3; Miguel De La Torre, *Doing Christian Ethics from the Margins* (Maryknoll, NY: Orbis Books, 2014), esp. chaps. 4, 5, and 9; and Michelle A. Gonzalez, *Shopping: Christian Explorations of Daily Living* (Minneapolis, MN: Fortress Press, 2010), esp. the introduction and chaps. 1 and 3. Worthy of note here too is the work of Kwok Pui Lan. For example, see her work with theologian Joerg Rieger, *Occupy Religion: Theology of the Multitude* (Lanham, MD: Rowman & Littlefield, 2012), esp. chaps. 1–4.

14. This is one of the notable differences between U.S. liberation theology and Latin American liberation theology. Latin American liberation theologies have shown a tendency to focus on poverty and economic inequality, while going easier on cultural injustice oftentimes. U.S. liberation theologies have tended to go the other way. We can and will find exceptions to this proclivity. On balance, however, this is a general tendency in these two streams of liberation theology.

15. For some examples of liberal/progressive theological works that have delved into the economic realm to deal with forms of economic inequalities, see Joerg Rieger, *No Rising Tide: Theology, Economics, and the Future* (Minneapolis: Fortress Press, 2009); Richard A. Horsley, *Covenant Economics: A Biblical Vision of Justice for All* (Louisville, KY: Westminster John Knox Press, 2009); Lisa Sowle Cahill, *Global Justice, Christology, and Christian Ethics* (New York: Cambridge University Press, 2013); Kathryn Tanner, *Christianity and the New Spirit of Capitalism* (New Haven, CT: Yale University Press, 2019); and Nimi Wariboko, *The Split Economy: Saint Paul Goes to Wall Street* (Albany, NY: SUNY Press, 2020).

ies scholars should connect our concerns and demands for cultural change to an equally resolute, principled, and well-reasoned concern and demand for socioeconomic change.

I have neither envisioned nor proposed an exclusive binary between cultural and socioeconomic forms of justice. I aspire to merge these two dimensions and conceptions of justice because many people in our social groups, communities, and society continue to suffer injustices that are traceable to both political economy and to culture simultaneously. Hence, my hope has been to promote the construction of theologies and religious studies colloquies that can tie together the problematics of recognition and redistribution and can, in this way, adopt the cause of a more comprehensive emancipatory project for justice.[16]

Attending to place and to place's epistemic input prompts me to consider another series of significant questions. Where does the impetus for this broader emancipatory political vision come from? What is the origin of this critical social-justice orientation that stays focused on matters of economic inequality? Why has it been so important to me that the forces that confine people in the quagmire of economic and material inequality not be forgotten, nor that the particular perils of economic hardship be ignored? The answer lies in Spanish Harlem. The attentiveness and focus being discussed arise out of the unparalleled education I received from and within Spanish Harlem on the social and economic consequences of excessive privilege and on the disadvantage of economic hardship.

I use language that confers agency or involvement on Spanish Harlem's behalf here because I want to emphasize the active role that it played in this whole affair. In fact, practically everything inside of it played a role in shaping my insight into the actuality and perils of economic inequality. The material configuration, location, and ethos of Spanish Harlem, including its preponderant architecture and building design or housing stock; its visible grittiness; its sociodemographic characteristics; its traffic patterns; its geographic setting within Manhattan and next door to Yorkville in the Upper East Side of Manhattan; even the struggles and diligence of its residents and

---

16. My language and thinking here are influenced by Nancy Fraser, *Justice Interruptus: Critical Reflections on the Postsocialist Condition* (New York: Routledge, 1997); Nancy Fraser, *Redistribution or Recognition?: A Political-Philosophical Exchange* (New York: Verso Books, 2003); Nancy Fraser, *Scales of Justice: Reimagining Political Space in a Globalizing World* (New York: Columbia University Press, 2010).

the reputation it wrestled with as a district all worked together to leave a mark on my psyche and to brief me on the subject of America's undeniable class divide. I would venture to say that no text or chart could ever match the knowledge and insight conveyed by Spanish Harlem's physical environment and borders. As a matter of fact, the teaching it provided me on the reality of inequality came prior to any book learning that I could acquire on notions of economic fairness and market economy. Long before I got the opportunity to read from and about Karl Marx, Friedrich Engels, Max Weber, Jane Jacobs, John Rawls, Michael Harrington, William Julius Wilson, Douglas Massey, and Nancy Denton during my middle and late college years, Spanish Harlem had already taught me much about the real-life consequences of economic disparity in a country that is often known for its excess. I remember well the exact location where much of this learning took place: it was on Ninety-Seventh Street and Park Avenue.

Briefly looking in two directions from that very spot reveals a prevalent, living, physical portrait of the divergent fortunes of the rich and the poor or near poor. From there, one experiences all that is needed to understand that gross inequality exists in the United States, and it is all that is needed to comprehend that such inequality leads to consequences in virtually every dimension of everyday life. Look toward the south, and you will see those elegant, kempt, well-maintained streets for which Park Avenue is generally renowned. Trash is hardly seen in that direction, and a manicured wide boulevard is lined with trees and greenery year-round. Tulips and cherry trees in the spring, begonias in the summer, hawthorn trees ablaze with red buds in the fall, and lighted fir trees in the winter grace the street.[17] Perish the thought, however, that the streets north of Ninety-Sixth Street and all through Spanish Harlem are accorded the privilege and benefit of such beautification. Things look good in those southerly Park Avenue streets. It all makes for an attractive scene in that direction, an eye-pleasing view without a doubt. Maintaining even this stretch is no mean feat, particularly in an overall gritty New York City.

Helping, too, are all of those door-person-attended luxury apartment houses on both sides of the avenue from Forty-Seventh Street to Ninety-

---

17. The Fund for Park Avenue is the New York City nonprofit organization that is responsible for planting and maintaining the trees and flowers on Park Avenue. The nonprofit accepts responsibility only for the "south side" streets of Park Avenue, between 54th and 86th Streets. The NYC Parks Department extends the landscape gardening and grounds-keeping up to Ninety-Sixth Street.

Sixth Street. Even when standing on Ninety-Seventh Street, it is plain as day that those houses are well-maintained, affording their occupants elegant and generous living spaces on top of the comfort, security, and luxurious appearance of the overall building. The streets to the south of Ninety-Seventh Street are well lit, and the wider boulevard and more open sight lines existing in that direction combine with the further brightness to engender a greater sense of safety on that side. The neighborhoods to the south also reap the visual and status benefits conferred by such iconic structures as the Met Life Building, the Helmsley Building, the Waldorf Astoria, and Grand Central Terminal, and also by the many glass-box skyscrapers that serve as headquarters for corporations and investment banks such as J.P. Morgan, Chase, UBS, Citigroup, Colgate-Palmolive, and Met Life.

Furthermore, the streets to the south remain relatively quiet, even in such a high-traffic city. The sound of sirens, whether from police, fire, or paramedic vehicles, are rare in that direction. Even cab drivers and regular motorists seem willing to hold back from honking their horns. That is because road signs posted by city administrators threaten to impose a fine on any motorist who dares to disturb the peace on "those streets" of Park Avenue. I never saw one of these signs north of Ninety-Seventh Street. The peace of the residents of Spanish Harlem and Harlem more broadly seems to be neither as precious nor as important.

All things considered, looking southward from Ninety-Seventh and Park reveals a picture of plushness, comfortability, security, and location-based privilege. It is, so to say, a veritable urban bliss. And so far, my description of the picture has said nothing of the chauffeured luxury vehicles and Lincoln Town Car taxis, the mink coats and men's designer jackets, the income of locals, the good home-value-appreciation rate, the weighty role of housing in the household wealth of residents, the quality of educational opportunities afforded to children of that area in its many prestigious private schools, the advantageous life chances for individuals because of a higher quality of public amenities, the inexplicable improved effectiveness of public servants such as the police, the lower exposure to street violence and gang activity, nor the availability of less toxic air inside the city. These are among the other trappings of fortune commonly enjoyed by residents of such affluent jurisdictions and are more generally known. The physical environment of an area, however, the look and sounds of a district or geographic region alone can tell a story. And the story observed and heard when looking to the south at Ninety-Seventh Street and Park Avenue tells of luxurious comfort, of placial or place-based privilege, of life in relative safety, and of material well-being.

One might consider life in that direction to be a matter of good fortune, perhaps even a blessing. On that account, it is nothing of which to be ashamed or by which to be troubled. The problem is that things in the other direction to the north don't feel, look, or sound the same. And the sight of the great divergence as well as the thought of its likely consequences for present and future life disturbs somewhat. Or it could at the very least. It disturbs all the more if one hazards a guess that the privilege enjoyed in one jurisdiction might have something to do with or may not be entirely unrelated to the disadvantage experienced in the other. This is when it is reasonable for one to want to stop and consider the reason for the troubling feeling in one's soul.

I used to stop by Ninety-Seventh Street and Park Avenue pretty regularly, often after school when I was growing up and all through the years I lived in Spanish Harlem.[18] It was only three blocks and two avenues away from my home. As Morpheus explained to Neo in *The Matrix* (1999), I think it was because I knew something. What I knew I couldn't explain in words at first, but I felt it and experienced or witnessed it there in that specific location: that there is something wrong with the world that is and that the transgression has something to do with structured social inequality. This feeling was there like a splinter in my mind, driving me mad, and this feeling or intuition brought me to Ninety-Seventh Street and Park Avenue over and over again to look in one direction, south, and then in the other, north.

Often, when looking at the neighborhood or the neighborhoods to the south, James Baldwin's question, "And why isn't it for you?" would cross my mind before I ever encountered it in the written word.[19] I asked this question because my neighborhood, seen to the north at Ninety-Seventh Street and Park Avenue, looked very different from the one bordering it to the south. It was and continues to be a neighborhood rich in history and cultural treasures, with a caring and a close-knit community. It is a likable, proud, and historic district without a doubt. It is home to a significant Puerto Rican diasporic community on top of that. Spanish Harlem looks very different from the more affluent and ritzy neighborhood bordering it to the south—

---

18. I still do this today whenever I visit my parents and my sister and her family living there.

19. James Baldwin, "A Talk to Teachers," in *The Price of the Ticket* (Boston: Beacon Press, 1985), 332.

Yorkville. One could tell just on the basis of sight and sound that the difference carried consequences for most aspects of everyday life.

Spanish Harlem has those old and poorly maintained tenement houses, several public-housing projects, and the unsightly, massive granite and steel viaduct that serves as the foundation for the elevated railway tracks of the Metro North Line, cutting right through Spanish Harlem and starting on Ninety-Seventh Street and Park Avenue. There is clearly less streetlight on Spanish Harlem's side of Park Avenue. Trash is more noticeable. The ugly stone and steel viaduct and the single-lane traffic pattern it imposes on the avenue in each direction from Ninety-Seventh Street until the Harlem River at 132nd Street replace the manicured, wide boulevard that is lined with trees and greenery south of Ninety-Seventh. There is no nonprofit organization like the Fund for Park Avenue to beautify the residential streets of Spanish Harlem. There are none of those road signs threatening to impose a fine on noisy impatient motorists and conductors of emergency vehicles. The streets are noisier from those drivers, the passing Metro North trains on the elevated railroad tracks, and the many pedestrians in the narrower and more congested streets.

Congested by vehicle, train, and pedestrian traffic, the district, Manhattan Community District 11, has also reported higher asthma rates than its southerly neighbor.[20] The asthma rates are just one of many potential health drawbacks of extended living in poorly maintained, densely inhabited, and frequently rat-, mice-, and roach-infested buildings. Instead of iconic, status and property value-raising structures, Spanish Harlem's residents can count on a higher degree of exposure to violence, gangs, and toxic air, all while having to get by without the limousines and chauffeured luxury vehicles you see south of Ninety-Seventh Street. Public transportation and the occasional taxi ride will have to do for Spanish Harlemites, though the Yellow Cab taxis have been known to avoid our part of town.

Focusing only on the inequality that one can see and hear as it is organized in space, on the physical environment's appearance alone, it becomes clear that the two sides of Ninety-Seventh Street and Park Avenue live recognizably different and unbalanced lives. On the strength of the physical environment alone, one can tell that the people living north of Ninety-Seventh Street must live, move, and have their being inside a neighborhood that isn't

---

20. Community Health Profiles 2015—Manhattan Community District 11: East Harlem, www1.nyc.gov; NYC—Manhattan Community District 11, 2018—East Harlem PUMA, NY, www.censusreporter.org.

as clean, nice-looking, quiet, pleasant, safe, well thought of, desirable, and rewarding as those who live to the south. Moreover, one can intuit that life north of that invisible-but-tangible boundary line on Ninety-Seventh Street is likely to be more onerous, fraught with danger, difficulties, and disadvantages, and more insecure or uncertain, particularly with regard to physical safety, material comfort, and well-being now and into the future, than life to the south.

There is something else we are likely to intuit when looking in two directions at Ninety-Seventh Street and Park Avenue, I believe: it is that the residential and lifestyle divergence we are taking note of in this social setting has been put in place, and I don't mean by God. One understands deep down inside that the visible situational differences neither dropped from the sky predesigned nor emerged suddenly, randomly, or without method here on Earth. It registers that they are the result of political, economic, and social forces and processes: the result of decisions and actions taken and not taken by individuals, agencies, and institutions of society over many years. One might imagine the list of main determinants and underlying drivers being long, and one wouldn't be wrong. Federal and local government leaders, agencies, and policies; business executives and financial firms; real-estate investors, developers, and speculators; corporate and commercial investors; private investors and organizations; urban planners; even the cultural power of consumer tastes and collective patterns of racial stigmatization and discrimination: all of these constituents, parties, and entities have played a role in producing the topography of privilege and privation, the topography of inequality that we can see, hear, and feel at Ninety-Seventh Street and Park Avenue.

The thought of the anthropogenic and/or manufactured nature of the placial inequality surveyed at this location should be enough to prompt the sentiment that what we are witnessing is not so much a tragedy as it is a scandal. The difference between tragedy and scandal is subtle but important. As Sasha Abramsky rightly notes, tragedy can lie outside the realm of the deliberate, the product not so much of poor judgment, failed policy, callousness, or a skewed moral compass as of "confounded bad luck or happenstance."[21] However, when inequality flourishes as a direct result of decisions taken or not taken by political and economic leaders and as a consequence of a deficit

---

21. Sasha Abramsky, *The American Way of Poverty: How the Other Half Still Lives* (New York: Bold Type Books, 2013), 11–12.

of collective responsibility, indifference, passivity, and bias, then "it acquires the rancid aroma of scandal."[22]

In addition to the numerous parties implicated in this scandal discussed above, we can also linger on the question of the factors and processes that were instrumental in creating the scandal, for they, too, are many. Scratching the general surface, we see that this scandal of divergence emerged through the inability of our socioeconomic institutions to deliver meaningful progress for each and every citizen and resident in the same manner; social policies that have failed in creating inclusive growth; the valuing of some people's labor more than that of others; and income inequality that has been allowed to grow increasingly extreme. Looking deeper reveals other factors, including the effect of dubious public and private sector disinvestment and investment patterns; the effect of discriminatory practices that put services (financial and otherwise) out of reach for residents of certain neighborhoods based on race or ethnicity and geographical area; the effect of the disgraced urban-renewal policies of the 1940s and 1950s; and the effect of uneven geographical development over long periods of time. It is important to consider also the established tendency among municipal governments of catering to the needs of affluent districts while neglecting those of low-income neighborhoods. In this case, we even have to account for grievous social practices and oppressive economic and labor factors that made it impossible for the predominantly brown, Black, and more variegated folks living north of Ninety-Seventh Street to live in other regions and neighborhoods and that made it necessary for them to cram into the tenements and projects of Spanish Harlem. Such relevant social practices include exclusionary zoning laws, the demand for cheap labor in cities, and the high cost burdens encountered by many in other residential areas. These practices are the result of an intricate and pernicious conflation of race, politics, economic privation, privilege, and opportunism. To this, we can add a dash of callousness, indifference, denial, gullibility, and misplaced blaming of the victims of poverty on the part of the American public, leading to a collective irresponsibility that tolerates levels of inequality that should be unacceptable.

It is quite the toxic brew that produced the state of things as they exist on Ninety-Seventh Street and Park Avenue all of this suggests. And there is no doubt that many ingredients, factors, and processes are involved in its making. One can even get an indication or inkling of the complexity of the situation right there in place. It shouldn't be too difficult for an observer to

---

22. Abramsky, *The American Way of Poverty*, 11–12.

see, for instance, that complexions in Yorkville immediately south of that Ninety-Seventh Street boundary line become considerably whiter. They are noticeably darker, browner, or more tanned in Spanish Harlem. This alone should be enough to remind one of what social theorists call the "intersectionality" of race and class.[23] It is a complicated, many-faceted mess for sure, in other words. But deep down one understands that money has much to do with it. One understands that money has been and continues to be a key factor in the creation of this place-based inequality. Even as an adolescent comparing the look of Yorkville and Spanish Harlem I knew it. Money has a lot to do with it.

Exploitation of people's labor for the benefit of others; working class jobs with stagnant wages; insufficient or no retirement funds; inadequate health insurance; the loss of blue-collar jobs due to automation, outsourcing, and the economic interests of big businesses and shareholder capitalism; government's general indifference to the loss of blue-collar jobs, and government's unwillingness to regulate the economic behavior of individuals and firms in the private sector; cutbacks in programs to protect low-income families and individuals from poverty and hardship; incomes that have continued growing more unequal to this day; and a vast difference in the way that the lives and communities of the rich and those of the poor or near poor are regarded and served by municipalities, urban planners, architects, businesses, community organizations, and investors: these are among the money matters that have mattered very much in generating the geographic disparity being considered. They are among the monetary or money-based reasons why things look so different in those two directions on Ninety-Seventh Street and Park Avenue.

I know that similar regional disparities can be seen elsewhere here in the United States and around the world, but there is something particularly notable to my having seen it and experienced it in the middle of Manhattan in New York City. After all, among other things, New York City is often and reasonably referred to as the financial capital of the world. In fact, if the New York City metropolitan area were a sovereign state, it would have the eighth-largest economy in the world, producing an estimated gross

---

23. See Kimberlé Crenshaw, *On Intersectionality: Essential Writings* (New York: New Press, 2017); Ange-Marie Hancock, *Intersectionality: An Intellectual History* (New York: Oxford University Press, 2016); Patricia Hill Collins, *Intersectionality as Critical Social Theory* (Durham, NC: Duke University Press, 2019); *Intersectionality: Foundations and Frontiers*, ed. Patricia R. Grzanka (New York: Routledge, 2019).

metropolitan product (GMP) of $2 trillion. New York City is also home to the highest number of billionaires of any city in the world.[24] It should be noted, however, that it is the borough of Manhattan specifically that carries the claim to fame with respect to financial means. This is understandable, seeing as it is anchored by Wall Street in the Financial District of Lower Manhattan, and because it serves as home to the world's two largest stock exchanges by total market capitalization, the New York Stock Exchange and the NASDAQ. What's more, as luck would have it, Yorkville in particular has been where Wall Street big shots, celebrities, and billionaire heirs love to mingle and reside. This placed them right there next door to my neighborhood in Spanish Harlem, immediately to the south of that imaginary but tangible boundary line I have been talking about on Ninety-Seventh Street. It is no wonder that Manhattan has been referred to as "Money Makin' Manhattan" by some.[25]

Not everyone was making or coming into money in Manhattan obviously, and this includes virtually everyone in El Barrio. The irony of life in a low-income, underprivileged, and underserved neighborhood in a city and region known for economic largesse was and is still hard to miss. This irony makes the reality of place-based inequality all the more telling, impactful, and unforgettable. Unlike most places in the United States, where at least a little bit of geographic distance exists between low-income and affluent neighborhoods, there is something to be said for the way in which the great place-based divergence of Park Avenue was and continues to be in such immediate proximity. In other settings, inequality can be hidden, unseen, passed over, or avoided because of even a small geographic distance. At Ninety-Seventh Street and Park Avenue in Manhattan, however, inequality is side by side, bordering itself, plain to see, and hard to miss. I definitely saw it, heard it, felt it, and experienced it on a daily basis while growing up in Spanish Harlem, and the experience had an impact on me, teaching me significant things.

Among the lessons the sight of that place-based inequality gave to me was the understanding that we really are not all equal or treated equally in

---

24. Borden Taylor and Hillary Hoffower, "The Top 10 Cities in the World for Billionaires, Ranked," in *Business Insider,* July 2, 2020, https://www.business insider.com.

25. "Money Making Manhattan" or "Money Makin' Manhattan" has been a rap nickname for the borough of Manhattan since the early 1980s. John "Mr. Magic" Rivas (1956–2009), a hip-hop radio DJ, is believed to have coined the term. The Beastie Boys, a hip-hop trio, used the term in the lyrics to "Super Disco Breakin'" (1998).

the United States. Living in Spanish Harlem and catching sight of the great divergence taught me to cast aside the myth of a classless U.S. society. U.S. residents live in a society that demonstrates its distaste for class divisions in a thousand informal ways, including even class division as a topic of discussion. But, as Timothy Noah quite rightly points out, "to dislike such divisions is not the same thing as to abolish them."[26] Abolition has eluded us across the years. What's more, at times, it seems that we are willing to accept, look past, deny, and even to reap the benefits of those divisions so far as possible. Despite our societal discomfitures, denials, and sheepishness around this matter, the truth is that unequal distribution of income and wealth, along with unequal distribution of property, land, power, voice, and opportunity, have always been common here.

From all indications, our economic divisions have become even greater during recent decades. The median U.S. American household is actually poorer in net worth today than it was in 2000, owing in part to significantly lower median wages for the majority of the population who lack a college degree, according to the Bureau of Labor Statistics.[27] More broadly, U.S. workers in general made only 12 percent more in 2018 than they did in 1978.[28] Meanwhile, rents for roughly the same period rose 45 percent; home sale prices by 83 percent; and health-care costs by 101 percent.[29] The cost of most everything else has increased exponentially as well. In the meantime, the wages paid to lower- and lower-middle-wage workers have not kept pace with inflation in our country, and they have not been even close. It is no wonder that financial insecurity has become a way of life for so many in the United States.

A full 38 percent of U.S. Americans have difficulty meeting their basic needs, according to a large Urban Institute study.[30] Sixty-nine percent of U.S. Americans have less than $1,000 in savings.[31] About 15.2 percent of the population fell below the woefully low federal poverty line in 2015, the

---

26. Timothy Noah, *The Great Divergence: America's Growing Inequality Crisis and What We Can Do about It* (New York: Bloomsbury Press, 2012), 38.

27. U.S. Bureau of Labor Statistics, January 2021, www.bls.gov.

28. Joanne Samuel Goldblum and Colleen Shaddox, *Broke in America: Seeing, Understanding, and Ending U.S. Poverty* (Dallas, TX: BenBella Books, 2021), 6.

29. Goldblum and Shaddox, *Broke in America*, 7, 52.

30. Signe-Mary McKernan, Caroline Ratcliffe, C. Eugene Steuerle, and Sisi Zhang, "Disparities in Wealth Accumulation and Loss from the Great Recession and Beyond," *Urban Institute* (April 30, 2014), https://www.urban.org.

31. "Survey: 69% of Americans Have Less Than $1,000 in Savings," *Forbes* (September 23, 2016), https://www.forbes.com.

bottom 25 percent having a mean net worth of negative $13,400, meaning that they owe more than they own.[32]

In 2007, Katherine Newman and Victor Chan estimated that there were fifty-four million near-poor Americans, a large and growing demographic of people living above the poverty line but only earning incomes between $20,000 and $40,000 for a family of four. These people are just one pink slip, divorce, or health crisis away from the edge and comprise an often-forgotten group of people they call "the missing class."[33] In 2016, the Coalition on Human Needs put the number of near-poor Americans at 95.2 million, defining the category as inclusive of those living below twice the poverty line, which stood at $24,563 for a family of four that year.[34] It is likely that even that number falls short of capturing the true picture of America's economic anxieties. I lean toward the more recent estimates put forth by Nicholas Kristof and Sheryl WuDunn in their eye-opening book *Tightrope*, where they mention a brittleness to life for about "150 million Americans."[35] We must never forget the further estimated 580,466 people experiencing homelessness on any given night in the United States, a rate of approximately seventeen people for every ten thousand in the general population.[36] After experiencing a slight dip in 2012 and 2013, that number has increased each year.

Covid-19 created a health and economic crisis in the United States and throughout the world. It made things all the worse for everyone at the bottom of America's working world, for the millions and millions who live "in the shadow of prosperity, in the twilight between poverty and well-being."[37] If anything, the pandemic simply exposed how thin the margins are for the average American. A superficially robust economy that has always done a lot more for those on top than everyone below cratered, burdened by a global virus outbreak for which our nation was regrettably unprepared.[38] When

---

32. "Income and Poverty in the United States: 2015," www.census.gov.

33. Katherine S. Newman and Victor Tan Chen, *The Missing Class: Portraits of the Near Poor in America* (Boston: Beacon Press, 2007), esp. 1–9.

34. *Coalition on Human Needs*, October 26, 2017.

35. Nicholas D. Kristof and Sheryl WuDunn, *Tightrope: Americans Reaching for Hope* (New York: Vintage Books, 2020), 17–18.

36. 2020 Annual Homeless Report to Congress, U.S. Department of Housing and Urban Development, https://www.huduser.gov.

37. David K. Shipler, *The Working Poor: Invisible in America* (New York: Vintage Books, 2016), 3.

38. I say superficially robust because the conventional ways we gauge the economy's health from month to month and from year to year whistle past the increasing

the pandemic led local and national governments to close businesses and issue stay-at-home orders, unemployment swelled to levels not seen since the Great Depression.[39] For white-collar workers who could work remotely, paychecks were more likely to keep coming in. A great many others were not as lucky. In April 2020, "the United States lost 7.65 million leisure and hospitality jobs, 2.1 million retail jobs, and 1.33 million manufacturing jobs."[40] As Joanne Goldblum and Colleen Shaddox note, "workers newly branded 'essential' continued to labor in grocery stores and nursing homes where they risked their lives for wages below what they needed to pay their bills."[41] Day-care providers, hospital attendants, delivery persons, transit workers, and various others join Goldblum and Shaddox's list.

In the last years and decades, things have only gotten worse for the majority of low- and lower-middle-income workers in the United States, but things have always been bad for the very many who find themselves "trapped for life in a perilous zone of low-wage work."[42] I saw it plenty in my years living in Spanish Harlem, where economic distress is not new. As these numbers show, economic distress is actually quite ordinary throughout the United States and has been ignored or denied. While so many hard-working and unemployed or underemployed people struggle to make ends meet and to gain a foothold on the elusive—maybe even faulty or deceptive—promise of the American dream, there are those who have been living it up without inter-

---

level of misery and despair felt by people in big pockets of the United States. The national GDP, which is still the gold standard for measuring a society's overall economic well-being, may indicate that an economy is robust and growing. But it presents a distorted picture as it represents the sum total of everything we produce over a given period. It doesn't measure such things as unpaid work, nor does it account for the adequacy of salary figures, employment benefits, health-care coverage, pensions, inflation rates, debt, etc. Even job aggregates and unemployment figures can fail to capture the true picture for they do not adjust for salary figures, employment benefits, health-care coverage, or pensions. Nor do these two measures account for frustrated job seekers who have given up on the possibility of landing a new position, or for formerly middle-class workers who have accepted more marginal positions that barely lift them out of poverty. For more on this issue, see Gene Ludwig, *The Vanishing American Dream: A Frank Look at the Economic Realities Facing Middle- and Lower-Income Americans* (New York: Disruption Books, 2020), esp. 10–15.

39. Goldblum and Shaddox, *Broke in America*, xvii.
40. Goldblum and Shaddox, *Broke in America*, xvii.
41. Goldblum and Shaddox, *Broke in America*, xvii.
42. Shipler, *The Working Poor*, 3.

ruption. For those in this small but powerful group, life seems to get better and better almost always, even during wide-reaching crisis moments, their lot becoming all the better quite possibly because it is often tied to and even dependent on the hardship, exploitation, and reduced circumstances of others. Even as President Joe Biden was announcing in an address to Congress that twenty million Americans had lost their jobs, *Forbes* was reporting that total billionaire wealth stood at $4.6 trillion as of the stock market close on April 28, 2021, up 35 percent, from $3.4 trillion, when markets opened on January 1, 2020, just as Covid-19 was beginning to take the world by storm.[43] In other words, U.S. billionaires got about $1.2 trillion richer during the pandemic. According to that *Forbes* report, three quarters of America's 722 billionaires are as rich, or richer, than they were before the pandemic—some by billions, tens of billions, or even more than one hundred billion dollars. They are beneficiaries, whether by intent or not, of economic and social policies that are designed to produce inequality.

Even as the earnings of most Americans have not kept pace with the cost of living, corporate profits have been rising consistently since the 1980s. The average worker may not have benefited from these profits, but "CEO pay rose 940 percent between 1978 and 2018."[44] Related to the salary of an average citizen, "the ratio of a CEO's pay to the average worker's pay has grown exponentially from 30-to-1 in 1978 to 270-to-1 today."[45] In 1965, the average chief executive earned about twenty times as much as the average worker. That divergence in pay has only grown since then. Kristoff and WuDunn offer a further perspective on this point: "A Walmart employee earning the median salary at the company, $19,177, would have to work for 1,188 years to earn as much as the chief executive did in 2018 alone."[46] The figure of 1,188 years is more than fifteen whole lifetimes for Spanish Harlem residents![47]

We need focus not only on the billionaires. In fact, we should not, for doing so could distract us from the broader scope of our country's growing

---

43. "How Much Money America's Billionaire's Have Made during the Covid-19 Pandemic," *Forbes* (April 30, 2021), https://www.forbes.com.

44. Goldblum and Shaddox, *Broke in America*, 6.

45. Ludwig, *The Vanishing American Dream*, 7.

46. Kristoff and WuDunn, *Tightrope*, 61.

47. K. Hinterland, M. Naidoo, L. King, V. Lewin, G. Myerson, B. Noumbissi, M. Woodward, L. H. Gould, R. C. Gwynn, O. Barbot, and M. T. Bassett, "Life Expectancy by Community District," in Community Health Profiles 2018, Manhattan Community District 11: East Harlem (2018): 20, https://www.nyc.gov.

inequality crisis. A good number of other Americans continue to get richer even as the majority of the population gets poorer and struggles mightily in consequence. More than 8 percent of adults in the United States, more than twenty million people, have enough assets to fit the definition of "a millionaire," according to the Global Health Report 2020 by Credit-Suisse. The United States also added 2,251,000 new millionaires from 2019 to 2020 alone, topping the list of countries with the most millionaires.[48] About 13.61 million households, more than 10 percent of households in the United States, have a net worth of one million or more, not including the value of their primary residence.[49]

We can question the fairness, reasonableness, soundness, and effectiveness of an economic and political system that allows some to prosper to this extent while subjecting the greater share of the population to a daily struggle for basic needs and resources. Our economic and political system has allowed income, overall wealth, and life opportunity to skew successively over time, with the rich getting richer and most everyone else falling behind, and that is the issue.

This is indeed an issue. The long-standing and growing inequality in our midst should be concerning. Economic fairness and equal or shared opportunity and hope are in question here. Witnessing countless individuals and families trapped in the quagmire of low wages and unemployment or underemployment, near the edge of poverty, and struggling through life in reduced circumstances while others accrue the spoils of prosperity in the world's richest nation evokes a moral concern. There can be no doubt also that the problems caused by our enduring and growing inequality weigh heavily on our social and political fabric. Distrust of our political and economic institutions; hostility toward government; polarization, racism, bigotry, and misplaced blame; the increasing use of opioids, drugs, and alcohol to deal with despair, anxiety, and frustration; growing suicide rates; and unfulfilled potential for many of our children because of variability and shortcomings in our health and education systems: these are among the societal complications occasioned by our mounting inequality.

Moreover, there is the matter of national pride, identity, and compe-

---

48. Global Wealth Report 2020, Credit-Suisse, https://www.credit-suisse.com.

49. 2020 Market Insights Report—Spectrem Group, https://www.einnews.com/pr_news/565666479/new-spectrem-study-reveals-significant-increases-in-number-of-millionaires. See also the U.S. Census Bureau—The Wealth of Households: 2017/Current Population Reports, www.census.gov.

tence or standing. The Gini Coefficient measures distribution of income and serves as a measure of income inequality for 159 countries. The United States' 0.480 in 2020 ranks us fifty-third overall and thirty-third among the thirty-seven countries in the Organization for Economic Co-operation and Development (OECD).[50] Income inequality in the United States is also the highest of all the G7 nations, according to data compiled by the Pew Research Center in 2020.[51] According to the Social Progress Index, which is based on research that covers 146 countries for which there is reliable data, the United States lags behind in other important social measures as well. We rank forty-first in child mortality, forty-sixth in internet access, forty-fourth in access to clean drinking water, fifty-seventh in personal safety, and thirtieth in high-school enrollment. Overall, the Social Progress Index ranks the United States twenty-eighth in well-being of citizens, behind all the other members of the G7.[52]

And as if all this weren't worrisome enough, it appears too that opportunities for upward mobility are becoming harder to find in our country. This is ironic and unsettling since upward mobility is America's supposed creed. Circumstances at the bottom might be hard, but a plucky young shoe-shiner or laborer, with his or her "eye on the main chance can rise in the world through hard work"[53] it is often said or thought. The narrative of upward mobility is an important part of the American Dream, but economic reality does not match these expectations. Only 8 percent of Americans born in the lowest fifth in income distribution ever make it to the highest fifth in income distribution in adulthood.[54] Even upward mobility within the lower or middle economic tiers is proving elusive. Recent polls and studies show that each consecutive generation of Americans is finding it harder to climb the economic ladder by earning higher incomes than their parents. Individuals born in 1980 have only a 45 percent chance of out-earning their parents at age thirty, compared to 93 percent for those born in 1940. As it stands

50. 2020, data.oecd.org.

51. Katherine Schaeffer, "Six Facts about Economic Inequality in the U.S.," Pew Research Center (February 7, 2020), https://www.pewresearch.org.

52. See Social Progress Imperative Global Index: Results at www.social progress.org/2020.

53. Noah, *The Great Divergence*, 28.

54. Mark R. Rank and Lawrence Eppard, "The American Dream of Upward Mobility Is Broken," *The Guardian* (March 13, 2021), https://www.theguardian.com; "Is the American Dream Over? Here's What the Data Says," *World Economic Forum* (September 2, 2020), https://www.weforum.org.

right now, it takes five generations for a low-income family to reach median income.[55] When you combine the stagnant and even declining prospects for upward intergenerational economic mobility with the higher levels of discontent and financial anxiety that many low- and lower-middle-income residents must contend with on a daily basis, on top of the rising threat of crime and violence being encountered in many regions of our country, it is easy to see why Americans were among the most stressed populations in the world, tied with Iranians, and more stressed than Venezuelans, according to a 2019 Gallup Report.[56]

All of this is undermining our nation's reputation and standing on the world stage, not to mention our competitiveness there as well. Furthermore, it suggests that living conditions have been getting more arduous, distressing, and uncertain for countless low- and moderate-income Americans even as the country's wealthy continue to prosper and improve their lot. Our incomes, riches, opportunities, living circumstances, and life prospects are drastically unequal, continuing a long-term trend in our country. Despite our reluctance to admit it and despite our tendency to wax lyrical about our land of plenty and opportunity, we have always been a nation of haves and have-a-lot-lessers or have-nots.

Class divisions have always been a part of the American economic and social landscape. The chasm between the people thriving in our country's economy and those unable to thrive has been visible all along, even in pockets of the most prosperous cities in the United States of America.

Living in Spanish Harlem, I witnessed inequality that was organized and fixed firmly in place. Between New York City's near bankruptcy in 1975 and the attempts at gentrification in El Barrio in more recent years, I experienced a revealing inequality that shaped the very physicality of our neighborhoods. I witnessed how inequality wrought financial insecurity and a life of struggle for basic needs, resources, status, and good future prospects for many, all while delivering the benefits of affluence, luxury, safety, exceptional schools, social networks, and a more assured future to others. I learned that economic inequality resulted in living separate and unequal lives. That boundary place in Spanish Harlem, Ninety-Seventh Street and Park Avenue, taught me that inequality is real.

There is an institutionalized divide between the wealthy and the poor or

55. "Is the American Dream Over?"; Hannah Ziady, "The American Dream Is Much Easier to Achieve in Canada," *CNN Business* (January 20, 2020).

56. See Gallup 2019 Global Emotions Report, https://www.gallup.com/.

near-poor in this country, and it severs that very spot. Experiencing this divide from an early age inspired me to question America's brash boast that we have no class system. While it is true that our country disallows hereditary titles of nobility and recognizes the sovereignty of the people, ours has never been a land of equity. Spanish Harlem taught me that our social class divisions are wide and cut deep, and it taught me to tune out America's euphoric hymn to work, rejecting the tendency to blame people for their economic hardship. Assuming that anyone can attain prosperity from hard work and deducing that the failure to do so reveals a personal fall from righteousness or innate character flaw rather than a malfunctioning political and economic system are two related and troublesome beliefs and traditions to which Americans have often adhered. Consequently, we end up blaming people living in poverty or near poverty for their suffering, deeming those excluded from the proceeds of prosperity as lazy, fundamentally weak, given to vice, or as inherently flawed in some other way. People with money are not the only ones who succumb to these beliefs, for the poor and the near-poor can and do perpetuate the narrative that a lack of work comes with a whiff of sinfulness.

As a resident of Spanish Harlem, however, I noticed that, often, work does not work. I remember repeated cases of my neighbors, fellow church-goers, and family members who worked, worked, and worked for most of their lives, clocking in five, six, and even seven days a week at a job or two. Yet, for all their effort, they never could get very far from where they started. They never could quite break away and move a comfortable distance from poverty or from living in near poverty. Hence, they found it hard to save, at times went without decent health care, lived in crumbling or forbidding housing, could not move to safe neighborhoods if they so desired, nor could they send their children to better nonpublic schools. When retirement age came around, it was not uncommon to hear them consider neighborhoods that were even more affordable than Spanish Harlem. They considered moving to the outer boroughs of New York City, to out-of-state regions of Connecticut or Florida, or back to Puerto Rico; the latter two options being popular destinations for members of my Puerto Rican community after retirement. But the reason they had to wander through a borderland of struggle their entire lives, while living on the margins of the world's richest nation and in the middle of "money makin' Manhattan," was because their jobs shared three unhappy traits: they paid low wages, offered little or no benefits, and led nowhere.[57]

---

57. Shipler, *The Working Poor,* esp. 3–12 and 39–76.

They were neither lazy, weak, inadequate, nor freeloaders at heart. My Boricua community and other fellow Spanish Harlemites flowed into and out of the 103rd, 110th, and 116th Street train stations every morning and evening, heading to or returning from work with bells on. The no. 6 train carried the masses of people who evoked pride in our place. "There goes Spanish Harlem off to work" or "back from work," I often thought upon witnessing the sight.

The small subset of the neighborhood's population who had to turn to public assistance through welfare and/or food stamps were usually low-income older people of retirement age or persons who had been denied access to income-generating labor altogether. Even among them, one got the sense of work being considered an honor, and being on welfare and other public benefits was deemed either as shameful, lamentable, or embarrassing; a certain and unfortunate sentiment that signaled their having succumbed to the harshness and lack of empathy permeating the American atmosphere. Many of them wound up working in the informal economy, doing laundry for neighbors, sewing jobs from home, and fixing discarded radios and televisions, among other things. Their prevailing attitude and accepted view show that not one of them wanted to scuffle about and that even those in this smaller group carried a good work ethic. They were joined in these sentiments by the hordes of other work-loving and hardworking Nuyoricans and Spanish Harlemites.

From my own experiences in the neighborhood and with the people of the neighborhood, I can say for sure that laziness, dependency, inadequacy, or bad choices were not the problem. The people in El Barrio struggled mostly because their labor was appropriated for the benefit of others. They struggled mostly because they were confined to poorly paid work. They struggled in numerous cases because they were denied access to income-generating labor altogether. They struggled on the whole because the political economy of the industrial empire that lured them to these parts with hopes of opportunity, access to paid work, an adequate material standard of living, and the possibility of meaningful social progress failed them. Instead, they came into a miasma of low income, insufficient health-care coverage, unemployment, layoffs, inferior public schools, distressed housing, underserved—therefore, decaying and unsafe—neighborhoods, a lack of resources, limited social mobility and political power, and, more generally, a life of struggle. To add insult to injury, they got to live right next to the affluent and high-opportunity neighborhood in the Upper East Side of Manhattan. They could witness each and every day that the reputed American Dream is only for some rather than for everyone.

From my own point of view, two images converge here: struggle and drastic inequality. The conditions of struggle were evident in the physical characteristics of Spanish Harlem and in the day-to-day lives of its residents. The drastic inequality of wealth, opportunity, dwelling places, resources, and living conditions that transpires regularly in regions of the United States was and is plainly displayed at Ninety-Seventh Street and Park Avenue. Both images remain engraved in my body and soul, in my heart and mind.

These mental images engendered a literary emphasis in time and are the main reason why I have given prominence to the topic of economic inequality in my writings and teaching. Bearing the impression of these place-based experiences and lessons in my heart and soul, I have chosen to bring attention to issues pertaining to political economy and class in hopes of raising awareness of the injustices of material inequality and in the hope that, in doing so, others will be persuaded to speak out on and grapple with the dilemmas of income, wealth, power, and assets inequality as well.

I know all too well that the disadvantage of material inequality is compounded for people oppressed by racism, ethnocentrism, sexism, and other forms of discrimination. Therefore, it is important to keep track of the different status inequalities lurking in our midst, standing at the ready to interrogate the institutionalized patterns, structures, and policies that produce and sustain them, with the hope of defending identities, ending cultural domination, and winning recognition where necessary. As I see it, we must be aware not to limit the grammar of our political claims-making to what I have called a cultural politics of identity and recognition, restricting our discursive activism to injustices that are traceable to culture in consequence. People suffer injustices that are traceable to political economy and the decision-making processes of governments, institutions, and corporations as well. Hence, we need an integrative perspective and a comprehensive political project that strives to address the cultural, political, and economic dimensions of social life and justice; all of this in high hopes of correlatively furthering the causes of recognition, representation, and redistribution.[58] Spanish Harlem taught me this.

Place—Spanish Harlem in this case—played an active role in the process of my attention to a critical social-justice perspective that closely monitors the problems of economic inequality. This thematic emphasis in my work

58. Fraser, *Scales of Justice*, esp. 1–29.

did not result from my experience and reasoning powers alone, for, if that were the case, I would retain all of the perceptual and epistemic agency in this matter, rendering the physical, social, and cultural environment of Spanish Harlem passive in the process. Everything about the place, including the physical characteristics of the neighborhood, the experience of the residents, and the geographical location of Spanish Harlem in Manhattan and next door to Yorkville, became influential toward my way of thinking, toward my beliefs about the world, and toward my intellectual choices. Spanish Harlem's physical, social, cultural, and geographical features carried information that impacted my perceptual and cognitive life, influencing and, to a certain extent, structuring my understandings of thought and belief. That the topics of economic inequality, poverty, and economic hardship were never discussed in my household only adds to my growing belief in the power of place. After all, when everything is taken into consideration, Spanish Harlem stands out as my first and foremost teacher on economic injustice.

Spanish Harlem taught me more than lessons on economic injustice, however. I see connections between El Barrio and the pragmatist tenor of my thinking and writing. I was a pragmatist well before I discovered and embraced the ideas and arguments of the central figures of the philosophical tradition of American pragmatism in college and graduate school.[59] That intellectual discovery and exploration proved to be exhilarating, soul-stirring even, yet Spanish Harlem had already pointed me in pragmatism's direction. My attraction to the ideas and arguments of these thinkers emerged through my experiences in and with Spanish Harlem.

I have been particularly attracted to pragmatist motifs that evade speculative or nonexperiential metaphysics and to the passion for historicist ways of thinking that focus on the ways and means by which people have, do, and can overcome obstacles, dispose of predicaments, and settle problematic situations in a given place at a given time. I keep in view in this regard the likelihood that life in a marginalized and disadvantaged inner-city neighborhood played a part in my penchant for reasoning processes that are earthbound and burdened with practicality. Given my strivings to survive and prosper in

---

59. I first got the chance to explore the work of such pragmatist thinkers as Charles Sanders Peirce, William James, John Dewey, W. E. B. Du Bois, Reinhold Niebuhr, Richard Rorty, Richard Bernstein, Cornel West, Susan Haack, and Cheryl Misak during my junior year in college, and then again with increased attention during my first year in Harvard Divinity School's Master's of Theological Studies program.

a part of town where the going was tougher and the complexions browner, it is not entirely surprising that I found little value in unhistorical and ethereal or otherworldly ruminations. Life in Spanish Harlem demanded a certain kind of in-the-moment attitude, resourcefulness, alertness, vigilance, and presence of mind. This is needed when safety is at issue, when life is lived on the edge, even if not by choice, and when life is a constant challenge amid the absence of affluence, privilege, public and private resources, and what I like to call favorable opportunities.

Under these circumstances, life has to be lived with a kind of existential urgency and with an on-the-ground disposition. In such circumstances, it helps to have a this-worldly hope. Considering this place, it is hardly surprising that I developed a fondness for pragmatic thinking and that I would be drawn to a philosophical tradition that grapples with the messiness and uncertainties of life without recoiling into metaphysical fantasy or wishful thinking; a philosophical tradition that tries to deploy thought as a weapon to enable more effective action.[60] Because of Spanish Harlem, the empirical emphasis and ameliorative impulse of American pragmatism appealed to me. Pragmatism was right in my perceptual and conceptual wheelhouse.

I recognize that others in situations like this or similar to this could settle upon a completely different outlook and way of thinking. Belief systems and mindsets are rarely predictable or straightforward, and I have no intention to promote an environmental determinism. What I propose is more in line with what Paul Vidal de la Blache once called an "environmental possibilism,"[61] which, as Christopher Preston explains, "gives the environment some role, but not a determinative role in shaping thought and belief."[62] In environmental possibilism, one can speak of perceptual and cognitive influence without erasing personal agency and autonomy and without discounting the impact of social, cultural, experiential, or other factors.

I suggest that Spanish Harlem influenced my way of thinking in a similar way. It played a part in an otherwise complex perceptual and conceptual process that incorporated other factors, among them my own volition and some

60. Cornel West, *The American Evasion of Philosophy: A Genealogy of Pragmatism* (Madison: University of Wisconsin Press, 1989); Michael Bacon, *Pragmatism: An Introduction* (Malden, MA: Polity Press, 2012); Cheryl Misak, *The American Pragmatists* (New York: Oxford University Press, 2013); and Albert R. Spencer, *American Pragmatism: An Introduction* (Malden, MA: Polity Press, 2020).
61. Paul Vidal de la Blache, *Principles of Geography* (New York: H. Holt, 1926).
62. Christopher J. Preston, *Grounding Knowledge: Environmental Philosophy, Epistemology, and Place* (Athens: University of Georgia Press, 2003), 98.

degree of randomness. This complex process played out a certain way in my case but could just as easily turn out differently in others, even others of my family, block, or neighborhood. The question of how we think and know is complicated. Nonetheless, in one way or another, places come to exert a subtle influence on how we think and know. Places shape our experiences and our understandings of thought and belief in consequence.

The favored religion of the place likewise contributed to my pragmatist leanings though in an unexpected and odd sort of way. In the previous chapter, I mentioned how Pentecostal Christianity held sway in Spanish Harlem. There used to be and pretty much still is a Pentecostal church in every other block of the neighborhood. Along with their loud, vivacious, and enthusiastic worship forms, these churches are known for their sermonic allusions to an afterlife—a heavenly realm free of suffering for those who have accepted God's gift of salvation through the atoning work of Jesus Christ. Even as a young fellow, I noticed how this message raised morale and inspired hope. As I said before, this is nothing to sneeze at in instances of sustained hardship caused by structural injustice. Consequently, I recognized the value of the heaven-focused theology I encountered in Spanish Harlem's Pentecostal community, but I did not necessary agree with it.

Disenchanted with the otherworldly focus of this theology, I went looking for Christian meaning systems that focused on the here and now. I became convinced that the primary task and purpose of religion ought to be the provision of meaning and direction in and for life here on Earth. This was doubly so under the circumstances of life in a disadvantaged neighborhood. If religion was to yield hope, it had better be a hope for living in this world. I found and relished this hope when I discovered liberation theology in my junior year of college. I pursued this hope further, going to divinity school to find the inspiring discursive tradition centered on the heights and depths of the human experience that characterized liberal Christianity. These early ruminations bear witness to the conceptual concerns, conclusions, and leanings of a budding pragmatist, and Spanish Harlem's ethos had something to do with their emergence.

With regard to my academic career, this pragmatist disposition shows up in what I write about, how I write, and in what I choose not to write about. Theories of divine reality and divine action are nowhere to be found in my writing. There aren't any soundings on the origins of creation, nor any inquiries into the divinity of Jesus, the immanent Trinity, the next world, nor eschatological life and experience. Evading abstract doctrine and speculative discourse on what is ultimately ineffable, inaccessible, insolvable, and mysterious, my writing is right at home with the tangible and the practical, attending to our subjective lived experiences.

The latter focus opens me to the contingency of the self, community, and the social world. It opens me to the revisability of theories, knowledges, beliefs, and all systems of values and principles of conduct. In my hands, theology becomes, at times, a mode of social and cultural criticism, and, at other times, it is a critical hermeneutics that interprets the meanings of a religious tradition in order to ascertain what it can mean for us today in the light of the best available contemporary theories and in consideration of today's pressing concerns. The ultimate goal in either case is a reflective method that enriches the human experience and helps us to deal with the pressing issues of our time.

Just as Spanish Harlem shaped my attention to economic inequality and pragmatism, El Barrio is a clear influence on the unequivocal Latino identification of my thinking and writing. Five of the seven volumes that I have published, and all but one of my printed articles, are directly related to the topic of Latinidad. My heritage and family context played a role in this work naturally, but we should not underestimate the role of Spanish Harlem, too.

The neighborhood communicated cultural meaning and connection by various means. For example, the Spanish and Spanglish that were regularly spoken there conveyed ethnic and cultural information. The music heard throughout the place—often in the form of salsa, merengue, boleros romanticos, trio music, Latin freestyle, hip-hop, or Latin world pop—did the same. To this we can add the murals and street art; the national flags on display, especially from Puerto Rico, Cuba, Mexico, and the Dominican Republic; the outdoor ads often written in Spanish and featuring Latino/a themes and Latino/a popular icons; the food, clothing, and leisure items sold in local stores; the myriad Spanish-language newspapers and magazines on offer; the bodegas, cuchifritos, and other types of Latino/a shops and restaurants. Even the fiery Pentecostal sermons delivered in Spanish during outdoor church services and the periodic Catholic street processions accompanied with hymns sung in Spanish amplified the common modes of expression and signification that served as perceptible markers of Latinidad in the neighborhood—as discernible and distinguishable markers of Latino/a life, culture, and identity in the district. Consequently, it was impossible to enter the neighborhood and not know that it was Latino/a. Similarly, it was difficult, if not impossible, to live in the neighborhood and not derive a sense of identity and a sense of community from it, especially if one was of Latino/a descent oneself. The physical and cultural features of the place combined to teach about traditions, about heritage, about affiliation, and about group status.

The neighborhood's primary identity, of course, was Puerto Rican, owing to the history and ascendancy of this community in the district. But a great number of Latino/as from other parts of Latin America and the Caribbean called Spanish Harlem home as well, increasing the Latino/a presence and influence in the neighborhood all the more. Given the normal social interaction between the different Latino/a subgroups living in the district, and given the gravitation toward general ethnic labels and social identities for groups in the United States, residents maintained a dual identity quite comfortably. One was Puerto Rican, or Cuban, or Mexican, or Dominican, and also Latino or Latina. While in the district, one felt sheltered and affirmed in one's cultural, ethnic, and racial identity. Because of crime, Spanish Harlem may have felt unsafe at times, especially at night, but it lacked neither a sense of community nor a sense of national, cultural, nor ethnic pride. Consequently, if one was Latino/a, one felt accepted and embraced in and by the neighborhood. One felt a sense of belonging.

All bets were off as soon as one ventured outside the boundaries of the district, however. There, one was fully aware of America's ongoing problem with racial and ethnic diversity, encountering racial or ethnic discrimination in overt or covert forms.

We, the people of the United States, often think of ourselves as a nation that welcomes and incorporates or "assimilates" difference, whether of the entering immigrant or of our long-standing citizens. The truth is, however, that Americans have always been more inclined to celebrate difference in the past tense than in the present. When encountered in real time, racial and ethnic difference is typically judged a nuisance or even a menace. If one is a person of color or a member of a racial or ethnic minority, one is likely to remember an unpleasant experience of racial profiling, discrimination, or even a hate crime, all for simply having the hallmarks of these identities or for having wandered into an area, neighborhood, or part of town where one's own kind is neither welcomed nor awaited. Even in cosmopolitan New York City, this antipathy was common. So long as I was in Spanish Harlem, I could see, feel, and know that my Puerto Ricanness, my Nuyoricanness, and my Latinidad were accepted, celebrated, and affirmed. The physical and cultural realities of the neighborhood made this clear.

Spanish Harlem's ethnic and cultural embrace has counted for a lot in my career. It taught me my sense of identity and pride as a Puerto Rican, as a Nuyorican, and as a Latino. It is a reason why I have followed Latino/a studies, Boricua literature, and Puerto Rican studies over the years. Spanish Harlem also provided me with a template for valuing cultural citizenship. Having sensed, received, and partaken of its ethnic, cultural, and racial embrace, I could recognize and ferret out hurtful and unjust patterns of insult, bias, degradation, and disrespect whenever and wherever they turned up. With its affectionate embrace and the opposite experiences of racial and ethnic discrimination outside of the neighborhood came the sense that the matter of a positive ethnic, cultural, and racial identity was not to be taken for granted, and the sense that this was something for which it was worth fighting, something worth preserving. This is why matters of cultural justice have remained on my radar screen.

Even when calling attention to the gravity of economic injustice, I've never lost sight of the need to address unjust social patterns of cultural subordination, nonrecognition, and disrespect. Frankly, I have never seen the two political projects as oppositional, which is why I have written on matters of culture and on matters of economy, on cultural politics and on social politics. The goal has always been an emancipatory discursive agenda that is broad enough to incorporate the political, economic, and cultural dimensions of justice and receptive enough to make allowances for the demands and goals of representation, redistribution, and recognition in relation to them.[63] I attribute such inclinations and ambitions to the influence of Spanish Harlem.

Sharing snippets of my personal history in El Barrio, I have turned the spotlight on the space of negotiation between human subjectivity and the physical places that we inhabit. Within my own narrative, these three overarching emphases and themes appear in my thought and writing and can be traced to El Barrio's active influence: (1) a critical social-justice orientation that stays focused on matters of economic inequality; (2) a pragmatist approach to things; and (3) an unequivocal Latino identification.

My life story is not, then, the focus here. Rather, the "marvelous potency of place" is the story.[64]

Places are highly influential over and constitutive of our identities and knowledge claims, both as individuals and as members of human collectives.

---

63. Fraser, *Scales of Justice*, esp. 1–29.

64. Aristotle, *Physics*, trans. R. P. Hardie and R. K. Gaye (Oxford: Clarendon Press, 1930), 208B 34.

We are prone to forgetting, overlooking, or neglecting this basic existential and epistemological fact. Especially in the orbit of our intellectual work, the power of place deserves recognition and careful consideration. In my own field of theology and my own subfield or subdiscourse of U.S. liberation theology especially, we have rightly identified race, gender, ethnicity, and class among the epistemic locations that a theologian or religious scholar and critic brings to his or her knowledge claims. In the last decade or so, we have thankfully begun to make space for the contributions that our particular fleshly bodies make to our perceptual experience and, hence, to our understandings of thought and belief. The centrality of place in human experience and subjectivity, however, has been patchy, episodic, or missed altogether. Now, we must consider how particular places possess their own epistemic value, figuring out the particular ways in which the places in which we live are at work, influencing what we think and write.

Our neighborhoods, just like the natural environments we inhabit, have intelligence, knowledge, and the ability to communicate ideas.[65] They generously share their epistemic appurtenances as well, even if we aren't always prompt to see them. We stand to gain much from a more deliberate and careful consideration of their role in shaping our thought, writing, and belief structures. One of the rewards could be a better understanding of the *topos* of our thinking—a better understanding of the place within which our thinking emerges.

Perhaps turning to place in this way could genuinely lead us to see the places that have been around us and within us all the time—to come back to place, or to a place, in a way that brings that place itself into view. Perhaps for the first time, it could bring us to know the places from which we come or the places in which we have lived and to know them with more attention to their features, character, and effects. Perhaps that would prompt us to be attentive to places and to care for places, understanding the importance of place in our narratives of ourselves and of our communities. Such reflection on the role of place in shaping our thoughts and beliefs could lead us to discover the true provenance of our thinking—specifically to discover the *placed* origin of our thinking. This learning would be significant. Even more,

---

65. Keith H. Basso, *Wisdom Sits in Places: Landscape and Language among the Western Apache* (Albuquerque: University of New Mexico Press, 1996), esp. 105–50; and Vine Deloria Jr., *God Is Red: A Native View of Religion* (New York: Putnam Publishing Group, 1973), esp. 61–76 and 271–86.

reflection on the perceptual and epistemic agency of place could bring us to a fuller understanding of who we are.

If we simply assume that who we are is something deep inside us, we ignore the furtive, vital, and shaping interaction that exists between our brain, bodies, and our physical environments. We ignore the multiple ways in which all of the physical material around us, including the built and natural environments, acts upon our bodies and minds. Our physical environment has such a constant moment-to-moment influence on who we are physically and cognitively that any tracing of who we are needs to look inwardly and outwardly—out toward the physical localities of significance that comprise some of the important factors relevant to who we are physically and cognitively.[66]

With Place in Mind and at the Center

An adequate account of our knowing and of our own work as intellectuals, activists, and human beings must take stock of the significance of our engagement with the places in which we dwell. Moreover, I hope it has become clear that the broader self-awareness and self-enlightenment are no small feat, particularly in today's intellectual climate in which a good deal of consideration goes toward uncovering the range of different epistemic locations or subjectivities that introduce values into our knowledge claims. This consideration should now point us in the direction of the significance of places, seeing as they make important contributions to how we think and how we see the world. One can even say that the places from which we come do some of our thinking and envisaging for us. The information that comprises our understandings of thought and belief relies not only on the information carried inside our brains and bodies but also on the information carried by the physical, geographical places we inhabit.[67] That being the case, we might as well include them as part of our critical self-inventories, indeed as part of who we are.

Attaining this wider, deeper self-awareness and meta-cognition would be worth the price of admission in itself. To this, we can also add the profit of

---

66. Michael Spivey, *Who You Are: The Science of Connectedness* (Cambridge, MA: MIT Press, 2020).

67. Spivey, *Who You Are*, esp. 73–146; Colin Ellard, *Places of the Heart: The Psychogeography of Everyday Life* (New York: Bellevue Literary Press, 2015), esp. 11–51; and Raymond W. Gibbs Jr., *Embodiment and Cognitive Science* (New York: Cambridge University Press, 2006), esp. 1–41.

discovering the place where our thinking and writing take place or origi-nate, the provenance of our thinking and writing. As the old Mastercard commercial used to say, all of this is priceless, and even further riches might be gained by theologians, religious studies scholars, and other academics in this process of reconsidering the character of place and the character of our encounter with place!

Recall the ways in which place matters. In chapter 1, I touched on various reasons why place matters: it is a necessary condition for life; it provides us with a sense of who we are; it impacts the products of the mind; it shapes our destinies, influencing the fates of individuals and groups; and the grievous experiences of displacement endured by numerous individuals and groups are factors that demonstrate that there are few topics and actualities that are as crucial, multifaceted, wide-ranging, or all-encompassing as place. This says nothing yet of the many challenges that places are facing here and abroad, including enduring homelessness, environmental deterioration, growing urbanization, and resource wars. These are portentous dynamics that are shaping and reshaping places and the lives of people living in places around the world. By engaging the topic and actuality of place, theology throws itself into one of the most pressing, multifaceted topics of our time, making itself more relevant for multifarious movements and conversations.

There is even more to be gained from a deliberate exploration of place and of place's centrality in human experience. For those of us whose work is centered on the interpretation of texts, the possibility exists for a kind of "topopoetic mode of reading"[68] that attends to the power of placial experi-ences in written works. By "topopoetic," I mean readings that pay heed to the physical setting of the considered text, not only to the words of a text or to the plot of a text's storyline. In these readings, the setting of a dialogue or narra-tive is not reduced to an expendable, passive, or ornamental backdrop for the written account's events or for the story's action. Instead, place is experienced as "one of the primary events of the story," and any action in the story would be looked on as "being shaped, at least partially, by the event of place."[69]

A topopoetic reading would be place-sensitive, appreciating the "land-guage"[70] of a text and the ways in which the vocabulary of a text is either

---

68. Steven Pultz Moslund, "The Presencing of Place in Literature," in *Geocriti-cal Explorations: Space, Place, and Mapping in Literary and Cultural Studies*, ed. Robert T. Tally Jr. (New York: Palgrave Macmillan, 2011), 29–46.

69. Moslund, "The Presencing of Place in Literature," 30.

70. Moslund, "The Presencing of Place in Literature," 38.

inspired by or affected by the physiognomy and cultural history of its physical setting. It would dwell on the natural and cultural landscape of a work; the trees, fields, vines, bushes, hills, mountains, valleys, rivers, deserts, life forms, and local climatic conditions of a work, as well as the broader human history associated with the particular local place from which the work gleans or proceeds. Such attention offers the possibility of a deeper understanding of and openness to the text and the world of the text. By opening up to the physical world of the texts we study, we could even wind up nurturing a "presence-based way of thinking" in our midst.[71] In a meaning-focused culture such as ours, in which the sensory dimension of our interaction with the world is so often underappreciated or ignored, that wouldn't be a bad thing at all. By focusing on the landguage and the physical emplacement of a text, we might find ourselves entering into the placial dimensions of the work, consequently experiencing our own emplacement in the world. We might find ourselves being taken "beyond the words," as Merleau-Ponty puts it, presencing not only the physicality of geographical places in the text but also the physicality of geographical places in our own lives.[72] In short, presence might occur or take over.

For those of us with an interest in the various doctrines or beliefs of a religious tradition, or in constructive and systematic theology, we face the possibility of a refreshing and timely reconfiguring of these traditional themes and pursuits. Take the concept, idea, or proposition of God, for instance. I see no reason why we cannot grow used to the practice of speaking of and thinking of God as Place. In the last six or seven decades, we have become more familiar with a great variety of metaphors in reference to God, each attempting in its own way to add to our rich palette of metaphors in reference to the ineffable reality of God, each also attempting to counterbalance the disproportionate influence of male-oriented and anthropocentric metaphors, and each trying to speak more directly to our current experiences and sensibilities. From the "Ground of Being" or simply "Be-ing" to "our power in mutual relation" or "serendipitous creativity" and "Mother, lover, friend," we have witnessed the incorporation of newfangled ideas and words to think and talk about God.[73] This conceptual and linguistic experimentation

---

71. Hans Ulrecht Gumbrecht, *The Production of Presence: What Meaning Cannot Convey* (Stanford, CA: Stanford University Press, 2004), esp. 1–20 and 51–90.

72. Maurice Merleau-Ponty, "The Prose of the World," *Tri-Quarterly* 20, no. 9 (1971): 16.

73. For the suggestion of these ways of thinking and talking about God, see

is both a good and a necessary thing. Since our theological ideas and statements about God cannot be viewed as literal inquiries into the transcendent and absolute nature of God but rather as symbolic, metaphorical, analogical, and therefore essentially imaginative renderings of God, it is important that the list of representational ideas and figures of speech we use in reference to God keep growing while remaining relevant, meaningful, and up to date. Accordingly, the metaphor of place merits consideration as a fitting, useful, and fertile metaphor in reference to God.

Within Jewish and Christian theological traditions, there is precedent for this very move. As philosopher Edward Casey notes, "we need only think of the fact that the Hebrew word *Makom*, the name of God, means precisely Place."[74] And various Jewish sources appear to establish the prevalence or commonness of talk of God as place in the past. Place as a synonym for God, writes Israeli, German, and Palestinian physicist Shmuel Sambursky, "became a generally accepted expression in the Hebrew language from the first centuries of the Christian era onwards."[75] Rabbinical commentaries appear to verify and explain the move. A rabbinical commentary on Genesis, for example, exclaims, "Why is God called place? Because He is the place of the world, while the world is not His place."[76] Philo of Alexandria follows suit when he states, "God himself is called place, for he encompasses all things, but is not encompassed by anything."[77] Casey notes that this train of thought was carried forward by the Cambridge Platonist Henry More, who makes the following assertion:

Paul Tillich, *Systematic Theology,* vol. 1 (Chicago: University of Chicago Press, 2012), esp. 235–70; Mary Daly, *Beyond God the Father: Toward a Philosophy of Women's Liberation* (Boston: Beacon Press, 1973), esp. 13–43 and 179–98; Carter Heyward, *The Redemption of God: A Theology of Mutual Relation* (Eugene, OR: Wipf & Stock, 2010), esp. 124; Gordon D. Kaufman, *In Face of Mystery: A Constructive Theology* (Cambridge, MA: Harvard University Press, 1993), esp. 322–40; and Sallie McFague, *Models of God: Theology for an Ecological, Nuclear Age* (Philadelphia: Fortress Press, 1987), esp. 78–90.

74. Edward Casey, *Getting Back into Place: Toward a Renewed Understanding of the Place-World* (Bloomington: Indiana University Press, 2009), 17.

75. Shmuel Sambursky, *The Concept of Place in Late Neoplatonism* (Jerusalem: Israel Academy of Sciences and Humanities, 1989), 15.

76. Cited in Sambursky, *The Concept of Place in Late Neoplatonism,* 15; and Casey, *Getting Back into Place,* 17.

77. Cited in Sambursky, *The Concept of Place in Late Neoplatonism,* 35; and Casey, *Getting Back into Place,* 17.

> There are not less than twenty titles by which the Divine Numen is wont to be designated, and which perfectly fit this infinite internal place (locus) the existence of which in nature we have demonstrated; omitting moreover that the very Divine Numen is called by the Cabalists MAKOM, that is Place (locus).[78]

If nothing else, these declarations seem to suggest that, at one time, God was referred to as Place.

We can, of course, draw attention to the biblical verses that refer to God as Place or that make allowance for the notion and allusion. These include the various Psalms that allude to God as "dwelling place" (Psalm 90:1; Psalm 91:9–10; Psalm 32:7; and Psalm 71:3); Deuteronomy 33:27–28, and Acts 17:28, where God is said to be the one in whom "we live and move and have our being." These written sources and references, and others like them, could be put to use in a constructive rendering of the concept of God. The idea of God as Place allows us to bring to mind and convey the sense of an all-encompassing, all-embracing entity or vital force; a sense of immanent transcendence; the notion of an interconnected otherness; and even the conception of God as the source, locus, and limit of all that exists. Within this framework, it could be said that "from God's Place the universe proceeds—and comes continually to end."[79] In short, the metaphor or analogy of God as place makes space for ways of thinking and talking about God that steer clear of anthropocentric and gender-biased tendencies, all while allowing for a relational conceptualization of divine transcendence.

Similarly, I think there is potential for a doctrine of creation that takes the scene, site, or place of creation into consideration. In doing so, creation would mean more than the created things—the waters, skies, landforms, animals, insects, trees, and human beings. After all, there can be no creation without a place for it. Things, and ultimately the world at large, needed to be brought into a place or into place and to be brought into being from somewhere (i.e., place). A place for and of creation was needed. And so, as Casey notes, one could say that, "if it is true that in the beginning was the Word, it is also true that in the beginning was the Place."[80] Either way, we are working toward the emplacement or placialization of the doctrine of creation as well as toward the further materialization or earthy grounding of the doctrine.

---

78. Casey, *Getting Back into Place*, 376.
79. Casey, *Getting Back into Place*, 18.
80. Casey, *Getting Back into Place*, 18.

In theological anthropology, I can envision new materialist and critical posthumanist theologies that attempt both to put us in our place and to put us back into place. Such theological anthropologies offer concepts and tools for reexamining human agency and humanity's relationship and intra-actions with one another and with other material forces and beings. These would continue to problematize two ontological assumptions that were common to Enlightenment-based thought and are still common to many modern Christian anthropologies: agency as a capacity belonging only to human beings and the presumption of human exceptionalism. These new theological anthropologies would proceed to make allowances for the formative powers possessed by nonhuman bodies and the world's mosaic of landscapes and physical locations; to encourage more astute, healthy, and sustainable engagements with the variegated, vibrant materiality that runs alongside, inside, and between us; and to re-envision human subjectivity and agency as a complex, circuitous, ongoing, and open-ended process invariably enmeshed in and distributed across a stunning assemblage and mosaic of material agencies.

Within the basic structure or direction of these more place-conscious and material-friendly theological anthropologies, I can envision sin as a breach of our corresponding harmonious relationship with the numerous and diverse places that emplace us and give rise to our very being; that allow us access to ourselves, to our better selves, to other persons, to what is other than human, to the world, and even to the place of places (i.e., God). Fittingly, redemption, atonement, or salvation would require our getting back into place and our getting back in place. They would require our determined effort to establish, maintain, and effect right relation with all of the places that situate us, that shape and form us, and that sustain us.

Along these lines, I can imagine those of us who are devoted to understanding the phenomenon of spirituality making every effort to extend the notion of sacred space to all of the immediate, palpable, sensed, and constantly changing geographical places that register in our memories and to which we have emotional and practical commitments.[81] A tract of land, a desert area, a forest, a garden, a seashore, a boat out at sea or on a lake, a temple, a cathedral, a chapel, a religious site, a neighborhood, a building, a café, a street corner, a yoga studio, a dance or music studio, a martial arts dojo, a gym, a classroom, and even a quiet corner of the room reserved for meditation can all hold and extend the best in us. They can evoke a sense of

---

81. I am borrowing here from language used by geographer Edward Relph in "Place and Connection," in *The Intelligence of Place*, 175–204.

balance, connection, and greater purpose, bringing us closer to the things that are dear to us and connecting us to the divine in according awe and respect. They all are or could become sacred places in this sense.

I can also envision those who are committed to the methods of practical theology taking advantage of a place-based approach to weave together theoretical insights with field-based inquiry, neighborhood or regional narratives, autobiography, and creative writing to arrive at a textured understanding of theological concepts. Turning to place offers something for everyone with regard to creative theological writing, justifying our dive into the topics of place, place experience, and place meaning all the more. Theology and religious studies scholars have vibrant opportunities to connect with one of the more crucial, multifaceted, and wide-ranging and all-encompassing topics of our time: the opportunity to explore the deep connections that exist between the different physical environments we inhabit and the character of our thought and beliefs; the opportunity to discover the back stories of their intellectual work, respecting the inexorable though often unpredictable and undetected placed origin of our thinking; and the opportunity to refresh the major themes and motifs of theology through a reconsideration of the topological aspects of human agency and experience.

Theology and religious studies could gain much in a move toward greater consideration of place and place experience with respect to the fields of theology and religious studies. The possibility also exists for a more personal or inner aspiration and attainment for those of us who are scholars of theological and religious studies. We could call it the realization of an inner disposition that informs and comes into view in our academic work. I am talking about the cultivation of a sense of place marked by a deeper consciousness of, responsiveness to, and appreciation for place.

This sense of place could take shape and become concrete or visible in a whole host of ways; in more ways than I can even imagine. Even so, in the interest of presenting some possible paths for application, I suggest a few possibilities for its unveiling and flowering here at the end of this book. I pose these possibilities in the form of a guiding question: How does one know when one's work is taking place seriously?

Some signs could look like this:

- We could find ourselves appreciating the ways in which the vocabulary of a text is affected by, or sometimes produced by, the physical environment of its setting.

- We could find ourselves dwelling on and appreciating the landscape and the environmental and natural features of a work instead of rushing to questions regarding the meaning and intention of the work and the politics of representation.
- We could find ourselves entering into the placial dimensions of a work, experiencing our own emplacement within the scene in the process.
- We could find ourselves reflecting on the ways in which the ideas and thinking process of a key figure of the past may have been influenced by the geographic region and location in which he or she lived.
- We could find ourselves thinking about the role that physical geographical location may have played in a historical development, or in the choosing of a particular ministerial path, or in the distinguishing characteristics of a social or religious movement.
- We could find ourselves giving some thought to our intellectual beginnings, to the placed origin or provenance of our thinking, and to the connections that may exist between the region(s) of our upbringing or the places in which we dwell and the character of our thinking and writing.
- We could find ourselves pondering how religious ideas, beliefs, rituals, and moral precepts can be developed or rethought in the light of the particularities of a particular place, and in a way that is both sensitive to and responsive to those particularities.
- We could find ourselves acknowledging and inquiring into our physical environment and our physical emplacement with renewed interest, showing a greater interest in the history of the places in which we find ourselves and a greater level of care and concern for their necessities and welfare.
- We could find ourselves being moved by and reporting on the many challenges places are facing and the many changes they are undergoing here and abroad.
- We could find ourselves showing understanding and empathy for those who endure experiences of transition and displacement whether due to migration, colonialism and imperialism, natural disasters, war, gentrification, redevelopment, and/or other destabilizing factors.
- We could find ourselves striving for creative space in our writing whether by means of narrative writing, autobiographical and episodic memory, stories of place, oral histories, ethnographies, show-and-tell methods, photography, song lyrics, or poetry, all in an attempt to capture and convey a sense of the complex history, vital materiality, and experience of place.

From my place, these are just some of the ways in which a heightened sense of place can arise and become evident in our lives and work. Each of these are just part of the rich depth of discovery, perception, insight, wisdom, and knowledge that abides in a more place-sensitive way of thinking, seeing, and understanding. It is little wonder that I find myself issuing this call (back) to place in hope that we, theologians and scholars of religion, will recognize the centrality of place in human experience and embrace it, letting in the intelligence of place.

I am confident that the more we can allow ourselves to explore the meanings and reaches of place, the more we will discover the extent to which we are touched and changed by the places in which we dwell.

Bibliography

Abram, David. *The Spell of the Sensuous*. New York: Vintage, 1996.

Abramsky, Sasha. *The American Way of Poverty: How the Other Half Still Lives*. New York: Bold Type Books, 2013.

Acosta-Belén, Edna, and Carlos E. Santiago. *Puerto Ricans in the United States: A Contemporary Portrait*. London: Lynne Rienner Publishers, 2006.

Alaimo, Stacy, and Susan Hekman, eds. *Material Feminisms*. Bloomington: Indiana University Press, 2008.

Aristotle. "Physics." In *Aristotle: Basic Works*. Trans. R. P. Hardie and R. K. Gaye. Oxford: Clarendon Press, 1930.

Augé, Marc. *Non-Places: Introduction to an Anthropology of Supermodernity*. London: Verso, 1996.

Ayala, César J., and Rafael Bernabe. *Puerto Rico in the American Century: A History since 1898*. Chapel Hill: University of North Carolina Press, 2007.

Bachelard, Gaston. *The Poetics of Space*. Boston: Beacon Press, 1994.

Bacon, Michael. *Pragmatism: An Introduction*. Malden, MA: Polity Press, 2012.

Baldwin, James. "A Talk to Teachers." In *The Price of the Ticket*. Boston: Beacon Press, 1985.

Barad, Karan. *Meeting the Universe Halfway: Quantum Physics and the Entanglement of Matter and Meaning*. Durham, NC: Duke University Press, 2007.

Barger, Lillian Calles. *The World Come of Age: An Intellectual History of Liberation Theology*. New York: Oxford University Press, 2018.

Bartholomew, Craig G. *Where Mortals Dwell: A Christian View of Place for Today*. Grand Rapids, MI: Baker Academic, 2011.

Basso, Keith. *Wisdom Sits in Places: Landscape and Language among the Western Apache*. Albuquerque: University of New Mexico Press, 1996.

Bauman, Zygmunt. *Liquid Modernities*. Cambridge, MA: Polity Press, 2000.

———. *Globalization: The Human Consequences*. New York: Columbia University Press, 1998.

Bell, Christopher. *East Harlem Remembered: Oral Histories of Community and Diversity*. Jefferson, NC: McFarland, 2013.

Bennett, Jane. *Vibrant Matter: A Political Ecology of Things*. Durham, NC: Duke University Press, 2010.

Bergman, Sigurd. *Religion, Space, and the Environment*. New York: Routledge, 2017.

———. ed. *Theology in Built Environments: Exploring Religion, Architecture, and Design*. New York: Routledge, 2017.

Bevans, Stephen B. *Models of Contextual Theology*. Maryknoll, NY: Orbis Books, 2002.

Bigwood, Carol. *Earth Muse: Feminism, Nature, and Art*. Philadelphia: Temple University Press, 1993.

Blangger, Tim. "Tito Puente Dips Jazz into Salsa." *The Morning Call* (October 7, 1990). www.mcall.com.

Bourgois, Philippe. *In Search of Respect: Selling Crack in El Barrio*. New York: Cambridge University Press, 2003.

Braidotti, Rosi. *Posthuman Knowledge*. Cambridge, MA: Polity Press, 2019.

Braun-Reinitz, Janet, and Jane Weissman, eds. *On the Wall: Four Decades of Community Murals in New York City*. Jackson: University of Mississippi Press, 2009.

Brueggeman, Walter. *The Land: Place as Gift, Promise, and Challenge in Biblical Faith*. Minneapolis, MN: Fortress Press, 2002.

Burrows, Edwin G., and Mike Wallace. *Gotham: A History of New York City to 1898*. New York: Oxford University Press, 2000.

Cahill, Lisa Sowle. *Global Justice, Christology, and Christian Ethics*. New York: Cambridge University Press, 2013.

Cardenal, Ernesto. *The Gospel in Solentiname*. Maryknoll, NY: Orbis Books, 1976.

Carrión, Arturo Morales. *Puerto Rico: A Political and Cultural History*. New York: W. W. Norton, 1983.

Casey, Edward. "How to Get from Space to Place in a Fairly Short Stretch of Time." In *Senses of Place*. Ed. Steven Feld and Keith Basso. Santa Fe, NM: School of American Research Press, 1996.

———. *The Fate of Place: A Philosophical History.* Berkeley: University of California Press, 1997.

———. *Getting Back into Place: Toward a Renewed Understanding of the Place-World.* Bloomington: Indiana University Press, 2009.

Cashin, Sheryll. *Place Not Race: A New Vision of Opportunity in America.* Boston: Beacon Press, 2014.

Cicero. *De oratore.* Trans. E. W. Sutton and H. Rackham. Loeb Classical Library. Cambridge, MA: Harvard University Press, 1942.

Chen, Xiangming, Anthony M. Orum, and Krista E. Paulsen. *Introduction to Cities: How Place and Space Shape Human Experience.* Hoboken, NJ: Wiley-Blackwell, 2018.

Cobb, Edith. *The Ecology of Imagination in Childhood.* New York: Columbia University Press, 1977.

Collins, Patricia Hill. *Intersectionality as Critical Social Theory.* Durham, NC: Duke University Press, 2019.

Coole, Diana, and Samantha Frost, eds. *New Materialisms: Ontology, Agency, and Politics.* Durham, NC: Duke University Press, 2010.

Copeland, M. Shawn. *Enfleshing Freedom: Body, Race, and Being.* Minneapolis, MN: Fortress Press, 2009.

Cox, Harvey. *Fire from Heaven: The Rise of Pentecostal Spirituality and the Reshaping of Religion in the Twenty-First Century.* Cambridge, MA: Da Capo Press, 1995.

Crenshaw, Kimberlé. *On Intersectionality: Essential Writings.* New York: New Press, 2017.

Cresswell, Tim. *Place: An Introduction.* Malden, MA: Wiley Blackwell, 2015.

Daly, Mary. *Beyond God the Father: Toward a Philosophy of Women's Liberation.* Boston: Beacon Press, 1973.

Dávila, Arlene. *Barrio Dreams: Puerto Ricans, Latinos, and the Neoliberal City.* Berkeley: University of California Press, 2004.

Dayton, Donald W. *Theological Roots of Pentecostalism.* Grand Rapids, MI: Baker Academic, 1987.

DeLanda, Manuel. *A New Philosophy of Society: Assemblage Theory and Social Complexity.* New York: Continuum, 2006.

———. *Materialist Phenomenology: A Philosophy of Perception.* New York: Bloomsbury Academic, 2021.

De La Torre, Miguel. *Doing Christian Ethics from the Margins.* Maryknoll, NY: Orbis Books, 2014.

Deloria, Vine, Jr. *God Is Red: A Native View of Religion*. New York: Putnam Publishing Group, 1973.

Diadato, Nazzareno, and Gianni Bellocchi. "Historical Perspective of Drought Response in Central-Southern Italy." *Climate Research* 49, no. 3 (October 2011): 189–200.

Dovey, Kim. *Becoming Places: Urbanism/Architecture/Identity/Power*. New York: Routledge, 2015.

Duany, Jorge. *Puerto Rico: What Everyone Needs to Know*. New York: Oxford University Press, 2017.

Dunbar-Ortiz, Roxanne. *An Indigenous Peoples' History of the United States*. Boston: Beacon Press, 2015.

Edensor, Tim, Ares Kalandides, and Uma Kothari, eds. *The Routledge Handbook of Place*. New York: Routledge, 2020.

Eliot, T. S. "Little Gidding." In *Four Quartets*. Boston: Mariner Books, 1943.

Ellard, Colin. *Places of the Heart: The Psychogeography of Everyday Life*. New York: Bellevue Literary Press, 2015.

Escobar, Arturo. "Culture Sits in Places: Reflections on Globalism and Subaltern Strategies of Localization." *Political Geography* 20 (2001): 139–74.

Espinosa, Gastón. *Latino Pentecostals in America: Faith and Politics in Action*. Cambridge, MA: Harvard University Press, 2016.

Fernández, Johanna. *The Young Lords: A Radical History*. Chapel Hill: University of North Carolina Press, 2020.

Fletcher, Karen Baker. *Sisters of Dust, Sisters of Spirit: Womanist Wordings on God and Creation*. Minneapolis, MN: Fortress Press, 1998.

Florida, Richard. *The New Urban Crisis: How Our Cities Are Increasing Inequality, Deepening Segregation, and Failing the Middle Class—And What We Can Do about It*. New York: Basic Books, 2017.

Fox, Nick, and Pam Alldred. *Sociology and the New Materialism: Theory, Research, Action*. London: SAGE Publications, 2017.

Fraser, Nancy. *Justice Interruptus: Critical Reflections on the "Postsocialist" Condition*. New York: Routledge, 1997.

———. *Redistribution or Recognition?: A Political-Philosophical Exchange*. New York: Verso Books, 2003.

———. *Scales of Justice: Reimagining Political Space in a Globalizing World*. New York: Columbia University Press, 2010.

Freeman, Lance. "Five Myths about Gentrification." *Washington Post* (June 3, 2016), https://www.washingtonpost.com/opinions/five-myths-about-

gentrification/2016/06/03b6c80e56-1ba5-11e6-8c7b-6931e66333e7_
story.html.

Freidenberg, Judith Noemi. *Growing Old in El Barrio*. New York: NYU
Press, 2000.

Freyer, Roland G. "Measuring Crack Cocaine and Its Impact." *Economic
Inquiry* 51, no. 3 (July 2013): 1651–81.

Gallagher, Winifred. *The Power of Place: How Our Surroundings Shape Our
Thoughts, Emotions, and Actions*. New York: HarperPerennial, 1994.

Gibbs, Raymond W. *Embodiment and Cognitive Science*. New York: Cambridge University Press, 2006.

Gibson, James J. *The Ecological Approach to Visual Perception*. New York:
Taylor & Francis, 2014.

Glazer, Nathan, and Daniel Patrick Moynihan. *Beyond the Melting Pot*.
Cambridge, MA: MIT Press, 1968.

Goetz, Edward G. *New Deal Ruins: Race, Economic Justice, and Public
Housing Policy*. New York: Cornell University Press, 2013.

Goldblum, Joanne Samuel, and Colleen Shaddox. *Broke in America: Seeing,
Understanding, and Ending U.S. Poverty*. Dallas, TX: BenBela Books,
2021.

Goldhagen, Sarah W. *Welcome to Your World: How the Built Environment
Shapes Our Lives*. New York: HarperCollins, 2017.

Gonzalez, Michelle A. *Shopping: Christian Explorations of Daily Living*.
Minneapolis, MN: Fortress Press, 2010.

Gorringe, T. J. *A Theology of the Built Environment: Justice, Empowerment,
Redemption*. Cambridge, UK: Cambridge University Press, 2002.

———. *The Common Good and the Global Emergency: God and the Built
Environment*. Cambridge, UK: Cambridge University Press, 2011.

Gregory, James N. *The Southern Diaspora: How the Great Migrations of
Black and White Southerners Transformed America*. Chapel Hill: University of North Carolina Press, 2005.

Grosz, Elizabeth. *The Incorporeal: Ontology, Ethics, and the Limits of Materialism*. New York: Columbia University Press, 2018.

Grzanka, Patrick R., ed. *Intersectionality: Foundations and Frontiers*. New
York: Routledge, 2019.

Gumbrecht, Hans Ulrecht. *The Production of Presence: What Meaning Cannot Convey*. Stanford, CA: Stanford University Press, 2004.

Hancock, Ange-Marie. *Intersectionality: An Intellectual History*. New York:
Oxford University Press, 2016.

Hayden, Dolores. *The Power of Place: Urban Landscapes as Public History*.
Cambridge, MA: MIT Press, 1995.

Hays, R. Allen. *The Federal Government and Urban Housing*. Albany, NY: SUNY Press, 2012.

Haraway, Donna J. "Situated Knowledges: The Science Question in Feminism and the Privilege of Partial Perspective." *Feminist Studies* 14, no. 3 (Fall 1988): 575–99.

Harvey, David. *Spaces of Global Capitalism: A Theory of Uneven Geographical Development*. New York: Verso, 2019.

Heidegger, Martin. *Being and Time*. Trans. John Macquarrie and Edward Robinson. New York: Harper & Row, 1962.

Heyward, Carter. *The Redemption of God: A Theology of Mutual Relation*. Eugene, OR: Wipf & Stock, 2010.

Hjalmarson, Leonard. *No Home Like Place: A Christian Theology of Place*. Farnham: Ashgate Publishing, 2003.

———, ed. *The Soul of the City: Mapping the Spiritual Geography of Eleven Canadian Cities*. Skyforest, CA: Urban Loft Publishers, 2018.

Hollenweger, Walter J. *Pentecostalism: Origins and Developments Worldwide*. Peabody, MA: Hendrickson Publishers, 1997.

hooks, bell. *Belonging: A Culture of Place*. New York: Routledge, 2009.

Hopkins, Dwight N. *Down, Up, and Over: Slave Religion and Black Theology*. Minneapolis, MN: Fortress Press. 2000.

———. *Black Theology: Essays on Gender Perspectives*. Eugene, OR: Cascade Books, 2017.

Horsley, Richard A. *Covenant Economics: A Biblical Vision of Justice for All*. Louisville, KY: Westminster John Knox Press, 2009.

Hubbard, Phil, and Rob Kitchin, eds. *Key Thinkers on Space and Place*. London: SAGE Publications, 2011.

Inge, John. *A Christian Theology of Place*. Farnham: Ashgate Publishing, 2003.

Isasi-Díaz, Ada María. "Mujeristas: A Name of Our Own." *The Christian Century* (May 24–31, 1989): 560–62.

———. *Hispanic Women: Prophetic Voice in the Church*. Minneapolis, MN: Fortress Press, 1992.

———. *En La Lucha/In the Struggle: Elaborating a Mujerista Theology*. Minneapolis, MN: Fortress Press, 1993.

———. *Mujerista Theology: A Theology for the Twenty-First Century*. Maryknoll, NY: Orbis Books, 1996.

———. "Un Poquito de Justicia—A Little Bit of Justice." In *Hispanic/*

Latino Theology: Challenge and Promise. Ed. Ada María Isasi-Díaz and Fernando F. Segovia, 325–39. Minneapolis, MN: Fortress Press, 1996.

Jacobsen, Eric O. *The Space Between: A Christian Engagement with the Built Environment.* Grand Rapids, MI: Baker Academic, 2012.

Kaufman, Gordon D. *In Face of Mystery: A Constructive Theology.* Cambridge, MA: Harvard University Press, 1993.

King, Ben E. "Spanish Harlem." On *Spanish Harlem.* Atlantic Records, 1961.

Kirby, Kathleen M. *Indifferent Boundaries: Spatial Concepts of Human Subjectivity.* New York: Guilford Press, 1996.

Kirby, Vicki. *Quantum Anthropologies: Life at Large.* Durham, NC: Duke University Press, 2011.

Knight, Cher Krause, and Harriet F. Senie, eds. *A Companion to Public Art.* Malden, MA: Wiley-Blackwell, 2016.

Kochar, Rakesh, and Richard Fry. "Wealth Inequality Has Widened along Racial Ethnic Lines since End of Great Recession." *Pew Research Center* (December 12, 2014). https://www.pewresearch.org.

Kristof, Nicholas D., and Sheryl WuDunn. *Tightrope: Americans Reaching for Hope.* New York: Vintage Books, 2020.

Lan, Kwok Pui, and Joerg Rieger. *Occupy Religion: Theology of the Multitude.* Lanham, MD: Rowman & Littlefield, 2012.

Lee, Anthony W. *Painting on the Left: Diego Rivera, Radical Politics, and San Francisco's Public Murals.* Berkeley: University of California Press, 1999.

Lemann, Nicholas. *The Promised Land: The Great Black Migration and How It Changed America.* New York: Vintage Books, 1991.

Leong, David P. *Race and Place: How Urban Geography Shapes the Journey to Reconciliation.* Downers Grove, IL: InterVarsity Press, 2017.

Loewen, James. *Sundown Towns: A Hidden Dimension of American Racism.* New York: Simon & Schuster, 2006.

Ludwig, Gene. *The Vanishing American Dream: A Frank Look at the Economic Realities Facing Middle- and Lower-Income Americans.* New York: Disruption Books, 2020.

Malpas, Jeff. *Place and Experience: A Philosophical Topography.* Cambridge, UK: Cambridge University Press, 1999.

Massey, Doreen. *Space, Place, and Gender.* Minneapolis: University of Minnesota Press, 1994.

———. *For Space.* London: SAGE Publications, 2005.

McFague, Sallie. *Models of God: Theology for an Ecological, Nuclear Age.* Philadelphia: Fortress Press, 1987.

Melendez, Miguel. *We Took the Streets: Fighting for Latino Rights with the Young Lords.* New Brunswick, NJ: Rutgers University Press, 2005.

Menin, Sarah, ed. *Constructing Place: Mind and the Matter of Place-Making.* New York: Routledge, 2003.

Merleau-Ponty, Maurice. "The Prose of the World." *Tri-Quarterly* 20, no. 9 (1971): 3–129.

Mignolo, Walter D. *The Darker Side of Western Modernity: Global Futures, Decolonial Options.* Durham, NC: Duke University Press, 2011.

Misak, Cheryl. *The American Pragmatists.* New York: Oxford University Press, 2013.

Monge, José Trias. *Puerto Rico: The Trials of the Oldest Colony in the World.* New Haven, CT: Yale University Press, 1997.

Moslund, Steven Pultz. "The Presencing of Place in Literature." In *Geocritical Explorations: Space, Place, and Mapping in Literary and Cultural Studies.* Ed. Robert T. Tally Jr., 29–46. New York: Palgrave Macmillan, 2011.

Morales, Ed. *Fantasy Island: Colonialism, Exploitation, and the Betrayal of Puerto Rico.* New York: Bold Type Books, 2019.

Nast, Heidi J., and Steve Pile, eds. *Places through the Body.* New York: Routledge, 1998.

Newman, Katherine S., and Victor Tan Chen. *The Missing Class: Portraits of the Near Poor in America.* Boston: Beacon Press, 2007.

Noah, Timothy. *The Great Divergence: America's Growing Inequality Crisis and What We Can Do about It.* New York: Bloomsbury Press, 2012.

Ogden, Laura A. *Swamplife: People, Gators, and Mangroves Entangled in the Everglades.* Minneapolis: University of Minnesota Press, 2011.

Orsi, Robert A. *The Madonna of 115th Street: Faith and Community in Italian Harlem, 1880–1950.* New Haven, CT: Yale University Press, 2010.

Pears, Angie. *Doing Contextual Theology.* New York: Routledge, 2010.

Pérez-Gómez, Alberto. "Place and Architectural Space." In *The Intelligence of Place: Topographies and Poetics.* Ed. Jeff Malpas, 157–76. New York: Bloomsbury Academic, 2017.

Pevar, Stephen L. *The Rights of Indians and Tribes.* New York: Oxford University Press, 2012.

Phillips-Fein, Kim. *Fear City: New York's Fiscal Crisis and the Rise of Austerity Politics.* New York: Metropolitan Books, 2017.

Pickering, Andrew. *The Mangle of Practice*. Chicago: University of Chicago Press, 1995.

Pinn, Anthony B., and Dwight N. Hopkins, eds. *Loving the Body: Black Religious Studies and the Erotic*. New York: Palgrave Macmillan, 2004.

Pinn, Anthony B. *Embodiment and the New Shape of Black Theological Thought*. New York: NYU Press, 2010.

Plunz, Richard. *A History of Housing in New York City*. New York: Columbia University Press, 2016.

Pred, Allan. "Place as Historically Contingent Process: Structuration and the Time-Geography of Becoming Places." *Annals of the Association of American Geographers* 74 (1984): 279–97.

Preston, Christopher J. *Grounding Knowledge: Environmental Philosophy, Epistemology, and Place*. Athens: University of Georgia Press, 2003.

Price, Patricia L. *Dry Place: Landscapes of Belonging and Exclusion*. Minneapolis: University of Minnesota Press, 2004.

Rae, Murray A. *Architecture and Theology: The Art of Place*. Waco, TX: Baylor University Press, 2017.

Ramirez, Daniel. *Migrating Faith: Pentecostalism in the United States and Mexico in the Twentieth Century*. Chapel Hill: University of North Carolina Press, 2015.

Rank, Mark R., and Lawrence M. Eppard. "The American Dream of Upward Mobility Is Broken." *The Guardian* (March 13, 2021).

Reid, Marcella Althaus. *Indecent Theology: Theological Perversions in Sex, Gender, and Politics*. London: Routledge, 2000.

———. *Liberation Theology and Sexuality*. Farnham: Ashgate Publishing, 2006.

Relph, Edward. *Place and Placelessness*. London: Pion Press, 1996.

———. "Place and Connection." In *The Intelligence of Place: Topographies and Poetics*. Ed. Jeff Malpas, 177–204. New York: Bloomsbury Academic, 2017.

Rieger, Joerg. *No Rising Tide: Theology, Economics, and the Future*. Minneapolis, MN: Fortress Press, 2009.

Rivera, Mayra. *Poetics of the Flesh*. Durham, NC: Duke University Press, 2015.

Rivera-Pagán, Luis N. "God the Liberator: Theology, History, and Politics." In *In Our Own Voices: Latino/a Renditions of Theology*. Ed. Benjamín Valentín, 1–20. Maryknoll, NY: Orbis Books, 2010.

Robbins, R. G. *Pentecostalism in America*. Westport, CT: Praeger, 2010.

Rodriguez, Clara E. "Forging a New, New York: The Puerto Rican Community, Post-1945." In *Boricuas in Gotham: Puerto Ricans in the Making of Modern New York City*. Ed. Gabriel Haslip-Viera, Angelo Falcón, and Félix Matos Rodriguez, 195–218. Princeton, NJ: Markus Wiener Publishers, 2004.

Rothstein, Richard. *The Color of Law: A Forgotten History of How Our Government Segregated America*. New York: W. W. Norton, 2017.

Sack, Robert David. *Homo Geographicus: A Framework for Action, Awareness, and Moral Concern*. Baltimore, MD: Johns Hopkins University Press, 1997.

Said, Edward W. *Beginnings: Intention and Method*. New York: Columbia University Press, 1985.

Sambursky, Shmuel. *The Concept of Place in Late Neoplatonism*. Jerusalem: Israel Academy of Sciences and Humanities, 1989.

Sanchez, José Ramon. "Housing Puerto Ricans in New York City, 1945–1984: A Study in Class Powerlessness." PhD diss., New York University, 1990.

Sánchez Korrol, Virginia E. *From Colonia to Community: The History of Puerto Ricans in New York City*. Berkeley: University of California Press, 1983.

Sanderson, Eric W. *Mannahatta: A Natural History of New York City*. New York: Harry Abrams, 2009.

Santana, Carlos. "Smooth." On *Supernatural*. Arista Records, 1999.

Schaeffer, Katherine. "Six Facts about Economic Inequality in the U.S." *Pew Research Center* (February 7, 2020). https://www.pewresearch.org.

Schacter, Rafael, and John Fekner. *The World Atlas of Street Art and Graffiti*. New Haven, CT: Yale University Press, 2013.

Schissel, Wendy, ed. *Home/Bodies: Geographies of Self, Place, and Space*. Calgary, Canada: University of Calgary Press, 2006.

Shipler, David K. *The Working Poor: Invisible in America*. New York: Vintage Books, 2016.

Seamon, David. *Life Takes Place: Phenomenology, Lifeworlds, and Place Making*. New York: Routledge, 2018.

Sexton, Patricia Cayo. *Spanish Harlem: Anatomy of Poverty*. New York: Harper & Row, 1965.

Sharkey, Patrick. *Stuck in Place: Urban Neighborhoods and the End of Progress toward Racial Equality*. Chicago: University of Chicago Press, 2013.

Sharman, Russell Leigh. *The Tenants of East Harlem*. Berkeley: University of California Press, 2006.

Sheldrake, Philip. *Spaces for the Sacred: Place, Memory, and Identity*. London: SCM Press, 2001.

———. *The Spiritual City: Theology, Spirituality, and the Urban*. Malden, MA: Wiley-Blackwell, 2014.

Shipler, David. *The Working Poor: Invisible in America*. New York: Vintage Books, 2005.

Smith, Neil. *Uneven Development: Nature, Capital, and the Production of Space*. Athens: University of Georgia Press, 2008.

Spencer, Albert R. *American Pragmatism: An Introduction*. Malden, MA: Polity Press, 2020.

Spivey, Michael. *Who You Are: The Science of Connectedness*. Cambridge, MA: MIT Press, 2020.

Stein, Samuel. *Capital City: Gentrification and the Real Estate State*. New York: Verso, 2019.

Sternberg, Esther M. *Healing Spaces: The Science of Place and Well-Being*. Cambridge, MA: Belknap Press, 2009.

Tanner, Kathryn. *Christianity and the New Spirit of Capitalism*. New Haven, CT: Yale University Press, 2019.

Taylor, Borden, and Hillary Hoffower. "The Top 10 Cities in the World for Billionaires, Ranked." *Business Insider* (July 2, 2020). https://www.businessinsider.com.

Thomas, Lorrin. *Puerto Rican Citizen: History and Identity in Twentieth-Century New York City*. Chicago: University of Chicago Press, 2010.

Thomas, Piri. *Down These Mean Streets*. New York: Vintage Books, 1997.

Thrift, Nigel. "Inhuman Geographies: Landscapes of Speed, Light, and Power." In *Writing the Rural: Five Cultural Geographies*. Ed. Paul J. Cloke and Marcus A. Doel, 191–250. London: Sage Publications, 1994.

———. *Non-Representational Theory: Space, Politics, Affect*. New York: Routledge, 2007.

Tillich, Paul. *Systematic Theology. Vol. 1*. Chicago: University of Chicago Press, 2012.

Townes, Emilie M. *Breaking the Fine Rain of Death: African American Health Issues and a Womanist Ethic of Care*. New York: Continuum Publishers, 1998.

Traub, Amy, and Catherine Ruetschlin. "The Racial Wealth Gap: Why Policy Matters." *Demos* (March 10, 2015). https://www.demos.org.

Trigg, Dylan. *The Memory of Place: A Phenomenology of the Uncanny.* Athens: Ohio University Press, 2013.

Tuan, Yi-Fu. *Topophilia: A Study of Environmental Perception, Attitudes and Values.* Englewood, NJ: Prentice Hall, 1974.

Tuana, Nancy. "Material Locations: An Interactionist Alternative to Realism/Social Constructivism." In *Engendering Rationalities.* Ed. Nancy Tuana and Sandra Morgan, 221–44. Albany, NY: SUNY Press, 2001.

Tuck, Eve, and Marcia McKenzie, eds. *Place in Research: Theory, Methodology, and Methods.* New York: Routledge, 2015.

Vale, Lawrence J. *After the Projects: Public Housing Redevelopment and the Governance of the Poorest Americans.* New York: Oxford University Press, 2019.

Valentín, Benjamín. *Mapping Public Theology: Beyond Culture, Identity, and Difference.* New York: Bloomsbury T&T Clark, 2002.

———. "Dialogic Mediations: Reflections on the Hopeful Future of U.S. Liberation Theology." In *The Reemergence of Liberation Theologies: Models for the Twenty-First Century.* Ed. Thia Cooper, 49–56. New York: Palgrave Macmillan, 2013.

———. *Theological Cartographies: Mapping the Encounter with God, Humanity, and Christ.* Louisville, KY: Westminster John Knox Press, 2015.

———. "What's 'Liberation' Got to Do with It?" *Reflections* (Spring 2017): 36–38.

Vega, Bernardo. "Memorias de Bernardo Vega." In *Puerto Rican Arrival in New York: Narratives of the Migration, 1920–1950.* Ed. Juan Flores. Princeton, NJ: Markus Wiener Publishers, 2005.

Vidal de la Blache, Paul. *Principles of Geography.* New York: H. Holt, 1926.

Villafañe, Eldin. *The Liberating Spirit: Toward an Hispanic American Pentecostal Social Ethic.* Grand Rapids, MI: Eerdmans, 1993.

Violette, Zachary J. *The Decorated Tenement: How Immigrant Builders and Architects Transformed the Slum in the Gilded Age.* Minneapolis: University of Minnesota Press, 2019.

Vitek, William, and Wes Jackson, eds. *Rooted in the Land: Essays on Community and Place.* New Haven, CT: Yale University Press, 1996.

Wagenheim, Olga Jiménez. *Puerto Rico: An Interpretive History from Pre-Columbian Times to 1900.* Princeton, NJ: Markus Weiner Publishers, 1998.

Wanzer-Serrano, Darrel. *The New York Young Lords and the Struggle for Liberation*. Philadelphia: Temple University Press, 2015.

Wariboko, Nimi. *The Split Economy: Saint Paul Goes to Wall Street*. Albany, NY: SUNY Press, 2020.

West, Cornel. *The American Evasion of Philosophy: A Genealogy of Pragmatism*. Madison: University of Wisconsin Press, 1989.

Whalen, Carmen Teresa. "Colonialism, Citizenship, and the Making of the Puerto Rican Diaspora: An Introduction." In *The Puerto Rican Diaspora: Historical Perspectives*. Philadelphia: Temple University Press, 2005.

Wilkerson, Isabel. *The Warmth of Other Suns: The Epic Story of America's Great Migration*. New York: Vintage Books, 2001.

Wilson, William Julius. *The Truly Disadvantaged: The Inner City, the Underclass, and Public Policy*. Chicago: University of Chicago Press, 1987.

———. *When Work Disappears: The World of the New Urban Poor*. New York: Alfred A. Knopf, 1996.

Wolfe, Patrick. "Settler Colonialism and the Elimination of the Native." *Journal of Genocide Research* 8, no. 4 (December 2006): 387–409.

Wright, Gwendolyn. *Building the Dream: A Social History of Housing in America*. Cambridge, MA: MIT Press, 1983.

Ziady, Hannah. "The American Dream Is Much Easier to Achieve in Canada." *CNN Business* (January 20, 2020). https://www.cnn.com.

Zipp, Samuel. *Manhattan Projects: The Rise and Fall of Urban Renewal in Cold War New York*. New York: Oxford University Press, 2010.

Zukin, Sharon. *Naked City: The Death and Life of Authentic Urban Places*. New York: Oxford University Press, 2010.

Index

Latino/as, and disadvantages of place, 38

liberation, and quest for justice, 4, 5

liberation theology
  as contextual, 7–13
  differences between U.S. and Latin American, 115n14
  disregard for place, 4, 8–10, 10–11n16, 11–13
  and "people/thing materialities," 9, 10, 11

Little Italy, in East Harlem, 63, 64, 65

Maduro, Otto, 1

Makom (Hebrew term), 145

Malpas, Jeff, on place and self-identity, 30

materiality
  loss of sense of, 13, 14, 21, 22
  vital, 14, 15

McKenzie, Marcia, on colonialism and displacement, 40

McKinley, President William, and annexation of Puerto Rico, 72

memory, influence of place on, 30–32, 108–10

Merleau-Ponty, Maurice, 144

Mexican Americans, in Spanish Harlem, 102, 103

Mignolo, Walter, and zero point epistemology, 7, 8

migration, and loss of sense of place, 24

minorities, racial and ethnic, experience of place, 33

More, Henry, on God as Place, 145, 146

Moser, Edvard and Britt, and "grid cells," 32

mujerista theology, 1

municipal government, and scandal of economic inequality, 121, 122

murals, and artistic creativity, 87, 88, 96

nature, human independence and separation from, 23

New York City
  economic inequality of neighborhoods in, 123, 124
  history of Puerto Rican settlement in, 68–70. *See also* East Harlem, history of Puerto Rican settlement
  as magnet destination for Puerto Ricans, 58

Newman, Katherine, on poverty in America, 126

Noah, Timothy, on U.S. class divisions, 125

Nuyorican literature, 55

O'Keefe, John, and "place cells," 31

Ogden, Laura, and place writing practices, 50

Operacíon Manos a la Obra/Operation Bootstrap, 76, 77

Pentecostal Christianity
  otherworldly focus of, 137
  in Spanish Harlem, 95, 137

Pevar, Stephen, effects of displacement on Indigenous peoples, 41, 42

Philo of Alexandria, on God as Place, 145

physical geography, as cross-disciplinary field of study, xiv, xv

place/places
  as agent, xviii, 9, 17, 23, 112